Dialectical Theology and Jacques Ellul

Dialectical Theology and Jacques Ellul

An Introductory Exposition

Jacob E. Van Vleet

Fortress Press
Minneapolis

DIALECTICAL THEOLOGY AND JACQUES ELLUL
An Introductory Exposition

Cover design: Erica Rieck

Library of Congress Cataloging-in-Publication Data
Print ISBN: 978-1-4514-7039-0
eBook ISBN: 978-1-4514-7979-9

The paper used in this publication meets the minimum requirements of
American National Standard for Information Sciences — Permanence of Paper
for Printed Library Materials, ANSI Z329.48-1984.

Manufactured in the U.S.A.

This book was produced using PressBooks.com, and PDF rendering was done by
PrinceXML.

Contents

Acknowledgements

I would like to thank Michael Gibson, editor of theology at Fortress Press, for his interest and confidence in this project from the beginning. Also, many thanks to Lisa Gruenisen, Anna Doherty, and Laura Neil for help with editing and formatting the manuscript at its various stages.

Numerous individuals assisted me over the years in researching and writing this work. I am tremendously grateful to my former professor and friend Claude Welch of the Graduate Theological Union at UC Berkeley for many hours of dialogue on Søren Kierkegaard, Karl Barth, and Jacques Ellul. If it were not for Welch, I may have never traveled down the path of Ellul studies. For reading and commenting on earlier drafts of this book, my sincere appreciation goes to Sean Kelly and Eric Weiss, both faculty at the California Institute of Integral Studies, and to David W. Gill of Gordon-Conwell Theological Seminary.

I am deeply thankful for the Humanities and Philosophy Department at Diablo Valley College. Jackie Halm has given me years of support and scheduling flexibility; Bob Abele has provided me with intellectually challenging conversation and scholarly motivation. Also, much gratitude to all my colleagues at DVC and other institutions, including Dennis Ean Roby, Steven Goodman,

Aaron Weiss, Art Mielke, Keith Mikolavich, Wayne Yuen, and Mickey Huff, among others.

Special appreciation also goes to my Bay Area and Los Angeles family for years of friendship and inspiration: Matt and Lena Reynoso; Zachary, Margarita and David Gordon; Jason Escalante; and Brad and Emily Nabors.

Finally, for the many years of careful editing, ceaseless encouragement, emotional support, and profound wisdom, I thank my dearest friend: my wife, Moriah.

Introduction

The Skeleton Key—Dialectical Hermeneutics

When I read *The Technological Society* for the first time, I was delighted, because I thought, "Here is someone who is saying what I have already been thinking."
–Theodore Kaczynski, 1998[1]

Throughout the eighteen-year search for the identity of "the Unabomber," the Federal Bureau of Investigation compiled very little concrete information about the perpetrator. One conclusion they did come to: the Unabomber was very familiar with the writings of the French philosopher and theologian Jacques Ellul. In letters to newspapers and in work subtitled *Industrial Society and Its Future*,[2] the Unabomber used an uncommon amount of Ellul's vocabulary. Also, his critiques of modern technological society were oddly consistent with Ellul's critique of technology.[3]

On April 3, 1996, Theodore Kaczynski was arrested in his cabin near Lincoln, Montana for murdering three people and injuring eleven. In pretrial interviews, Kaczynski acknowledged Ellul's

---

1. Theodore Kaczynski, quoted in Alston Chase, *Harvard and the Unabomber: The Education of an American Terrorist* (New York: Norton, 2003), 294.
2. Theodore Kaczynski, *The Unabomber Manifesto: Industrial Society and Its Future* (Berkeley: Jolly Roger, 1995).
3. See Chase, *Harvard and the Unabomber*, chapter 1.

immense influence on his thinking, along with his reverence for Ellul. In fact, before Ellul's death in 1994, Kaczynski briefly corresponded with him. According to Kaczynski's brother, Ellul's book *The Technological Society* had become his "bible."[4] When the FBI searched his cabin, they discovered a small but impressive library containing several books by Ellul. However, none of Ellul's theological works were found, only his philosophical and sociological work concerning technology.[5]

While Kaczynski was quite familiar with Ellul's thought, it seems as if Kaczynski failed to read a vital portion of Ellul's work, his Christian writings. As a confirmed agnostic wanting nothing to do with any type of institutional religion, Kaczynski limited himself to a reading of Ellul that was incomplete, and therefore insufficient. Like many others, Kaczynski failed to understand this: in order to understand correctly Ellul's work, one must grasp his distinctly dialectical methodology and worldview. By doing so, one is able to grasp both Ellul's philosophy and his theology in a clear, integrated, and complete way.[6]

By interpreting Ellul's work in the same narrow way that Kaczynski did, one comes to see Ellul as merely a neo-Luddite or a fatalist calling for a complete overthrow of "the system." In fact, even historian Lewis Mumford describes Ellul's work as "fatalistic."[7] Postmodern philosopher of technology Andrew Feenberg also dismisses Ellul's work as "pessimistic" and "deterministic."[8] Indeed, if one reads only Ellul's work on technology, one will most likely agree

---

4. Ibid., 332.
5. Ibid., 92–93.
6. David W. Gill also makes this claim in "The Dialectic of Sociology and Theology in Jacques Ellul: A Recent Interview" (interview and paper given at the American Academy of Religion Annual Meeting, November 21, 1988).
7. Lewis Mumford, *The Myth of the Machine,* vol. 2, *The Pentagon of Power* (New York: Harcourt Brace Jovanovich, 1970), 290–91.
8. Andrew Feenberg, *Questioning Technology* (London: Routledge, 2000), 9.

with Mumford, Feenberg, and many others who respect Ellul as a founder of the philosophy of technology, but fail to take his work seriously because they mistakenly believe it offers no solutions to the problems raised by technology.[9]

Ellul published over fifty books in his lifetime, and almost everything he wrote was either philosophical or theological in nature.[10] To use an analogy he was fond of, Ellul's work was like the two parallel rails of a train track, one rail being theological, the other philosophical.[11] Clearly, no train can move ahead on just one rail. For every philosophical work Ellul wrote, he wrote a theological counterpart to it. This was central to his dialectical methodology. For example, the counterpart to *The Technological Society* is *The Meaning of the City*, a biblical study of cities from Genesis to Revelation. In addition, *The Politics of God and The Politics of Man*, a study of 2 Kings, was written as a dialectical counterpart to *The Political Illusion*.[12] For Ellul, the dialectical tension between his two strands of work was constant and acted as the conjoiner between them.[13]

The purpose of this study is to establish the necessity of being acquainted with both sides of Ellul's work by way of his dialectical methodology. If one reads only his philosophical work, it will seem to offer no solution. If one reads only his theological work, it will seem shallow. If, however, one is familiar with Ellul's conception of

---

9. See Mumford, *The Myth of the Machine*; Feenberg, *Questioning Technology*.
10. In the following, I refer to Ellul's non-theological work as "philosophy." Ellul was primarily a historian and sociologist, but his work concerning technique is highly philosophical in nature. Likewise, Ellul maintained that he was not a theologian, but as we will see, this is clearly not the case. So, for the purposes of clarity, I will address the two veins of Ellul work as philosophy and theology, respectively.
11. For Ellul's discussion of his dialectical methodology, see Jacques Ellul, "On Dialectic," in *Jacques Ellul: Interpretive Essays*, ed. Clifford G. Christians and Jay M. Van Hook (Urbana: University of Illinois Press, 1981), 291–308.
12. Ellul published *The Technological Society* in 1964 and *The Meaning of the City* in 1970, as well as *The Political Illusion* in 1967 and *The Politics of God and the Politics of Man* in 1972.
13. Ellul, "On Dialectic."

dialectic—the hermeneutical key to his work—one will gain a full and coherent understanding. By weaving together Ellul's most significant philosophical and theological works with the thread of dialectic, I seek to accomplish this task.

In chapter 1, I discuss the three primary intellectual influences on Jacques Ellul: Søren Kierkegaard, Karl Marx, and Karl Barth. I explain how Marx's dialectical view of history, as well as his critique of capitalism, influenced Ellul's sociological and philosophical hermeneutics. Also, I describe how Kierkegaard's philosophical anthropology and his emphasis on paradox, combined with Barth's notion of dialectical inclusion, influenced Ellul's theological hermeneutics.

Ellul's notion of dialectic as worldview and methodology are discussed in chapter 2. By looking at the process of history and the Hebrew and Christian Scriptures, we learn how Ellul defended his dialectical position. Additionally, I explain how Ellul's conception of dialectic influences his Christology.

Ellul's relation to other dialectical theologians, as well as his conception of God, is detailed in chapter 3. Also presented is an important discussion of two of Ellul's key distinctions: religion and revelation, and seeing and hearing. Finally, the logic behind Ellul's belief in universal salvation is outlined and explained.

In chapter 4, Ellul's philosophy of technology, including his conception of technique, is described. As the most important concept in Ellul's oeuvre, technique's conditions, characteristics, and ethical entailments are presented. Included in this chapter are brief considerations of two thinkers who share with Ellul a deep concern with the technological society, Herbert Marcuse and Martin Heidegger.

The subjects of chapter 5 are propaganda and politics. As two spheres within the realm of technique, propaganda and politics comprise the biggest threats and temptations to Christians. Also considered herein are the inherent physical violence in current political systems, and the innate psychological violence in modern propaganda.

Finally, in chapter 6, I return to Ellul's theology. By presentation and analysis of his concept of hope, his defense of nonviolence, and his theory of universal reconciliation, I demonstrate that Ellul's work—theological and philosophical—forms a coherent whole, united by his dialectical outlook.

1

———

Primary Influences on Ellul's Dialectical Worldview

Before delving into the details of Ellul's thought and works, we must seek to understand Ellul's background and central influences. What sort of family life shaped Ellul? From whom does Ellul derive his foundational ideas? How does he differ from these thinkers? In this chapter I will briefly discuss Ellul's biography as well as three main thinkers who influenced Ellul greatly: Marx, Kierkegaard, and Barth.

Brief Biographical Sketch of Jacques Ellul

Jacques Ellul was one of the first philosophers to devote his entire academic life to researching and writing on the effects of technology. Ellul published over fifty books in his lifetime and hundreds of essays. The common theme throughout all of his philosophical and theological work was technology (or, *la technique*). His first full work on the issue was *La Technique ou l'enjeu du siecle* published in France in 1954 (*The Technological Society*, 1964), and his last was *Le bluff technologique* in 1988 (*The Technological Bluff*, 1990).[1] In fact, Ellul stated in an 1981 interview, "I have not actually written a wide variety of books, but rather one long book in which each 'individual book' constitutes a chapter."[2] Other philosophers, such as Heidegger and Jaspers, had occasionally written on technology. However, Ellul was the first to focus consistently on technology throughout the entirety of his work.[3]

Ellul was born an only child in 1912 to Joseph and Martha Ellul in Bordeaux. Ellul's father was a nonpracticing Greek Orthodox Austrian, and his mother was a deeply religious Protestant of Jewish descent. Joseph forbade his wife to discuss religion with young Jacques, so that his son might freely decide for himself what he should believe.[4]

As a teenager, Ellul taught German, French, Latin, and Greek lessons in order to financially support his family, which had little money. In his late teens, Ellul underwent two conversions. The first came in 1930 when he borrowed *Das Kapital* from the library while attending the faculty of law. Ellul states, "In 1930 I discovered Marx. I read *Das Kapital* and I felt I understood everything. I felt that at last I knew why my father was out of work, at last I knew

---

1. *La Technique* was translated into English by John Wilkinson and published as *The Technological Society* (New York: Vintage) in 1964. *Le bluff technologique* was translated into English by Geoffrey W. Bromiley and published as *The Technological Bluff* (Grand Rapids, MI: Eerdmans) in 1990.

2. Jacques Ellul and Patrick Troude-Chastenet, *Jacques Ellul on Politics, Technology and Christianity* (Eugene, OR: Wipf & Stock, 1995), 12.

3. For a thorough discussion of the history of the philosophy of technology, with many references to Ellul, see Andrew Feenberg, *Questioning Technology* (London: Routledge, 2000).

4. The biographical information summarized in this section comes from Jacques Ellul, *Perspectives on Our Age: Jacques Ellul Speaks on His Life and His Work*, trans. Joachim Neugroschel (Toronto: Canadian Broadcasting Company, 1981); Jacques Ellul, *In Season, Out of Season: An Introduction to the Thought of Jacques Ellul*, trans. Lani K. Niles (San Francisco: Harper & Row, 1982); and Andrew Goddard, *Living the Word, Resisting the World: The Life and Thought of Jacques Ellul* (Carlisle, UK: Paternoster, 2002).

why we were destitute. I had finally found *the* explanation."[5] For Ellul, Marx was an astonishing discovery that suddenly explained the reality of the world both personally and universally. He read Marx's works not simply as an economic theory or an exposure of the mechanics of capitalism, but as an entire worldview that encapsulated the progression of history and shed light on his own family life. Later, Ellul would go on to teach university courses on Marx for thirty-five years.[6]

The second conversion was Ellul's encounter with the Christian faith. Ellul recognized early on that Marx's theory did not answer existential questions regarding life, death, love, and so on. At the age of twenty, Ellul embraced Christianity. He considered his conversion very personal and always refused to discuss it in detail. However, in a 1981 interview, he explained,

"I became a Christian in 1932. From that moment on I lived through the conflict and the contradiction between what became the center of my life—this faith, this reference to the Bible, which I henceforth read from a different perspective—and what I knew of Marx and did not wish to abandon."[7] From an early age, Ellul's thought was clearly shaped by Marx and by his Christian faith. These two factors, in combination with his encounter with Karl Barth, which will be discussed later, would shape Ellul's dialectical method.[8]

In 1936, Ellul received a doctorate in law from the University of Bordeaux. The following year he began teaching at Montpellier and the University of Strasbourg at Clermont-Ferrand. In 1940, he was fired because of his open resistance to Marshal Petain's government.

---

5. Ellul, *Perspectives on Our Age*, 5.
6. See Ellul's lengthy discussion of Marx's influence in Jacques Ellul, *Jesus and Marx: From Gospel to Ideology*, trans. Joyce Main Hanks (Grand Rapids: Eerdmans, 1988).
7. Ibid., 14.
8. Geoffrey Bromiley also maintains this in "Barth's Influence on Jacques Ellul," in *Jacques Ellul: Interpretive Essays*, ed. Clifford G. Christians and Jay M. Van Hook (Urbana: University of Illinois Press, 1981), 32–51.

At that time, Ellul and his wife, Yvette, moved back to Bordeaux. Later that year, the Germans arrested Ellul's father; Yvette was also targeted because she was born in Holland but carried a British passport. Ellul and his wife then escaped from Bordeaux into the Martres countryside for three years. During this time, Ellul pastored a small church of peasants and supported his family by growing corn and potatoes and tending sheep.[9]

In 1944, Ellul and his family returned to Bordeaux once again, where he served a two-year stint as deputy mayor. Three years later, he accepted a post at the Institute of Political Studies in Bordeaux—a position he would maintain until his retirement in 1980. In 1990, Ellul's wife died and in 1994 he passed away.[10]

Marx

It might be surprising for some to read Ellul's writings and find that Marxist themes permeate nearly all of his work. As one of Ellul's earliest intellectual influences, Marx played a significant role in Ellul's thought throughout his career. In Ellul's words,

> Thus, for me, Marx was an astonishing discovery of the reality of this world, which, at that time, few people condemned as the "capitalist" world. I plunged into Marx's thinking with an incredible joy. . . . As I became more and more familiar with Marxist thought, I discovered that his was not only an economic system, not only the profound exposure of the mechanics of capitalism. It was a total vision of the human race, society and history.[11]

This is not to say that Ellul is a Marxist. Ultimately, he accuses Marx of slipping into ideology and of making unfounded assumptions

---

9. For the history of Ellul's life, see Goddard, *Living the Word*.
10. Ibid., 37.
11. Ellul, *Perspectives on Our Age*, 5.

about the nature of history and society. Ellul is also, of course, quite critical of Marx's strictly materialistic interpretation of reality. Still, it would be difficult to overstate Marx's immense influence on Ellul. Therefore, in order to fully grasp Ellul's theology and philosophy, one needs to understand Marx's thought—particularly his prophetic critique of capitalism and his dialectical understanding of history. This crucial familiarity with Marx is neglected in much of the secondary scholarship on Ellul. In the following, I will discuss some central themes and their relation to Ellul's methodology and overall worldview, beginning with Marx's theory of history.[12]

The Dialectical Movement of History

Marx viewed history as moving in a linear direction. His historical materialism, one of the most contentious aspects of his thought, holds that material and economic forces determine individual and collective consciousness in a dialectical manner. For example, the economic sphere first shapes how individuals view the world, giving them a framework and value system; then, this value system is projected by the individual onto reality in order to make sense of it. This projection furthers harmful social and cultural spheres of class structure, as well as values and historical consciousness.[13]

Capitalism is a logical outcome of this dialectical process. According to Marx, history progresses in a dialectical manner back and forth through six successive stages of greater and lesser freedom. The first stage was a primitive form of communalism. With its lack of rigid class structure, the democratic nature of ancient tribes, and shared property, this era provided relative freedom to the individual.

---

12. A helpful work on Marx's understanding of history is Gerald Cohen, *Marx's Theory of History: A Defense* (Princeton: Princeton University Press, 2000).
13. See ibid., 28–55.

Eventually, this communalism gave rise to ancient societies that were heavily dependent on slaves. As illustrated in ancient Greece and Rome, this second stage included a strict class structure and was often totalitarian rather than democratic. Furthermore, these slave-based societies introduced the notions of private property and imperialism to the Western world.[14]

Feudalism necessarily followed primitive communalism and slave-based societies. This stage in history is seen quite clearly in the so-called Dark Ages and the medieval period of European history. It was during this era that slavery waned and aristocratic and theocratic regimes began to dominate. According to Marx, feudalism was a type of "proto-capitalism," and it gave rise to the industrial-technological revolutions of the seventeenth and eighteenth centuries, and concurrently to the rise of capitalism.[15]

The phase of history in which we are now living is the capitalist stage. For Marx, capitalism is an economic system motivated primarily by profit. As the driving force in the capitalist system, the need for greater profit gives rise to the production of more and more artificial needs. With the rise in artificial needs comes the rise in competition and the exploitation of the working class. For both Marx and Ellul, capitalism necessarily leads to less freedom and to the dehumanization of the individual. In Marx's view, however, capitalism will eventually break down and move into the next two successive periods of history: socialism and communism.[16]

14. Ibid.
15. Ibid.
16. Marx intentionally did not give a detailed description of socialism and communism, due to his belief that historical progress would ultimately determine what form each would take. He did, however, describe socialism and communism as the two successive stages of history immediately following capitalism. Socialism, for Marx, was characterized by the social ownership of private property. Communism was characterized by the complete abolition of private property and socioeconomic class distinctions. See "Communism" and "Socialism" in *A Dictionary of Marxist Thought*, ed. Tom Bottomore (Oxford: Blackwell, 1991).

While Ellul does not adopt Marx's deterministic view of history's next stages, he expands on and develops Marx's critique of capitalism. For Ellul, it is not only capitalism that leads to the loss of freedom and dehumanization, it is also *technique*. Perhaps the most important concept in Ellul's work, technique refers primarily two aspects of modernity. First, it refers to the modern mindset guided by a desire for greater efficiency, instrumentality, and control. Second, technique refers to the technological milieu of contemporary industrial society. Overall, technique is the pernicious force underlying modern forms of capitalism, socialism, and other economic systems. As the foundation beneath our values and intellect, technique leads to grave alienation. (More will be said about technique in a later chapter.)

Technique aside, Marx's theory of history—in which freedom varies between time periods—influenced Ellul greatly.[17] As we will see, this is echoed in Ellul's view that history and reality are comprised of what he called necessity (the realm of technique) and freedom (the realm of the spirit). Furthermore, Marx's dialectical view of history ends in freedom: a classless, stateless society. Similarly, for Ellul, history ends in universal salvation and redemption for all, the ultimate freedom. Alongside Marx's view of history, other aspects of his philosophy were also of key significance for Ellul: namely, Marx's theories of alienation and ideology, which drive his critique of capitalism.

---

17. Some thinkers, such as Karl Popper, are primarily occupied with the falsification of Marx's theories; see Popper's *Hegel, Marx, and the Aftermath*, vol. 2, *The Open Society and Its Enemies* (Princeton: Princeton University Press, 1971). Ellul is not concerned with this approach. See Ellul's discussion of Marx's claims in Jacques Ellul, *What I Believe*, trans. Geoffrey W. Bromiley (London: Marshall, Morgan, & Scott, 1989), 89–103.

Alienation and Ideology

It is important to realize that for Ellul, Marxism is not to be confused with Soviet or French communism. These forms of communism, according to Ellul, are ideologies that have strayed far from the work of Marx.[18] Authentic Marxism, in Ellul's view, is a philosophy that unites with the poor and works to overcome ideology and alienation. Siding with the oppressed and exploited is a hallmark of Ellul's work, as it was with Marx. Both agree that the capitalist system necessarily oppresses and exploits. Furthermore, it causes individuals to live in a state of alienation.[19]

Marx understood alienation to be a state of being in which individuals were separated from their true nature, others, the fruit of their labor, the means of production, and the natural world.[20] More importantly, the essential characteristic of alienation is a lack of freedom. Marx states, "Just as alienated labor transforms the *free* and self-directed activity into a means, so it transforms the species life of man into a means of physical existence."[21]

For Marx and Ellul, one of the consequences of the capitalist system—which is itself a consequence of technique—is alienation, that is, a loss of freedom.[22] Individuals no longer have the choice to work or not, to pay their bills or not, to get involved in politics or not; the choice has been made. They are necessarily involved in a system that excludes freedom. This does not mean that freedom is unobtainable. For Ellul, capitalism—or any other economic system—can coexist

18. The influential Frankfurt School philosopher and Marxist, Erich Fromm, argues in favor of this line of thinking. See his excellent book, *Marx's Concept of Man* (New York: Continuum, 2004).
19. See Ellul, *Jesus and Marx.*
20. See Marx's "Economic and Philosophical Manuscripts" in *Marx's Concept of Man,* ed. Erich Fromm (New York: Continuum, 2004), 73–151.
21. Ibid., 85; italics added.
22. Ellul states, "We must recognize the truth in Karl Marx's observation that money in the capitalist system, leads to alienation," Jacques Ellul, *Money and Power,* trans. LaVonne Neff (Downers Grove, IL: InterVarsity, 1984), 20.

with freedom, but only if one lives a life according to the Spirit, as a follower of Christ.[23] (This will be explained in further detail when we specifically discuss Ellul's theology.)

The concept of alienation is of primary importance in Ellul's principle work on ethics, *The Ethics of Freedom*. Ellul observes that alienation is found throughout the Judeo-Christian Scriptures as well as human history. According to Ellul, alienation is a type of slavery. This is not a literal conception of slavery, as was the case with the ancient Israelites or in ancient Greece, but a spiritual and psychological state of being. He explains, "Alienation means being possessed externally by another and belonging to him. It also means being self-alienated, other than oneself, transformed into another."[24] This alienation is experienced at a subjective level and, for each individual, is unique.[25]

For Ellul, there are three common factors involved in alienation, which characterize the state of being in the realm of technique. First, there is a loss of autonomy. This is seen clearly in the necessary involvement of individuals in society. As stated earlier, there is no longer a choice to be part of the economic, political, or technological systems; one is already involved. Second, true knowledge has been replaced with ideology, or false consciousness. Evidence of this is found in various religious and political ideologies that abundantly flourish—often without question—in many sectors of society. Finally, individuals are no longer able to think for themselves. Following the first two factors involved in alienation, many have lost the ability to think critically and analytically.[26]

---

23. A full account of this is found in Jacques Ellul, *The Ethics of Freedom*, trans. Geoffrey W. Bromiley (Grand Rapids: Eerdmans, 1972).
24. Ibid., 24.
25. For a fuller discussion of the subjectivity of alienation, see Ellul, *The Ethics of Freedom*, chapter 1.
26. Ibid., 29.

All of these factors are related to another significant concept in both the writings of Marx and the work of Ellul: ideology. As stated earlier, ideology is false consciousness, or a lack of true knowledge concerning reality. Moreover, ideology is an inherited, unquestioned, unchallenged belief system. It is the opposite of self-reflection or self-examination, and is a blind, dogmatic faith in a particular system of thought. Two spheres of society where ideology is the most common are the political and the religious.[27]

What is the solution to alienation and ideology? For Marx, it will come from the revolution of the proletariat and the next stages of history. For Ellul, alienation and ideology can only be overcome by submitting to the Spirit. Through Christ, one can live in the world, but also be free of the necessities that are forced on the individual. Ellul's conception of freedom through Christ will be explained in detail later. For now, it is imperative that we recognize the vital influence of Marx upon Ellul. This is a central key to understanding Ellul's philosophy and theology. For brevity's sake, we will leave our discussion of Marx by reminding the reader of the three primary ideas that Ellul takes from Marx: his critique of capitalism, his concept of alienation, and his theory of ideology. These are crucial to Ellul's sociological and philosophical discussions of technique.

Kierkegaard

In contrast with Marx, Kierkegaard's relation to Ellul is far better known and documented.[28] This is partly due to the "safe" nature of Kierkegaard among evangelical Protestants, who seem to be Ellul's

---

27. Ellul discusses ideology at length throughout *The Ethics of Freedom*.
28. For a discussion of the relationship between Kierkegaard and Ellul, see Vernard Eller, "Ellul and Kierkegaard: Closer than Brothers," in Christians and Van Hook, *Jacques Ellul: Interpretive Essays*, 52–66.

primary readers. Kierkegaard is viewed in this light because he had relatively little to say about politics and economics, which are controversial and touchy subjects with many evangelicals today. As Marx had a great influence on Ellul's *sociological* hermeneutics, Kierkegaard had an immense influence on his *theological* hermeneutics.[29] Concerning Kierkegaard, Ellul states, "I was captivated by Kierkegaard because what he said went straight to my soul. Quite abruptly I realized that reasoning with the intellect alone and reasoning based on living experience are simply worlds apart. My passion for Kierkegaard . . . has remained with me throughout my life."[30]

Kierkegaard was the essential dialectical thinker. Throughout nearly all of his work, he continually emphasizes the dialectical relationships between various aspects of reality, including objective and subjective truth, time and eternity, God and humans, Christendom and Christianity, the crowd and the individual, and so on. Kierkegaard understands dialectic to be a necessary theoretical tool for understanding the world and one's place in it. Further, he sees reality as being constituted by opposing dialectical categories of existence (e.g., faith and reason, eternity and time, etc.), which require the individual to constantly live in an existential tension.[31]

---

29. According to Ellul, he read every work of Marx and all of Kierkegaard's writings. These were the only two authors about whom he could say this. See Goddard, *Living the Word*, 16.
30. Ellul and Troude-Chastenet, *Jacques Ellul on Politics*, 54.
31. Many of the distinctions that Kierkegaard made, Ellul updates and revises. For example, Kierkegaard's distinction between Christendom and Christianity is updated in Ellul's work *The Subversion of Christianity*. Also, Kierkegaard's distinction between time and eternity is utilized uniquely in *Reason for Being*.

Dialectical Anthropology: Freedom and Necessity

Perhaps the most striking symmetry between the work of Kierkegaard and Ellul is found in their philosophical anthropology. For both thinkers, a human being is a combination of freedom (spirit) and necessity (matter). These are contradictory elements and in constant tension, but they can and must coexist. Throughout his work, Kierkegaard presupposes this relationship, as does Ellul.

In *Either/Or: A Fragment of Life* and in *Concluding Unscientific Postscript*, Kierkegaard discusses the four stages or spheres of human existence: aesthetic, ethical, religiousness A, and religiousness B.[32] The aesthetic stage of human existence is characterized by a preoccupation with immediate sensual pleasure and satisfaction. The ethical stage is distinguished by a strong sense of duty and moral obligation to others and oneself. Religiousness A is a spiritual frame of mind found in various cultures that recognizes the divine in nature and oneself. Religiousness B, however, refers specifically to the Christian faith that, in Kierkegaard's view, is unique and only accessible through revelation. For Kierkegaard, at different times in one's life, one may oscillate between these various spheres of existence. The most important feature of these stages is this: all aspects of human existence, from the most banal, to the most spiritual, require a *choice* from the individual. Choice unites the individual with the world; it unites freedom with necessity, the abstract and spiritual with the concrete and material. Kierkegaard views humans as living constantly within this dialectical tension. Humans live on the boundary between freedom and necessity, and through their choices, move in the direction of one or the other, to a greater

---

32. Søren Kierkegaard, *Either/Or: A Fragment of Life*, trans. Alistair Hannay (New York: Penguin, 1992), 381–591. *Concluding Unscientific Postscript to Philosophical Fragment*, trans. Howard V. Hong and Edna H. Hong (Princeton: Princeton University Press, 1992), 432–525.

or lesser degree.[33] Kierkegaard explains, "Flesh and blood or the sensate—and spirit are opposites. Thus it is easy to see what it is to be spirit, that it is to will voluntarily that which flesh and blood shrink from most—for spirit and flesh and blood are just as opposite as, to use an old adage, the ends of a sack."[34] We see that for Kierkegaard, humans are made up of two components: spirit and flesh. (In other places he refers to this distinction in terms of transcendence and immanence, or possibility and actuality.) These refer to the paradoxical constituents of human existence—the fact that humans are both immaterial and material. It is important to understand that for Kierkegaard, this is not simply an abstract way of viewing reality. Rather, these are concrete, qualitative categories of existence.[35]

Ellul inherits this dialectical logic from Kierkegaard, and applies it to the realms of technique and the spirit. However, in Ellul's theology, instead of choice, hope is the unifying factor. Furthermore, many additional Kierkegaardian tenets continue to play central roles in Ellul's work. This will become clearer when the details of Ellul's theology are discussed.[36]

Paradox

Another central idea in the work of Kierkegaard that Ellul adopts and develops is the notion of paradox. A paradox is an apparent contradiction, containing a truth. According to Kierkegaard, reality is comprised of factors that are contradictory, yet still coexist.

33. See discussions by Kierkegaard of the stages of life in his *Either/Or: A Fragment of Life* and in his *Journals and Papers*, trans. H. Hong and E. Hong (Bloomington: Indiana University Press, 1967–1978), volume 4.
34. Kierkegaard, *Journals and Papers*, 4:250.
35. A helpful work on Kierkegaard's logical categories is Arnold B. Come's *Trendelenburg's Influence on Kierkegaard's Modal Categories* (Montreal: Inter Editions, 1991).
36. Ellul's fullest account of hope is in his work *Hope in Time of Abandonment*, trans. C. Edward Hopkin (New York: Seabury, 1963).

Humans are excellent examples of paradoxes, being made up of spirit and matter. But for Kierkegaard, the *ultimate paradox* is the "God-man": Jesus Christ. Kierkegaard maintains that Christ is the greatest paradox because he was and is fully God and fully human, immanent and transcendent, temporal and eternal. Following this, Kierkegaard makes the distinction between quantitative logic and qualitative logic. The former refers to a logic which is limited to empirically verifiable results. Qualitative logic, conversely, refers to a type of reasoning which transcends the superficiality of physicalism; it is a logic which recognizes the subjective and often paradoxical nature of human experience—a logic which embraces, rather than dismisses, mystery. Kierkegaard writes, "Christianity entered into the world not to be understood, but to be existed in. This cannot be expressed more strongly than by the fact that Christianity itself proclaims itself to be a paradox. . . . That the Son of God became man is certainly the highest metaphysical and religious paradox."[37] Christ as paradox permeates both Kierkegaard's and Ellul's work. Not only does Christ signify a reality that transcends human logic and thus cannot be discussed fully in human language; Christ also represents the prototype of the dialectical nature of reality. This conception also greatly influenced Karl Barth, who is the third main influence upon Ellul.[38]

Barth

According to Ellul, one of the most instrumental thinkers to shape his dialectical worldview after Marx and Kierkegaard was Karl Barth. It was through Barth that Ellul discovered a unique way of interpreting the Judeo-Christian Scriptures, a new hermeneutical path that would

37. Kierkegaard, *Journals and Papers*, 3:404–1.
38. See Bromiley, "Barth's Influence on Jacques Ellul."

remain a constant element of Ellul's theological work.[39] According to Ellul scholar Patrick Chastenet,

> Barth's thinking enabled Ellul to avoid the "either-or" dilemma of the non-believers, and helped him handle the "already" and the "not-yet," in other words the promise and its fulfillment. But above all, the Swiss theologian enabled Ellul to understand the central idea of the Biblical message essentially formulated in dialectic terms: the free determination of man in the decision of God.[40]

Kierkegaard had already presented a dialectical view of reality that took into account contradictory factors such as freedom and determinism. Barth, however, developed and expanded this dialectic in articulate and insightful ways, which confirmed and encouraged Ellul's dialectical proclivities. Perhaps the most influential aspect of Barth's hermeneutics, however, was his theory of dialectical inclusion.[41]

Dialectical Inclusion

Throughout his work, Barth highlighted theological contradictions and paradoxes. He also worked to demonstrate that in Christianity, every aspect of reality is taken into account. Furthermore, each aspect is related to every other aspect: apparent opposites, such as faith and reason, impossibility and possibility, separation and reconciliation, are all seen as dynamic, interrelated aspects of the whole in Christianity.[42]

Scholar George Hunsinger describes Barth by way of analogy:

---

39. Ellul and Troude-Chastenet, *Jacques Ellul on Politics*, 5.
40. Ibid.
41. A thoughtful discussion of dialectical inclusion is found in George Hunsinger, *How to Read Karl Barth: The Shape of His Theology* (New York: Oxford University Press, 1991), part 1.
42. Karl Barth, *Church Dogmatics: A Selection*, trans. and ed. G. W. Bromiley (Louisville: Westminster John Knox, 1961), 29–35.

Like Mozart, Barth preferred to work with sharply contrasting themes resolved in higher unities and marked by regular recapitulations. Themes or fragments of themes, once dominant, are constantly carried forward into new settings where other themes take the ascendancy. Materials are constantly being combined, broken up, recombined, and otherwise brought into contrapuntal relationship. . . . The task of theology, in this view, is to describe as carefully as possible, from many different angles, the network of interconnections which constitute its . . . totality.[43]

This analogy is also applicable to the work of Ellul, with his notable inspiration from Barth. Barth's (and Ellul's) methodology, which seeks to show interconnections and strives toward synthesis, is known as dialectical inclusion.

Ultimately, for Ellul, this approach maintains that all aspects of reality are united in Christ and the Trinity, both of which unite all opposites. Furthermore, for Barth and for Ellul, God and reality can only be fully understood through a Trinitarian lens. This lens is a central hermeneutical tool that Ellul inherits from Barth.[44] Ellul's theology and even his philosophy are guided by this dialectical principle of inclusion, which will be expanded upon in more detail in a later chapter.[45]

It is of the utmost importance to recognize the influence of Marx, Kierkegaard, and Barth on the thought of Jacques Ellul. When the guidance of these thinkers is not recognized, Ellul's work may seem shallow and lacking in foundation. In contrast, a familiarity with Marx, Kierkegaard, and Barth's thought and impact on Ellul will

---

43. Hunsinger, *How to Read Karl Barth*, 28–29.
44. Concerning Barth's view of the trinity, Hunsinger writes, "As revealed in Trinitarian self-disclosure, God's identity in and with Jesus Christ is ineffaceably mysterious—concealed in the midst of disclosure and disclosed in the midst of concealment. God's self-disclosure is thus at the same time God's self-concealment," *How to Read Karl Barth*, 37. Ellul would most certainly agree with this description.
45. See Jacques Ellul, "On Dialectic," in Christians and Van Hook, *Jacques Ellul: Interpretive Essays*, 291–308.

make his work appear coherent and more complete. Furthermore, one must always keep in mind Ellul's conception of dialectic. This is the theoretical framework upon which his entire system is based.

2

———

Ellul's Dialectical Worldview

After examination of the background and influences that shaped Ellul's thought, we can now take a closer look at his dialectical method. Here, we not only find echoes of his past studies and experiences, but the many ways his methodology permeates his unique scholarship.

Ellul's philosophy and theology can be difficult to penetrate. Not only is he overly verbose and repetitive in many of his writings, he also occasionally contradicts himself. Ellul recognized these tendencies, but did not work to repair or clarify them.[1] After all, the very presence of these apparent stumbling blocks—of tension and contraction—holds the unifying guide to Ellul's work: his dialectic. The foremost Ellul scholar, David W. Gill, writes:

> If there is one characteristic which permeates every thought and every analysis rendered by Jacques Ellul, it is that his work is thoroughly

1. Like Kierkegaard, Ellul often employs paradoxical language and seemingly contradictory concepts. See Jacques Ellul, "On Dialectic," in *Jacques Ellul: Interpretive Essays*, ed. Clifford G. Christians and Jay M. Van Hook (Urbana: University of Illinois Press, 1981), 291–308.

dialectical. . . . Contradiction, opposition, and paradox are ever-present in anything Ellul has in view. Axiomatic-deductive, linear logic is rejected. Rationalistic "scientism"–the worship of empirically demonstrable facts (and nothing else)–is damned. Understanding, whether of Christianity or society, results from a true perception of the various antithetical factors and forces at work.[2]

Dialectic is the skeleton key to Ellul's philosophy and theology; it is the hermeneutical principle by which one can clearly and coherently explore all of Ellul's work. In fact, Ellul's conception of dialectic is both a worldview and a methodology. I will now explain this by discussing the key ideas in Ellul's insightful and often-neglected essay "On Dialectic."

Dialectic in History

Dialectic comes from the Greek word *dialegesthai*, which means "to dialogue."[3] It also connotes contradiction. There have been many competing definitions of dialectic. From Socrates and Plato to Kant, Hegel and Marx, various intellectuals have arrived at different conclusions concerning dialectic. As previously mentioned, Ellul's notion of dialectic stems from Marx, Kierkegaard, and Barth. While Ellul shares many similarities with these thinkers, he extends and develops the concept of dialectic in a new and comprehensive manner.[4]

According to Ellul, reality (the external world) is something with which humans enter into a dialogue. Reality exists as both separate and not-separate for humans; it is knowable and comprehensible, yet

2. David W. Gill, *The Word of God in the Ethics of Jacques Ellul* (London: Scarecrow, 1984), 157.
3. David Roochnik, *Retrieving the Ancients* (Oxford: Blackell, 2004), 7.
4. A helpful overview of the various definitions of dialectic we find in the aforementioned thinkers can be found in Errol E. Harris, *Formal, Transcendental, and Dialectical Thinking: Logic and Reality* (Albany: State University of New York, 1987).

also unknowable and incomprehensible. These fundamental aspects of reality are always inextricably linked. Thus, the basic structure of reality is dialectical.[5]

Ellul maintains that reality includes the logical and the illogical, the rational and the irrational. For example, if one looks at the world through the eyes of a twentieth-century scientist, then one will understand the rational side of reality; it is seen as causal, linear, and orderly. Conversely, if one looks at the world through the eyes of an existentialist, one will understand the irrational or absurd side of reality, which is seen as noncausal, nonlinear, and disorderly. The important point is this: reality contains both aspects—the sensical and the nonsensical, or as Ellul puts it, the "Yes and the No."[6] Ellul explains,

> Put a positive charge next to a negative one and you have a powerful flash, but this is a new phenomenon excluding neither the positive nor the negative. Can we be sure, then, that positive and negative factors in thought cancel one another, that one cannot maintain a No at the same time as a Yes? But these two questions show at once that there are two aspects of dialectic—a dialectic of ideas, but perhaps also a dialectic of facts, of reality.[7]

Ellul goes on to argue that reality (which is not limited to the physical, external world, but includes human thought, ideas) is comprised of contradictory factors that coexist. It necessarily follows that a comprehensive philosophical or theological system must take into account both constituents of reality: rational and irrational. Ellul agrees with Plato's statement, "The dialectician is one who sees the totality."[8]

---

5. Ellul, "On Dialectic."
6. Ibid., 293.
7. Ibid.
8. Plato, *Republic*, book 4, as quoted by Ellul, "On Dialectic," 293.

Ellul argues that there have been two primary interpretations of the nature of reality, beginning with the pre-Socratics. The first view, influenced by thinkers like Heraclitus, states that the nature of reality is always in a state of flux; therefore, true (immutable) knowledge can never be obtained. This perspective influenced many in Western thought, primarily Nietzsche and the existentialists. The second perspective, influenced by Parmenides, maintains that reality is unchanging and static. This view has also been extremely influential, particularly among many Platonists and certain religious thinkers. Ellul believes that both strands of thought are correct. Reality is comprised of changing and unchanging factors.[9] This belief is of utmost importance to remember when reading Ellul's philosophical and theological writings.

David Lovekin, in his book *Technique, Discourse, and Consciousness*, argues that Ellul's dialectic is informed primarily by Hegel.[10] It would be more accurate to state that Ellul was influenced primarily by Kierkegaard's dialectical method, which was informed by and shares similarities with Hegel's system, but also has key differences. Ellul is sympathetic to Hegel's logic, while also critical of it. He argues that Hegel's system requires all aspects of reality to be in a state of change. In other words, if two factors ultimately end in a synthesis, then they cannot remain unchanged—change is necessitated through the final movement. In contrast, Ellul believes that reality consists of factors that are ultimately synthesized, and it also consists of factors that remain separate and distinct.[11] For this reason, Ellul rejects Hegel's

9. Ellul states, "Reality includes not only contradictory elements, but also a permanent process of change" ("On Dialectic," 294).
10. David Lovekin, *Technique, Discourse, and Consciousness: An Introduction to the Philosophy of Jacques Ellul* (London: Associated University Press, 1991), 24.
11. Ellul, "On Dialectic." See Lovekin's discussion of Ellul and Hegel in *Technique, Discourse, and Consciousness*, 1–20. Ellul's is clearly a Kierkegaardian critique of Hegel's logic. However, Ellul's reading of Hegel is questionable. It is possible that Ellul's main source of knowledge concerning Hegel was via Kierkegaard. For an excellent overview of Kierkegaard's logic and critique

logic. He states, "One might also think of a living organism in which forces are constantly at work. Some of these forces tend to keep the organism alive, while others tend to destroy and disaggregate it; and at each instant there is a synthesis of the two groups of forces that produces the state of the live body at a given moment."[12] In this example, Ellul maintains that there are three factors that comprise reality: positive, negative, and a combination of positive and negative. This certainly sounds very Hegelian, but Ellul insists that his logic is more accurate and comprehensive, and thus ultimately quite different, than Hegel's.[13]

Ellul was also greatly influenced by Marx's conception of dialectic. As we have seen, Marx argued that history was moving dialectically from societies ruled by the bourgeoisie to societies ruled by the proletariat. He believed that the historical process evolves by way of a series of conflicting factors and ultimately ends with a new and more beneficial human society. For this reason, Marx (and Ellul) maintained that history can only be understood by looking at the conflicts within society. These represent the inherent tensions that force change, development, and social progress.

Like Hegel and Marx, Ellul believes there are contradictory factors that exist inherently in society. Hegel believed that history was producing better societies; Marx argued that history would ultimately end in a peaceful, communal state of existence for all. While Ellul appreciates both of these views, he does not accept these conclusions. Instead, he maintains that the very idea of "progress" is itself an ideology.[14]

---

of Hegel, see Arnold B. Come's *Trendelenburg's Influence on Kierkegaard's Modal Categories* (Montreal: Inter Editions, 1991).

12. Ellul, "On Dialectic," 294.

13. Jacques Ellul, *What I Believe*, trans. Geoffrey W. Bromiley (London: Marshall, Morgan, & Scott, 1989), 31.

14. Ibid., 34. Concerning Ellul's view of Hegel's dialectic, David W. Gill writes, "In general terms, Ellul agrees with Hegel's description of the 'positivity of the negativity.' That is, the negative

Furthermore, Ellul believes that Hegel and Marx both fall into a sort of deterministic mindset that excludes the dialectical category of possibility. According to Ellul, the category of possibility includes both freedom and necessity as essential components of reality. Because of possibility, the future can never be known in advance. Thus, Ellul argues that Hegel, Marx, and many of their followers are misguided.[15]

Hegel does a superb job of synthesizing opposites and reconciling differences. In fact, Hegel's approach seems more coherent than Ellul's. But Ellul insists that reality's constituents cannot always be synthesized; indeed, quite often they cannot be. Ellul's philosophical and sociological methodology is one of a phenomenologist. He simply describes reality as it presents itself to consciousness.[16] This is one reason why Ellul does not try to iron out the contradictions and paradoxes that present themselves. Rather, he embraces reality as it appears: both rational and irrational.[17] Later, however, we will see that Ellul is closer to Hegel than he admits.

pole of any dialectic has a positive value. The end of dialectical contradiction and interaction is the end of life, whether on an individual or a social level. Life implies movement, change, and development through the interplay of opposing forces. Change in this manner is not necessarily progress. On this point Ellul disagrees with both Hegel and Marx" (*The Word of God in the Ethics of Jacques Ellul*), 158.

15. Ellul, *What I Believe*, 30–34, 294–96.

16. Ellul maintains this in ibid., 29–34. Ellul rarely refers to reality as *dialectical*, but instead he simply refers to it as *dialectic*. This is intentional. Ellul believes that if reality were truly dialectical, this would always entail synthesis to a greater or lesser degree. But for Ellul, synthesis is not a necessary component of our present reality. It is a possibility, but not a necessity. For Ellul, dialectic may or may not encompass a dialectical process; thus, he employs the term *dialectic* rather than *dialectical*.

17. Wilkinson correctly argues this point in his introduction to Jacques Ellul, *The Technological Society*, trans. John Wilkinson (New York: Vintage, 1964).

Dialectic in the Hebrew and Christian Scriptures

It is necessary to understand Ellul's methodological approach to the Hebrew and Christian Scriptures in order to fully grasp the depth of his theological writings. According to Ellul, dialectic appears first in ancient Hebrew thought. He maintains that in the Hebrew Scriptures there is a clear presentation of human consciousness coming to terms with the often contradictory nature of the spiritual and material worlds. Ellul does not argue that there is an explicit theory of dialectic found in ancient Judaism, but that the principle of dialectic unambiguously appears in this tradition.[18] He argues, "The Hebrews formulated God's revelation dialectically without examining what they were doing intellectually, without working out the noetic aspect."[19] In other words, Ellul argues that the Hebrews experienced reality as it presented itself to them: as a dialectic. They did not rationalize it away or deny its contradictions. Rather, they embraced the paradoxical nature of reality and described it. In this sense they were some of the first phenomenologists.[20]

Ellul discusses several examples of dialectic in the Hebrew Scriptures in order to support his claim. First, the ancient Hebrews state that a unique, transcendent Being exists outside human history, and at the same time inside human history. They describe their God as one who actively moves through history with them. Conversely, God is described as not being restricted to the temporal realm. This Being is known and unknown to them; he is one who participates, and one who does not. God is an active dialogue partner and a silent dialogue partner. This dialectical relation culminates in the incarnation of Jesus Christ, whom a small group of Hebrews believed to be fully God and fully human, fully transcendent and immanent.

18. Ellul, *What I Believe*, 35–42.
19. Ibid., 36.
20. Ibid., 37.

Ellul goes on to argue that in Christianity, we encounter the most fully developed understanding of dialectic, because of its insistence upon the dual nature of Christ.[21]

Second, Ellul maintains that dialectic is evident in recurring processes located in the Hebrew and Christian Scriptures. For example, the process of "command– disobedience– judgment– reconciliation" is a dialectical movement that is found throughout these sacred texts.[22] This is clearly illustrated in the story of the Exodus. Here, the Hebrew people fail to follow the command of God (disobedience), they are sentenced to slavery in Egypt (judgment), and finally they are reconciled to God as they return to the Holy Land. In the Christian Scriptures this process also continually takes place. For example, Jesus's parable of the prodigal son clearly demonstrates this dialectical process. According to Ellul, the sacred narratives within the Judeo-Christian Scriptures always end in reconciliation. Furthermore, Ellul maintains that *all* things ultimately end in reconciliation.[23] It is clear that this reconciliation might also be called a synthesis. So, despite his insistence that his dialectical methodology is fundamentally different than Hegel's, we can see that they are more similar than not.

A third aspect of dialectic found in the Scriptures, according to Ellul, is the relation of the part to the whole. According to Ellul, the remnant is always dialectically related to the sum, and vice versa. It follows that reconciliation is always the outcome for the part as well as the whole. He explains,

---

21. Ibid., 35–42.
22. Ibid. It is important to recognize that the Christian Scriptures for Ellul arise out of the Hebrew worldview. First-century Christians were primarily Jewish. Thus, Ellul does not see a sharp division between the Hebrew Scriptures and the New Testament. He sees similar patterns of thought and dialectic in both.
23. Ibid., 35.

The election of the chosen people implies the reintegration of the human race. The election of the remnant implies the reintegration of all Israel. The election of Jesus implies the reintegration of the remnant. From the biblical standpoint, then, the development of judgment is never a mechanism to separate the good and the bad (as though these were simply rejected, excluded, eliminated, etc.). It is an election of the bad mediated by the good.[24]

Here, Ellul is arguing that the part and the whole can never be understood apart from each other: what applies to one applies to both. For Ellul, dialectic necessarily involves a constant tension between the part and the whole, but it always ends as one—part and whole together in fulfillment and reconciliation.[25]

Following this dialectical path of reasoning, Ellul maintains that salvation is universal. In other words, the process of being reunited with God is the logical and necessary outcome of the historical process. Universal salvation is certainly not a dominant belief within Christian circles, and many have rejected Ellul's theological works because of his affirmation of this doctrine. In any case, Ellul remained firm and fast in his conviction: all things—humans, animals, the earth—will ultimately be reunited with God. More will be said concerning Ellul's universalism in a later chapter of this work.[26]

As a final summary, dialectic in Ellul's work includes the following principles:

1. Reality includes a permanent process of change.
2. Reality includes contradictory elements that cannot be synthesized.

24. Ibid., 301.
25. See Jacques Ellul, *The Humiliation of the Word*, trans. Joyce Main Hanks (Grand Rapids: Eerdmans, 1985), 268–69.
26. It would be a mistake to take Ellul's theology to simply be an updated version of Augustinianism. Ellul's dialectical conception of reality and his universalism seem to situate him on the periphery or even outside Augustinian circles of thought.

3. Reality includes noncontradictory elements that can be synthesized.
4. All constituents of reality end in reconciliation.

These key principles comprise Ellul's dialectical worldview.[27] One might object to this schema by arguing that if principle four is correct, then principle two cannot be (or vice versa). Even though all things end in reconciliation, Ellul maintains that there are certain constituents of reality that cannot be reconciled at this time or by human effort; for example, the technological realm and the transcendent realm, or human and divine realms. This is clearly demonstrated in the two veins of Ellul's writings. His philosophical and sociological works portray a world dominated by technique, artificiality, and necessity, whereas his theological work presents a reality constituted by spirit and freedom. Both strands of Ellul's work represent a reality that exists in dialectical tension, but, according to Ellul, neither of these realities can be reconciled by humanity.[28] Yet this is not to say that there will never be reconciliation. Ellul firmly believes the opposite.

> It is absolutely necessary that this dialectical factor exist. If the technological system is total, then this factor has to exist *outside* it. But only the transcendent can be outside it. For me then, the transcendent is, in the concrete situation which technology has put us, the necessary condition for the continuation of life, the unfolding of history.[29]

In this passage, it is clear that even though irreconcilable factors exist, the transcendent will ultimately make possible a future state of existence that will reconcile all constituents of reality. Ellul does not clearly describe this state of existence, or how to get there, but he

---

27. See Ellul, "On Dialectic"; Ellul, *What I Believe*, 29–34, 214–23.
28. Ellul, *What I Believe*, 42.
29. Ibid., 308.

nonetheless argues that it is a logical and necessary entailment of the dialectical nature of reality.

In conclusion, in Ellul's understanding of dialectic, he views reality as made up of contradictory forces always in tension. At the same time, he believes that history is moving toward a goal of reconciliation. He states,

> There is always *one* history (not two, a secular and a sacred), made up of conjunction, opposition, and contradiction of the independent work of man and the "relational" work of God. All history in every real and concrete event is an expression of this double force. . . . As in the dialectical crisis, no one factor is suppressed, but both are integrated into a synthesis.[30]

It is clear from these statements that Ellul's theory of dialectic dominates his worldview. Furthermore, it is impossible to have a worldview without it affecting one's methodology. Thus, both the worldview and the method of Ellul's work are dominated by dialectic.

Dialectic as the Key to Understanding
Ellul's Philosophical and Theological Work

As stated earlier, many who read Ellul's work are not familiar with his dialectic. I firmly believe that this lack of familiarity has led many to become alienated from either Ellul's philosophical or his theological work. It is my goal to not only present key ideas found in Ellul's writings, but also to continually demonstrate how dialectic is the thread that unites Ellul's entire system together and is the key to understanding all of his philosophical and theological work. In the following, I will briefly give some examples of dialectic in Ellul's

30. Ellul, *The Humiliation of the Word*, 304.

work, which will make clear the necessity of being familiar with it when approaching his writings.

Ellul's best-known book is *The Technological Society* (*La Technique*), first published in 1954. This brilliant work systematically describes and analyzes the role of technique in the modern world. Many have interpreted this book as taking a pessimistic attitude toward technique, but Ellul argued that it was primarily a phenomenological work that aimed at describing the underbelly of the technological realm. In it, he primarily presents the negative effects technique has had on society, human consciousness, and nature. Technique, according to Ellul, dominates and controls everything that crosses its path; it subsumes and transforms all that touches it. This leaves technique looking like a monolithic, one-dimensional entity. But this is not the case. When we approach technique in a dialectical manner, we see that technique can never be fully understood without a comprehension of those opposing factors that exist in tension with it.[31]

For example, according to Ellul, technique strips humans of freedom. It demands specific rules of efficiency that govern all arenas of contemporary society. Once technique takes over, humans must submit to it and end up existing in a realm of necessity. However, the opposing factor that exists in tension with necessity is freedom. (Necessity and freedom represent two contradictory factors that partially comprise dialectic.) Technique represents a determined milieu that excludes free agency. Conversely, out of their desire and in their search for freedom, humans continue to look to technique for fulfillment. In other words, human freedom—in part—propagates technique while at the same time limiting itself to the realm of necessity.[32]

31. See Ellul, *The Technological Society,* 79–135.

A concrete example of this dialectical relationship can be seen by looking at the Internet. The World Wide Web provides the user with the ability to cross geographic and cultural boundaries quite easily and efficiently. It also enables the user to freely and instantly communicate with friends and loved ones. So, in a sense, technique is creating a society where more people have this freedom. However, according to Ellul, technique is only creating the freedom necessary to submit to itself. That is, the freedom offered by the Internet requires a computer, an Internet connection, and the knowledge to use it. This is a limited freedom. True freedom would not involve one becoming ensnared by a technological device. This example illustrates the need to understand the dialectically opposed but interrelated factors involving the categories of necessity and freedom.

In his work *The Ethics of Freedom* (1976), Ellul offers one theological counterpart to much of his sociological and philosophical work concerning technique. According to Ellul, true freedom is only found in the Transcendent. Humans in modern society are not free because they have allowed themselves to be controlled by technique. Ellul calls this "slavery" or "alienation."[33] He writes, "He (the worker) is a man completely shut off from himself. He has become an appendix of the machine. . . . Alienation today is not that of misery or social inferiority. It has taken a more profound and total sense. It extends to more than the economic sphere. It is a psychological or moral problem."[34] The reality of alienation is a result of the realm of necessity, which itself is a characteristic of technique. Technique may provide individuals with limited freedom, but according to Ellul, they are still alienated.

---

32. See Ellul, "On Dialectic"; Daniel B. Clendenin, *Theological Method in the Theology of Jacques Ellul* (Lanham, MD: University Press of America, 1987), 26–42.
33. Jacques Ellul, *The Ethics of Freedom*, trans. Geoffrey W. Bromiley (Grand Rapids: Eerdmans, 1972), 23.
34. Ibid., 26.

For Ellul, the sphere of necessity makes way for the possibility of freedom. However, this possibility is not yet a complete actuality. Only through a relationship with the Transcendent can one break free from necessity and enter into complete freedom. The Transcendent is fully manifested in Christ. Furthermore, Christ embodies all four principles of dialectic. First, God, in Christ, is continually involved in a process of creative self-revelation. In other words, God is always acting in new and unpredictable ways; God is both immutable and mutable. Second, Christ is comprised of contradictory factors that cannot be synthesized: the human and the divine. Third, Christ's dual nature demonstrates that the material and the spiritual can, at some level, be synthesized into a whole. Finally, Christ's life and resurrection bring reconciliation to all things.[35]

The doctrine of the Trinity is central to Ellul's worldview and shapes nearly all of his work—philosophical and theological. We should remember that, for Ellul, the Trinity is a concrete manifestation of dialectic, and is also the fullest revelation of God. In fact, Ellul argues that Christians should refer to themselves first as Trinitarians rather than monotheists. He explains, "Creation by the Father, the incarnation of the Son, and transfiguration by the Spirit are the architecture of revelation. . . . Monotheism engenders authoritarianism and totalitarianism both ecclesiastically and politically. Trinitarian thinking ensures at the same time both divine and human liberty."[36] This radical conviction lies at the heart of Ellul's project. It demonstrates clearly that Ellul firmly believes that dialectic should be foundational—especially in religion. Furthermore, a nondialectical understanding of religion (that is, the worldview of technique) will result in a one-dimensional society of religious exclusivists.[37]

---

35. Ellul discusses his conception of the Trinity in *What I Believe*, 167–88.
36. Ibid., 178.

As we have seen, Ellul's dialectical theology shaped all of his intellectual work. The clearest example of this is in his book *Hope in Time of Abandonment* (1973), which Ellul considered to be his most important theological work. In it, we see a vivid dialectical understanding of reality. For example, Ellul argues that the realm of technique is the realm of the "closed" rather than the "open" (the spiritual realm). In the closed milieu, humans are restricted by institutions of domination, ideologies of control, and religions of fear. This sphere continues to limit and stunt the psychological and spiritual growth of humanity.[38]

Humans are restricted precisely because technique has determined human consciousness and behavior. There is rarely any true spontaneity, creativity, or freedom. Instead, humans think in certain preordained categories and act in predetermined modes of behavior. Because of this stifling, humans begin to look for an open sphere of existence. They look for freedom in new forms of technology, consumerism, and television, according to Ellul. Within this sphere of technique, however, freedom cannot be found. Only through the spiritual can one escape the realm of necessity. But how can one connect to the spiritual? Ellul maintains that the dialectical link between the closed and open realms is *hope*. Hope is not an impractical emotion or an abstract concept. For Ellul, hope is a living reality that should be enthusiastically embraced and lived out. As the title of his book suggests, we are living in an age of abandonment—a hopeless age where nearly every aspect of life has been abandoned to technique. Hope is the only true response to the domination of technique.[39] At first glance, this seems like an overly simplistic and

---

37. Ibid., 29–34, 188–210. Ellul believes that fundamentalism, in all religions, is primarily a result of nondialectical thinking.

38. Jacques Ellul, *Hope in Time of Abandonment,* trans. C. Edward Hopkin (New York: Seabury, 1963), 3.

39. Ibid, 4.

naïve response. However, upon further investigation into the nature of hope, we will see the dialectical coherence of Ellul's claim.

Hope, according to Ellul, is the "impossible possibility," the "antiobject," and the "antidiscourse."[40] It is not an object to be studied or a fixed theoretical concept. Rather, hope is a reality that is existentially encountered and acted out. Ellul does not clearly and specifically define hope, because he maintains that this would "systematize" hope.[41] Despite this insistence, Ellul does refer to his theology as a "theology of hope." He does believe, however, that his is a theology that is not fixed or immutable. Rather, it is one that is in a state of flux and is "unstructured."[42]

In order to fully understand how hope is the dialectical link between the realm of technique and the realm of freedom, we need to briefly discuss Ellul's conception of history. According to Ellul, history moves dialectically along two tracks, one spiritual and one material. Within the spiritual historical progression, there are two primary movements: presence and promise. The movement of presence denotes specific historical periods when God is "strikingly and unquestionably present."[43] Clear examples of these periods can be found in the Judeo-Christian Scriptures as well as in the individual experiences of the believer. Conversely, there are periods in history where God is silent, where God has "abandoned" humanity. These are periods of simultaneous abandonment and promise, such as our current moment in history. According to Ellul, "Such is the basic spiritual reality of our age. God is turned away. God is absent. God is silent."[44] This "turning away" is not a punishment for human behavior or a rejection of humanity by God, but a moment in history

40. Ibid., 174–75.
41. Ibid.
42. Ibid.
43. Ibid., 176.
44. Ibid., 111.

when God has chosen to remain silent. Ellul argues that there have been many moments of God's silence throughout history, especially as seen in the Judeo-Christian Scriptures. Our moment is not unique in this sense. Ellul quotes Paul Tillich to explain this age of silence:

> The Spirit has shown to our time and to innumerable people in our time the absent God and the empty space that cries in us to be filled by Him. And then the absent one may return and take the space that belongs to Him, and the Spiritual Presence may break again into our consciousness, awakening us to recognize what we are, shaking and transforming us.[45]

Like Tillich, Ellul firmly believes that history is constituted by presence and absence. However, Ellul also maintains that Tillich has oversimplified the situation by implying that humans merely need to wait for God to appear again. According to Ellul, the absence of God is also a demand: a demand to combine faith and action—praxis—with active hope. Hope can thrive only in a period of absence and silence.[46]

Not only is hope demanded from God's silence, it is also the dialectical link between absence and presence. In order to explain this, Ellul turns to Jewish theologian André Neher: "God has withdrawn in silence, not in order to avoid man, but, on the contrary, in order to encounter him. But it is an encounter of silence with silence. . . . The dialectic which links God with man is no longer positive. . . . It is a negative dialectic."[47] Silence has its dialectical counterpart: action. Furthermore, action must be motivated by

---

45. Paul Tillich, quoted in Ellul, *Hope in Time of Abandonment,* 111–12. In several places throughout Ellul's work, he enthusiastically quotes Tillich. It is important to remember that Ellul's theology shares similarities with Tillich, but ultimately it is much closer to Barth. Ellul's fundamental assumptions about the nature of reality, his methodology, and his rejection of the analogia entis in favor of the analogia fidei situate Ellul squarely within the Barthian tradition. However, Ellul's anarchism and universalism place him in a unique theological category that is not easily classifiable.

46. Ellul, *Hope in Time of Abandonment,* 177.

47. André Neher, quoted in Ellul, *Hope in Time of Abandonment,* 178. This passage is taken from Neher's brilliant book *The Exile of the Word: From the Silence of the Bible to the Silence of Auschwitz,* trans. David Maisel (Philadelphia: Jewish Publication Society, 1981).

confident hope in God. According to Ellul, this action is comprised primarily of prayer, fellowship, and local political engagement. He explicitly outlines these entailments of hope in his books *Prayer and Modern Man* (1970) and *Anarchy and Christianity* (1988). These will be further discussed in the final chapter of this work.

To summarize, the closed realm of technique coexists with the open realm of the spirit. The closed sphere is one of necessity and determination; the open sphere is one of freedom. Each realm also has its own historical progression. Within the spiritual progression, there are two movements, presence and promise (absence). This current age is a movement of absence: a period of God's silence. This moment in history is transcended by the dialectical link of active hope. More importantly, active hope also acts as the connector between the closed and the open realms, between necessity and freedom.[48]

As I have clearly demonstrated, in order to fully understand Ellul, one must first understand his conception of dialectic, as well as the central ideas found in his philosophical *and* theological writings. Without this knowledge, one's understanding of Ellul will certainly be superficial and inadequate, and one will miss the very motivating force behind Ellul's scholarship. Many philosophers, theologians, and social theorists today read only one side of Ellul's work. Even worse, they fail to grasp Ellul's dialectical worldview and methodology, let alone to see the world dialectically. Recalling Kaczynski, we can imagine how a truly comprehensive familiarity with Ellul's work and worldview could have likely led Kaczynski to a different philosopher for intellectual and moral support.

In the following chapters, not only will I make use of Ellul's dialectical method in order to weave together the most important

---

48. According to Ellul, only through Christ can one transcend the realm of necessity (technique). Ellul expands on this in *The Ethics of Freedom*.

aspects of his philosophy and theology, but I will also explain these aspects. For example, Ellul's conception of technique and its consequences will be discussed at length. Also, I will briefly present Ellul's critique of modern politics and propaganda, and explain Ellul's Christian anarchism. (Along with his conception of dialectic, Ellul's writings on anarchism and nonviolence are perhaps the most neglected part of his oeuvre.) Finally, I will present and explain Ellul's universal soteriology—a central aspect of his theology that has also been neglected and misunderstood by many.[49]

---

49. One of the few adequate discussions of Ellul's soteriology is found in Darrell Fasching, "The Ethical Importance of Universal Salvation," *The Ellul Forum* 1 (1988): 5–9.

3

———

God, Salvation, and Freedom

In order to understand Ellul's theology, we need to understand his place within the twentieth-century theological tradition. As stated earlier, Ellul's theological methodology was primarily influenced by Kierkegaard and Barth.[1] All three thinkers are often referred to as *dialectical theologians.* This particular Protestant theology proceeds from six axiomatic principles that separate it from other forms of Christian theology.[2]

1. Ellul refuses to call himself a theologian or a philosopher, in the same way that Kierkegaard refused these titles. In any case, Ellul wrote many profound books of theology and biblical studies showing deep insight into the Christian tradition. There is no doubt that Ellul was not only a historian, sociologist, and philosopher; he was also a theologian.
2. Dialectical theology is also sometimes referred to as *crisis theology.* Though it shares some similarities, dialectical theology is not to be confused with the *radical orthodoxy* movement or *liberation theology.*

Ellul and Dialectical Theology

The first principle of dialectical theology is the *absolute transcendence of God*.[3] For dialectical theologians, God is not identified with the natural world in any way, shape, or form. God is radically different from the earth or the cosmos. This differs from certain theologies that maintain that the cosmos is God's body or that human beings collectively comprise the mind of God.

The second principle is the *absolute separation between God and humans*. Following Kierkegaard's statement that there is an "infinite, qualitative distinction" between the Divine and humans, dialectical theologians emphasize the radical otherness and freedom of God. This entails that God is not limited to human systems of logic or categorization. Furthermore, God's actions are unpredictable and are ultimately beyond the scope of human reason.[4]

The third principle is the distinction between *religion and revelation*. Kierkegaard, Barth, and Ellul all believe that God is only knowable through God's self-revelation.[5] This can only be understood and appropriated through grace by faith. Religious adherents—even those within the Christian tradition—often make the false assumption that humans can know God by their own effort alone. In contrast, dialectical theology emphasizes that this is impossible.[6]

At this point, it might be tempting to assume that Kierkegaard, Barth, and Ellul are simply following Reformation thinkers such as Calvin and Luther. There is a key difference, however. Calvin, Luther, and many others within the Christian tradition argue that God can be known by looking to nature or natural laws as guides.

---

3. For a brief discussion of these characteristics of dialectical theology, see Chad Meister and J. B. Stump, *Christian Thought: A Historical Introduction* (New York: Routledge, 2010), 448–53.
4. Ibid., 449.
5. Ibid., 450.
6. Ibid.

This approach is common within Christianity, as exemplified by Thomas Aquinas. Known simply as *analogia entis*, or the analogy of (from) being, this method of understanding begins with human reason and the natural world. According to the analogia entis, by a systematic observation and description of nature (the physical world), one can make inferences about God's being. For example, one might see order and precision in nature and assume that God acts in an orderly and precise way.[7]

The analogia entis method of knowing God is rejected prima facie by dialectical theologians such as Kierkegaard and Ellul for two primary reasons. First, this methodology, a key component of natural theology, reduces and restricts God to the realm of human logic, which is always limited by space and time. In contrast, dialectical theologians underscore the radical alterity between God and humans, which always transcends human logic and rationality.[8] Kierkegaard's emphasis on "the Paradox" is a fine example of this view.

Second, the analogia entis can lead to problematic ideological interpretations of God. For example, if God can be known through nature, then many different and opposing conclusions about God might be reached, including interpretations about God that might preclude the uniqueness of Christianity. Dialectical theologians instead emphasize the *analogia fidei*, the analogy of (from) faith, rather than the analogia entis. The analogia fidei states that humans can know nothing about God's being if using their own natural reason alone. Instead, knowledge of God comes exclusively through God's

---

7. For an excellent work on the analogia entis and the analogia fidei, sprinkled with fascinating facts about Protestant views on the topic, see Keith L. Johnson, *Karl Barth and the Analogia Entis* (London: T & T Clark, 2011). Also, see George Hunsinger, *How to Read Karl Barth: The Shape of His Theology* (New York: Oxford University Press, 1991), 7–20. For a discussion of Aquinas on natural law and the analogia entis, see Brian Davies, *The Thought of Thomas Aquinas* (Oxford: Clarendon, 1993), 21–35, 70–75.
8. See Karl Barth, *Epistle to the Romans*, trans. Edwyn C. Hoskyns (Oxford: Oxford University Press, 1960), 10.

self-revelation in Christ. The analogia fidei undeniably corresponds with the dialectical theologian's conviction that only by faith in God's revelation can one know anything about God. This faith is subjective in the sense that it cannot be empirically verified by human reason alone, and it is objective in the sense that it is grounded in what is unconditionally, eternally true. The analogia fidei is a crucially important aspect of dialectical theology and one that often places it outside mainstream forms of Christian theology.

The fourth guiding principle is that *one's relationship with God is ultimately subjective*. Echoing Kierkegaard's statement that "subjectivity is truth," dialectical theologians maintain that religious discourse is fundamentally limited to the individual experience of the believer and to the community of the faith. This is not to say that religious experience is foundationless or untrue. On the contrary, the dialectical theologian maintains that only through faith can one truly enter into an authentic relationship with the living God. However, since this relationship is essentially subjective, it is largely incommunicable and unquantifiable.[9] This is why most dialectical theologians are equally opposed to all forms of both dogmatism and apologetics.[10]

The fifth principle is an emphasis on *God's gift of self-disclosure as found in the Judeo-Christian Scriptures*. Like many within the Protestant tradition, dialectical theologians maintain that Holy Scripture is the best guide for understanding God. Furthermore, it is through the Word of God—the communication of God through Scripture and Jesus Christ—that one can develop one's relationship with God. However, it is important to note that, while dialectical

9. Jacques Ellul, *What I Believe*, trans. Geoffrey W. Bromiley (London: Marshall, Morgan, & Scott, 1989), 167.
10. Jacques Ellul discusses his disgust of apologetics in *Living Faith: Belief and Doubt in a Perilous World*, trans. Peter Heinegg (San Francisco: Harper & Row, 1983), 131–32.

theologians look to the Bible as the primary source of God's revelation, they are not inerrantists or literalists.[11]

The sixth and final principle concerns methodology. Dialectical theologians hold that *the best way to understand ourselves and God is through a dialectical method*. As we know from our study of Ellul so far, this view sees reality as essentially comprised of seemingly contradictory factors. Only by recognizing these opposing aspects and their relation to each other will one be able to see the "whole" or reality as it truly is. This is why Kierkegaard often focused on paradoxes and why Ellul emphasizes the dialectic of necessity and freedom.[12]

These six principles must continually be kept in mind. After all, it is safe to say that Ellul falls squarely within the camp of dialectical theology, so familiarity with its framework is essential when approaching his work.[13]

God

Primary to Ellul's theology is his conception of God. Throughout Ellul's work, God is usually discussed in one of four ways. These are as follows: God as Wholly Other, God as living, God as Trinity, and God as love.

---

11. Meister and Stump, *Christian Thought*, 449.
12. See Julia Watkin, *Historical Dictionary of Kierkegaard's Philosophy* (Lanham, MD: Scarecrow, 2001), 65, 189.
13. Though there are certainly dissimilarities between Kierkegaard, Barth, and Ellul, the similarities outweigh the differences.

Wholly Other

Ellul explains the first and most fundamental of these aspects of God—Wholly Other—in this way: "The point is that if God is God, I cannot know anything about him on my own, and even less can I say anything about him. God is Wholly Other. If he were not, he would not be God."[14]

This emphasis on the unknowability of God is similar to Barth's famous statement in his *Epistle to the Romans*: "If I have a system, it is limited to a recognition of what Kierkegaard called the 'infinite qualitative distinction' between time and eternity, and to my regarding this as possessing negative as well as positive significance: 'God is in heaven, and thou art on earth.'"[15] For Barth and Ellul, who clearly both follow Kierkegaard, God is unknowable in terms of human rationality. In other words, by using deductive logic and scientific methods, one can never understand the essence of God or the motivations of God's actions. This is why Ellul is opposed to natural theology and its proponents. Aquinas and other natural theologians maintain that a partial knowledge of God's characteristics can be known by way of deduction and analogy. As mentioned previously, this approach is generally referred to as a form of analogia entis: analogy from being. Aquinas argued that a sustained reflection on nature would lead one to systematically deduce, by way of analogy, certain aspects of God's nature. Barth was a strong opponent of the analogia entis, maintaining that it involved anthropomorphism and that it restricted the freedom of God.[16] For these same reasons, Ellul rejects natural theology, instead relying on revelation and

---

14. Ellul, *What I Believe*, 171.
15. Barth, *Epistle to the Romans*, 10.
16. See Karl Barth and Emil Brunner, *Natural Theology: Comprising "Nature and Grace" by Professor Dr. Emil Brunner and the Reply "No!" by Dr. Karl Barth*, trans. Peter Fraenkel (Eugene, OR: Wipf & Stock, 2002).

faith—analogia fidei—for true knowledge of God. In his typically dialectical fashion, Ellul explains:

> I cannot have a single coherent image of God. I cannot say at a given moment that God is simply this or that for me. He is, but he is also other things at the same time which may finally be the opposite. I cannot attempt a synthesis or reconciliation between the different elements in which I believe I can understand God. I thus renounce here any attempt at intellectual coherence.[17]

Here, Ellul is referring to human rationality and its inability to lead to a full knowledge of God. When used alone to comprehend God, human knowledge will lead to confusion.[18]

However, Ellul maintains that one can know God through God's self-revelation.[19] Echoing Pascal, Kierkegaard, and other Christian existentialists and mystics, Ellul says that a deeper knowledge of God is possible. This intuitive level comes through revelation and is accepted by faith. The most basic way this occurs is through hearing and experiencing what Ellul calls the living Word of God.[20]

The Living Word of God

For Ellul, God is living. God is unknowable by way of human knowledge, yet God is knowable through God's self-revelation—communication—in the Scriptures and in the person of Christ. According to Ellul, by "hearing" the Word of God, whether in the Scriptures or in the life and teachings of Christ, one can authentically experience God. This method is the surest way of

17. Ellul, *What I Believe*, 169.
18. Ibid., 169–74.
19. Ibid., 174.
20. A good anthology of existentialism, which includes a discussion of Pascal and Kierkegaard, is Walter Kauffmann, ed., *Existentialism: From Dostoyevsky to Sartre* (New York: New American Library, 1975).

knowing God for Ellul. Experiences like those of Pascal are legitimate and can point humans in the right direction, but ultimately, the Word of God must be relied upon for concrete certainty.[21]

For Ellul, the phrase "Word of God" does not simply connote the sacred writings of Judaism and Christianity. Instead, the Word of God refers to the living, dynamic, ever-present, self-revealing of God to specific individuals. Thus, the Scriptures are "living" in the sense that God continually speaks through them, no matter the reader's point in history or place on the globe. The same is true of Christ. God has chosen to perpetually and progressively reveal himself through Christ to all who encounter him. So, when Ellul speaks of the Word of God, he is speaking of a living, active, time-transcendent God.[22]

Many evangelicals speak of the Word of God, but their conception is usually quite different than Ellul's. They often have in mind the Bible as a merely physical object containing historical facts about divine occurrences, and they believe that God's revelation occurs through the *reading* of the Bible. In contrast, Ellul maintains that the Word of God cannot be limited to a historical document; this would constrain the living God. Furthermore, Ellul stresses the *hearing* or experiencing of the Word of God, rather than the mere reading of the text. As a living force, the Word of God must be actively encountered.[23]

As a central avenue for communication with God, the Scriptures are viewed very highly by Ellul. The Scriptures hold the utmost authority—far more authority than ritual or dogma. Taken with his skepticism of natural theology and his refusal of the reliability of

21. Blaise Pascal, *Pensées,* trans. A. J. Krailsheimer (New York: Penguin, 1995).
22. Ellul, *What I Believe,* 167–88.
23. Ellul is critical of evangelicals like Billy Graham, who focus of the "image" of the text rather than on hearing the Word of God. See Jacques Ellul, *The Humiliation of the Word,* trans. Joyce Main Hanks (Grand Rapids: Eerdmans, 1985), 202. This criticism alone places Ellul outside mainstream evangelicalism, despite the fact that he is often embraced by evangelicals and sometimes labeled as one.

religious tradition, this might cause the reader to assume that Ellul is some sort of narrow-minded biblicist. However, this could not be further from the truth. Let us recall that Ellul's view of Scripture was informed primarily by Barth. Concerning Barth's understanding of Scripture, Francis Watson says,

> The Bible is not read, and must not be read, in a timeless, ahistorical vacuum. Nor is there much trace in Barth of conservative Protestant anxieties about biblical inerrancy, inspiration, non-contradiction, or historicity. . . . The Bible must be attended to because it *speaks* of this divine particularity, both in its content and in its form. . . . The truthfulness and trustworthiness of the Bible are therefore guaranteed by its *intrinsic* relationship to the truthfulness and the trustworthiness of the divine self-disclosive speech-act that takes place in Jesus.[24]

For Barth and Ellul, the Scriptures are the Word of God in that they contain God's revelation: divine communication. The Scriptures are not the Word of God in and of themselves. If approached in this manner, the Bible will be seen as divine and will lead to bibliolatry. Ellul refuses to divinize the Scriptures, but because they act as a conduit for the living God, he looks to them as a central guide for his theology.[25]

The Trinity

Along with the Scriptures, the Word of God connotes the God expressed in the doctrine of the Trinity. According to Ellul, the central revelation of God has taken place in Christ, who was and is Father, Son, and Holy Spirit—three in one. Following the

---

24. Francis Watson, "The Bible," in *The Cambridge Companion to Karl Barth*, ed. John Webster (Cambridge: Cambridge University Press, 2000), 59–61.
25. See also Geoffrey W. Bromiley, "Barth's Influence on Jacques Ellul," in *Jacques Ellul: Interpretive Essays*, ed. Clifford G. Christians and Jay M. Van Hook (Urbana: University of Illinois Press, 1981), 32–51.

proclamation of the Nicene Creed, Ellul maintains that the Trinity is not only a symbolic representation of God; it is also the very real, concrete, dynamic reality of God's being. The ontological status of God can therefore only truly be understood in terms of the Trinity. Ellul says, "The word of God is fully expressed, explained, and revealed in Jesus Christ, and only in Jesus Christ, who is himself, and in himself, the Word."[26]

Andrew Goddard maintains that the doctrine of the Trinity, though of great importance to Ellul, is not a central structuring element in Ellul's theology.[27] While this may be true, dialectic is of central importance, and the Trinity perfectly exemplifies the four aspects of dialectic.[28] Furthermore, the Trinity comprises the essence of God's self-revelation, which is a fundamental constituent of Ellul's theology. Ellul says, "The trinity is not a matter of theological accommodation to difficult problems. It is not a human invention. It belongs to the very essence of biblical revelation."[29] For Ellul, reality can only be understood by way of dialectic, and God can only be understood by way of God's self-revelation, which in itself is dialectical. Thus, although the Trinity does not play an explicitly central role in Ellul's theology, it is fundamental in the theoretical framework that underlies Ellul's entire theological project.[30]

In addition to speaking of God as Wholly Other, the living God, and God as Trinity, Ellul continually refers to God as love. The clearest example of Ellul's radical understanding of love is found in his universal soteriology, which will now be explained.

---

26. Jacques Ellul, *To Will and To Do*, trans. C. Edward Hopkin (Philadelphia: Pilgrim House, 1969), 27.

27. Andrew Goddard, *Living the Word, Resisting the World: The Life and Thought of Jacques Ellul* (Carlisle, UK: Paternoster, 2002), 63.

28. See chapter 1 for a discussion of dialectic in relation to the Trinity.

29. Ellul, *What I Believe*, 178.

30. Ibid.

Universalism

One of the most neglected aspects of Ellul's theology is his soteriology. This omission is odd, especially considering the absolutely central role of universalism to Ellul's theology. Recalling Ellul's dialectic, we remember that all things end in reconciliation. This means that history, nature, and humanity will all be reconciled in God. This is, in essence, Ellul's soteriological position.[31]

Following the Judeo-Christian doctrinal tradition, Ellul maintains that God is omnipresent, omniscient, and omnibenevolent. Expanding upon this view, Ellul points out that if God is truly omnipresent, the realm of hell, a place of eternal judgment, cannot exist.[32] For Ellul, the concept of hell is a logical contradiction if God's attributes are taken seriously. Here, even though he is critical of philosophical and theological systems, Ellul shows himself to be a devotee of deductive logic. (In fact, this use of logic is a hallmark of Ellul's work.) Ellul validly concludes that hell cannot be a realm of existence; it cannot even be a realm of nothingness, as some theologians have maintained.[33]

Ellul is critical of annihilationism in all forms. He states, "Death cannot issue in nothingness. This would be a negation of God himself."[34] Furthermore, Ellul believes the concept of nothingness to be empty and ultimately meaningless. He argues that this idea is simply an abstract "philosophical or mathematical concept" that bears no relation to concrete reality.[35] If God is all and is in all, then hell as a realm of nothingness or as a state of permanent annihilation is logically excluded.

31. Ellul's fullest account of universalism is in ibid., 188–209.
32. Ibid.
33. Ibid.
34. Ibid., 189.
35. Ibid.

Here, Ellul may seem to be deviating from his dialectical method. However, his four principles of dialectic do include constituents of reality that are mutually exclusive and cannot be synthesized. For example, Ellul maintains that God, in the final analysis, is reconciliation and synthesis. In the end, God unites all of creation, including that which was formerly irreconcilable—both being and nothingness.[36]

Also, it should be remembered that for Ellul, God is omnibenevolent. Therefore, all are loved by God—including those things that might seem unlovable. This act of loving is in itself an act of reconciliation.[37] Many within Christian theological circles argue that if God is just, there must be eternal punishment. Ellul maintains that this type of argument for hell and eternal wrath is flawed and based on an ill-conceived notion of justice.[38] Furthermore, it is an argument with implicit assumptions regarding heaven.[39] Conversely, Ellul's own dialectical worldview is much more inclusive and less polarizing, and based on coherent and sound logic.

Ellul's conception of God does not allow for the eternal separation of humans from God. This may be confusing for some who are familiar with the Reformed tradition with which Ellul was associated. Ellul was certainly influenced by Calvin, though he claimed that he was no longer a Calvinist after he studied Barth.[40] According to Calvin, some individuals are predestined to eternal life, and some to eternal death. Ellul disagrees, maintaining that the doctrine of predestination is correct, but that it has been misinterpreted by those within the Reformed church, including Calvin. He says, "There is

---

36. Jacques Ellul, "On Dialectic," in Christians and Van Hook, *Jacques Ellul: Interpretive Essays*, 291–308.

37. Ellul, *What I Believe*, 190.

38. Ibid., 192.

39. Ibid., 191.

40. Jacques Ellul, *Perspectives on Our Age: Jacques Ellul Speaks on His Life and Work*, trans. Joachim Neugroschel (Toronto: Canadian Broadcasting Company, 1981), 17.

indeed a predestination, but it can be only the one predestination to salvation. In and through Jesus Christ all people are predestined to be saved."[41] This predestination ultimately means that humans have no free choice concerning reconciliation. They cannot choose salvation or damnation, heaven or hell.

Ellul argues that God, being love and reconciliation, has determined by his very nature that salvation is for all. It is not a matter of faith or deeds, of belief or piety; it is a matter of God's very being.[42] Here we see that, for Ellul, the Christian message is essentially one of radical grace, acceptance, and inclusivity. Salvation does not concern the free decisions of humans, but the free decision of God. This decision has been made, once and for all. Ellul puts it succinctly: "A theology of grace implies universal salvation."[43]

In addition to his arguments from God's attributes, Ellul references the Scriptures to defend his conviction in universal salvation. He maintains that many have interpreted the Scriptures incorrectly, confusing and conflating judgment and condemnation with damnation. While there are many instances of judgment and condemnation in the Judeo-Christian Scriptures, there are very few (if any) examples of eternal damnation. Ellul recalls several examples in the Hebrew Scriptures where the Israelites are judged or condemned by God. However, in all of these examples, there is always redemption.[44]

Likewise, in the New Testament, there are several parables concerning hell, rejection from the marriage feast, and the place of "weeping and gnashing of teeth."[45] Ellul maintains that the error

---

41. Ellul, *What I Believe*, 192.
42. For a helpful discussion of Calvin's theology, see Michael Sudduth, "John Calvin," in *The History of Western Philosophy of Religion*, ed. Graham Oppy and Nick Trakakis (New York: Oxford University Press, 2009), 47–64.
43. Ellul, *What I Believe*, 195.
44. Ibid., 194–95.
45. Luke 13:28, NRSV

of believing in a literal hell comes, in part, from a misreading of select parables such as these. Ellul's view is that these parables are for instruction and pedagogical purposes, and they should not be taken in a crudely literal manner.[46]

In the Pauline Epistles there are also references to hell and eternal damnation. For example, in 1 Cor. 6:9 (NRSV), Paul writes, "Do you not know that wrongdoers will not inherit the kingdom of God?" This clearly implies that some will never see heaven. In contrast, Paul also states in Rom. 7:14-24 (NRSV) that all "sin dwells within me" and "the evil I do not want is what I do." By acknowledging that he is a sinner just as others are sinners, Paul's implication is clear: all are sinners, and the message of Jesus is that all are forgiven. Therefore, Ellul reasons that even though all are sinners and cannot inherit the kingdom of God, all people are also ultimately saved by grace.[47]

Ellul also relies heavily on John 3:16 (NRSV) to defend his position. This well-known passage states that "God so loved the world that he gave his only son, so that everyone who believes in him may not perish, but may have eternal life." Ellul goes on to contend that only an overly simple and naive interpretation of this passage supports a belief in eternal damnation.[48] If God is love, and loved the world enough to sacrifice Jesus, then it must have been for all, not only for a select few. For Ellul, to "perish" is to live in this world without knowledge of God—without hope. On the other hand, "everlasting life" is a life lived with knowledge of God's love and grace. This is true hope, and it mirrors our ultimate future reality with God.[49]

For Ellul, the difference between Christians and non-Christians is simply a matter of knowledge of one's salvation. Those who know

46. Ellul, *What I Believe*, 195.
47. Ellul also argues against eternal damnation by making a distinction between the flesh and the spirit, maintaining that evil does not constitute one's true self. See Ellul, *What I Believe*, 198.
48. Ibid., 202.
49. Ibid., 182.

God and recognize the reality of Christ live in hope. This hope is directed toward God and the final reconciliation of all things. Those who are not aware of God's work and plan place their hope in transitory aspects of technique.[50]

Salvation, reconciliation, and redemption are for all, according to Ellul. He is unequivocal in his rejection of eternal damnation and a literal hell. Throughout Christian history there have been others, like Ellul, who argue for universalism, but most Christians do not.[51] For example, in his insightful work on Ellul's methodology, Daniel Clendenin writes, "The most glaring inconsistency in Ellul's theological dialectic is his nearly unqualified affirmation of universal salvation of all people beyond history, a doctrine which Ellul says he accepted as a result of his reading Barth."[52] Clendenin argues that Ellul's universalism is problematic for three reasons. First, Ellul's use of Scripture to defend his position is selective, leaving out passages that contradict universalism. Second, the theory of universal salvation implicitly denies humans free-will. Third, universalism makes everyone a Christian, stripping humans of their individuality and heterogeneity.[53]

Ellul arrives at the conclusion of universalism from two primary premises. First, as stated earlier, Ellul interprets God's love to be all-inclusive and universal. This would leave out the possibility of anyone or anything escaping God's love. Second, following methodologically from the fourth principle of Ellul's dialectic, reconciliation, universalism is the necessary outcome.[54] Still, many

---

50. Ibid., 203.
51. For an excellent history and overview of universalism, see Gregory MacDonald, ed., *All Shall be Well: Explorations in Universal Salvation and Christian Theology, from Origen to Moltmann* (Eugene, OR: Wipf & Stock, 2011).
52. Daniel B. Clendenin, *Theological Method in the Theology of Jacques Ellul* (Lanham, MD: University Press of America, 1987), 135.
53. Ibid., 138–40.
54. Ellul, *What I Believe*, 207.

(like Clendenin) remain unconvinced, maintaining that this position is contradictory and illogical.[55]

I will not present a systematic defense of Ellul's position; this has already been done.[56] I will point out, however, that Clendenin's type of criticism is commonly encountered when discussing universalism. Yet, from a scriptural, logical, and dialectical stance, one can also coherently defend universalism, as Ellul does. Christians who have done this include Origen, Johannes Scotus Eriugena, and Karl Barth, to name a few.[57]

Religion and Revelation

In order to better understand Ellul's theology, I must first explain the distinction between religion and revelation. This is of primary importance in Ellul's theology, and it provides a vital foundation for his worldview. Furthermore, the dialectic between religion and revelation is a hermeneutical key to his Christian writings.

According to Ellul, religion is entirely a social construct. It consists of rituals, beliefs, and theology that connect humans to others, the past, nature, and the Divine. Religion also provides structure and order, making the universe comprehensible.[58]

Furthermore, Ellul maintains that religions always center on something "higher," be it a Divine being, a prophet, or a sacred order. Here Ellul is following the traditional definition of religion, *re-ligare*, which means to "re-tie" or "re-bind." In this case, religion binds

---

55. It is not my intention to defend Ellul from his opponents. A back-and-forth of arguments and counterarguments could continue ad infinitum. Instead, as stated at the outset, I am simply presenting Ellul's philosophy and theology in a sympathetic manner.

56. See Darrell Fasching, "The Ethical Importance of Universal Salvation," *The Ellul Forum*.1 (1988): 5–9.

57. See MacDonald, *All Shall Be Well*.

58. Ellul, *Living Faith*, 133.

the individual or the community to something greater. Moreover, religion is a system created by human beings for the primary purposes of making sense of reality, and providing meaningful connections. Both of these aspects of religion are efficacious and beneficial to humanity.[59]

If religion is the realm of humanity, revelation is the realm of the spirit. According to Ellul, religion is a movement by humans to reach the Divine, while revelation is a movement of the Divine to reach humans. Following Ellul's high Christology, it only makes sense that Christ is the unique example of the Divine reaching out to humans. This movement, while being paradoxical and ultimately incommunicable, is the essence of revelation. Ellul explains revelation as follows: "Never in any way, under any circumstances can we ascend to God, howsoever slightly. God has chosen to descend and to put himself on our level. . . . I would go so far as to say that *this* is what revelation is all about."[60] For Ellul, the Judeo-Christian Scriptures are full of clear examples of God descending to the human level, illustrating divine revelation.[61] Revelation is purely an act of grace, which in no way can be understood without God's assistance. In this respect, Ellul follows in the steps of Kierkegaard and thinkers within the existential and dialectical theological movements of the twentieth century, who emphasize that God cannot be fully known unless God chooses to reveal God's self. This sort of revealed theology stands in stark opposition to natural theology.[62] Ellul maintains that religion

---

59. Ellul follows Barth in his distinction between religions and revelation. Concerning Barth's distinction, Paul Tillich writes, "Barth did all this in the name of his fundamental principle, the absoluteness of God. God is not an object of our knowledge or action. . . . All our attempts to reach God are defined as religion, and against religion stand God's acts of revelation. Here began the fight against the use of the word 'religion' in theology," *Perspectives on Nineteenth and Twentieth Century Protestant Theology*, ed. Carl E. Bratten (New York: Harper & Row, 1995), 240–41.

60. Ellul, *Living Faith*, 137–38.

61. Ellul, like Barth, usually reads these examples of God descending to the human level in a particular—Christological—way.

is quite inferior to revelation, and that natural theology epitomizes religion. Concerning Teilhard de Chardin, who falls squarely into the Catholic tradition of natural theology, Ellul states, "Teilhard describes a process of ascent that leads humankind to the encounter with Christ the Last Word. . . . There you have the sum total of religion, completely legitimate and useful, indispensable to the person at whom the belief is aimed. It inspires belief, and then belief makes the person a participant in the phenomenon of religion."[63] Ellul claims that Teilhard and other natural theologians have systematized and dogmatized the movements and acts of God. In doing so, they strip God of freedom and limit God by their own epistemological presuppositions. Conversely, revelation places no constraints upon God, and makes no totalizing claims about God. Furthermore, it correctly recognizes that God is radically free and unpredictable and that human knowledge of God, without the aid of revelation, ultimately falls short.[64]

As aforementioned, God's self-revelation is found throughout the Judeo-Christian Scriptures; according to Ellul, this revelation lies at the heart of these traditions. Recognizing the revelation within Scripture frees one from restricting dogma and rituals found within most forms of Judaism and Christianity. Because of this, whereas religion unites and brings order, revelation does the opposite: "Revelation leads to the affirmation of powerlessness, the

---

62. Explaining natural theology, Rudolf Bultmann states, "God is assumed to be knowable to man 'by the light of natural reason' (*lumine naturalis rationis*); that is to say, his existence as the 'originator and avenger of the natural moral law' is knowable. Proof is deduced from the creation and the doctrine provides the foundation for dogmatics, since the propositions of the natural knowledge of God which are reached by rational arguments function as the 'preamble for faith,'" *Faith and Understanding*, trans. Louise Pettibone Smith (Philadelphia: Fortress, 1987), 313. This is an excellent definition of natural theology, and one that Ellul would agree with. Ellul opposes natural law on the conviction that God can only be known through grace, by faith.

63. Ellul, *Living Faith*, 137.

64. Ibid.

destabilization of human communities, the shattering of unity, the invalidating of the law, the impossibility of establishing an explicit, definitive content for faith."[65] This lack of order and unity can easily be viewed as negative, but not for Ellul. This is precisely the exciting, unpredictable aspect of revelation. Guided not by technique or necessity, revelation is governed by the freedom of God's choice. Conversely, religion is always steered by the spirit of technique, and thus always has at its core a thirst for power. Ellul explains, "In that religion ascends, it always expresses itself in a show of power. . . . On the contrary, the revelation of God . . . guides humankind in the direction of powerlessness, toward the choice to abandon human means of domination in order to become a people that entrusts itself to God's hands."[66] Without a doubt, the freedom of God is restricted in religion. In Ellul's view, Christianity has largely become a religion and is no longer authentic. Ellul refers to this inauthentic form of Christianity as Christendom.[67] This echoes Kierkegaard's distinction between Christendom and Christianity.[68] In his works *The Subversion of Christianity*, and *The New Demons*, Ellul maintains that the faith of the early Christians is "completely opposite" of the forms of Christendom existent in the modern world: the difference between the ancient faith and Christendom is "not just deviation but radical and essential contradiction and real subversion."[69]

65. Ibid., 141.
66. Ibid., 142–43.
67. Jacques Ellul, *The Subversion of Christianity*, trans. Geoffrey W. Bromiley (Grand Rapids: Eerdmans, 1990), 10–11; *The New Demons*, trans. C. Edward Hopkin (New York: Seabury, 1975), 1–17.
68. Kierkegaard said, "I dare claim *a priori* that this corruption is without analogy in the history of religion: the corruption consists in this—that Christianity continues to survive after it has been made into the opposite of what it is to be Christian," *Journals and Papers*, trans. H. Hong and E. Hong (Bloomington: Indiana University Press, 1967–78), 1:164. See also Kierkegaard's *Attack on "Christendom,"* trans. Walter Lowrie (Princeton: Princeton University Press, 1968).
69. Ellul, *Subversion of Christianity*, 3.

In short, Ellul maintains that Christianity, by the second and third centuries, became a "religion of the masses," a religion of "imperialism," and "fashionable."[70] This eventually led to the forms of Christendom we have today. Christendom now is not a faith of "grace, joy, liberation and hope," as the early church was.[71] Rather, it is a religion guided by the values of technique, and it exists in the realm of necessity.

In contrast, revelation exists in the realm of the spirit, where God's radical freedom and actions cannot be predicted or systematized. This, in turn, gives humans more freedom.[72] In the realm of necessity, human freedom is profoundly limited. In the realm of the spirit, humans can gain freedom from God. One of the first steps to gaining one's freedom is to be able to *hear* the living Word of God.

Seeing and Hearing

Our two primary sources of knowledge are sight and hearing. According to Ellul, one of the unsettling deficiencies of our modern world is the emphasis on sight over hearing. This is a result of technique. Ellul maintains that this emphasis has distorted our worldview, leaving us with a very fragmentary understanding of reality. In his work, *The Humiliation of the Word*, Ellul makes a persuasive case for recovering the lost art of hearing. By analyzing Ellul's arguments herein, we will better understand Ellul's distinctions between religion and revelation, Christendom and Christianity. Ellul's discussion of seeing and hearing also gives us unique insight into his dialectical worldview.[73]

70. Ibid., 27–34.
71. Ibid., 29.
72. Ibid., 149.
73. Ellul, *Humiliation of the Word*, 5–36.

Eyesight helps the individual understand reality by small, incremental experiences. It also helps one situate oneself in the world by providing reliable information to the subject. Eyesight also necessarily makes the subject the center of his or her world. According to Ellul, our images of reality directly condition our actions. Thus, sight organizes not only the external world, but also our internal understanding of the world. Ellul says, "Without space, no action is possible."[74] In other words, sight and action, though seemingly very different, are interconnected in a reciprocal relationship. This relationship always requires one's interpretation, which further relies on both sight and empirical experience.[75]

Because of sight, and its concomitant, action, humans have achieved mastery over a great part of the natural world. In fact, technique requires sight and action just as all technological progress does. For Ellul, sight is "the organ of efficiency."[76] Other senses, such as touch or taste, are far more inefficient conduits of information. For this reason, sight and technique are always closely related. Ellul writes, "The visual image potentially contains within itself all the traits and characteristics of what later become the experience, experimentation, and organization of technique."[77] He also maintains that one's images of the world always presuppose various interpretations of reality—some valid, others invalid. For instance, one's society and culture always influence one's perception. In this way, sight helps provide us with a place in the world, but this placement is always subjective and relative to a greater or lesser degree. While sight aids in situating us, it can also lead to "paths of separation and division, of intervention and efficiency, and of artificiality."[78] This is the path that we are on today, according to

74. Ibid., 7.
75. Ibid.
76. Ibid., 11.
77. Ibid.

Ellul. Furthermore, we have given primacy to seeing, while neglecting another central aspect of human existence: hearing.[79]

The domain of sight is space. The domain of sound is time. Therefore, in order to truly understand our place in the universe we need both senses to work in harmony. Because we have been conditioned by technique to want immediate results, we focus on what we can see, what is tangible and concrete. Ellul maintains that we have lost our sense of hearing, of truly listening. He encourages us to return to a balance of seeing and hearing by remembering what speech is. He explains, "Speech is basically presence. It is something alive and is never an object. It cannot be thrown before me and remain there. Once spoken, the word ceases to exist, unless I have recovered it."[80] As presence, speech contains the "word." The word is a fluid, living, act of communication. It is directed toward someone and requires response. It presupposes dialogue and exchange. It is often interpreted differently by various people, and this is what gives it a subjective quality. Ellul believes that we need to be open to the word, wherever it comes from, being willing to respond to it and engage it.[81]

When Ellul discusses hearing, he is not referring to one-directional communication or the dissemination of facts. Rather, Ellul is referring to interpersonal dialogue between humans and the Wholly Other. As many ancient Greek philosophers upheld, dialogue is the bearer of truth. The truth can only be partially understood if it is approached by sight alone. Only by being open to hearing the spoken word can one grasp truth in its fullness.[82]

78. Ibid., 12.
79. Historian Martin Jay accuses Ellul of forcing his readers to accept a "rigid dichotomy" between seeing and hearing. Jay also reduces Ellul's work to an "anti-modernist" project that is "hostile" to images (*Force Fields: Between Intellectual History and Cultural Critique* [New York: Routledge, 1993], 103–5). Clearly, Jay is not familiar with Ellul's dialectical methodology.
80. Ellul, *Humiliation of the Word*, 15.
81. Ibid., 15–21.

According to Ellul, the word entails three qualities: discussion, paradox, and mystery.[83] If there is *discussion*, there must be interlocutors; if these are present, then there is the possibility of an open exchange between them. This exchange assumes the possibility of freedom. For Ellul, this is one of the vital aspects of the word: it opens the door to human freedom. Wherever there is truly authentic dialogue, freedom exists.[84]

Clearly there is no freedom in the realm of necessity. However, freedom can be actualized anywhere humans begin to truly dialogue with each other and with God. Ellul explains, "Language is an affirmation of my person, since I am the one speaking, and it is born at the same time as the faint belief, aspiration, or conviction of liberty. The two are born together, and language is a sign bearing witness to my freedom and calling the other person to freedom as well."[85] Sight cannot bring freedom; it can only inform and situate the subject in the world. In contrast, hearing is inextricably linked to dialogue and language. As a bearer of the word, language is not only a sign of freedom; it brings freedom.

Freedom is also related to the second characteristic of the word: *paradox*.[86] For Ellul, the word is always intertwined with ambiguity, manifold meanings, and multiplicity.[87] This exemplifies the inherent freedom of the word, yet it is something that physical objects in the world cannot embody. He writes, "The word is always paradoxical because it corresponds to our ambiguity as persons."[88]

---

82. Ibid., 16–17, 25–26.
83. Ibid., 23.
84. Ibid., 220–21.
85. Ibid., 24.
86. Recall the earlier discussion of Kierkegaard's influence on Ellul. For Kierkegaard, "the Word" is Christ who is "the Paradox."
87. Ellul, *Humiliation of the Word*, 25.
88. Ibid.

Lastly, the word is characterized by *mystery.* As the word opens dialogue between two people, it inexorably points to the mysterious nature of others. Ellul explains, "The most explicit and best-explained word brings me back to mystery. This mystery has to do with the other person, whom I cannot fathom, and whose word provides me with an echo of his person, but only an echo. I perceive this echo, knowing that there is something more."[89] The word reminds us that there is much we do not know about others, ourselves, and the world. In this sense, it invokes a sense of wonder, of the mysterious. This open-endedness mirrors the freedom the word provides. We must recall that this mystery, along with dialogue and paradox, is not characteristic of the world of necessity; it belongs only to the spoken word.[90]

When we reconsider Ellul's four principles of dialectic, we see hearing and seeing in their own dialectical relationship. For instance, one of the constituents of reality is that it is static, and sight helps us to understand our limited and determined nature in the world: our necessity. Another component of reality is flux. Here we can recall that the word is dynamic and always in a state of change; it represents the mutability of our situation. When sight and the word are combined, we have a synthesis of fixity and fluidity, the third principle of dialectic. Finally, dialogue, which is presupposed by the word *language,* brings authentic freedom by reconciling speaker and hearer, subject and object, in a continually reciprocal relationship.[91]

Ellul reminds us that we should integrate sight with sound, seeing with hearing. As with his dialectical worldview, wholeness cannot occur without the two. He encourages us to listen to the word of others, but more importantly to the Word of God: Jesus Christ. Ellul

89. Ibid.
90. Ibid., 220–21.
91. Ibid., 215–16.

believes that through the Word, humans can escape the chains of necessity and live in freedom.

Freedom in Christ: The Answer to Alienation

As we have seen, the milieu of technique is the realm of necessity—a place that exploits and alienates. Technique and its entailments, such as the dominance of our society by capitalism and money, lead to this alienation. According to Ellul, alienation is a modern form of slavery, the opposite of freedom.[92] Alienation, however, is not only a result of capitalism. It is also a consequence of organized religion.[93]

On the one hand, Ellul believes that religion is "undoubtedly man's greatest achievement."[94] The world's religious traditions have provided extraordinary accounts of the origins of the world, profound psychological theories, insightful ethical codes, and beautiful art and architecture, among many other contributions. Yet, institutional religion has also exploited, enslaved, marginalized, and murdered millions. Echoing Marx, Ellul says, "Religion is the heart of a world without heart and the spirit of an age without spirit, but this means that it is the final and most total deception, for in this world without a heart or spirit it gives man the illusion of heart and spirit, preventing him from perceiving the truth."[95] Ellul maintains that religion is, in essence, idealism. It refuses to see and accept the inhumanity of the world caused by technique. Instead, it creates a false image of reality for its adherents, keeping them blind and ignorant. For instance, it is common to hear that our future in heaven—where angels and saints await us—matters far more than our

92. Ibid., 24.
93. See Ibid., 1–25.
94. Ibid., 25.
95. Ibid., 25–26.

own life on earth. This type of religious idealism causes alienation, stripping us of freedom.[96]

For Ellul, there are four central aspects of alienated human experience. These four factors are the direct entailments of technique. The first aspect is "the experience of the powerlessness of each of us in the world."[97] In the sphere of technique we are essentially ineffective. This is clear when we look at global politics, economic systems, and the development of technology. Most of the time, it makes no difference what an individual might think or do. Technique dominates all arenas of society with no regard to the agency of individuals.

Second, individuals experience the "absurd" nature of our modern world. In other words, we see and feel meaningless events and products created by technique everywhere. We cannot escape from these absurdities; we must live with them. One example of this is found in the mass media. Serious journalism has been overshadowed by superficial stories aimed at manipulating the public. This aids in creating a society without intellectual or moral depth.[98]

Third, the experience of alienation reminds individuals that they are abandoned. Recognizing their powerlessness to change the situation, along with the profound meaninglessness inherent in modern society, individuals are reminded that they are truly alone. This deepens and extends the problem of alienation.[99]

Fourth, by stripping individuals of meaning and the power to act, an attitude of indifference is fostered. Following from the first three aspects of alienated experience—powerlessness, absurdity,

---

96. Here, it is helpful to recall Ellul's distinction between religion and revelation.
97. Jacques Ellul, *The Ethics of Freedom*, trans. Geoffrey W. Bromiley (Grand Rapids: Eerdmans, 1972), 29.
98. Jacques Ellul, *Propaganda: The Formation of Men's Attitudes*, trans. Konrad Kellen (New York: Vintage, 1962), 47.
99. Ellul, *The Ethics of Freedom*, 33–34.

abandonment—is a sense of hopelessness and despair. This response is only logical; it is a product of the realm of necessity. Ellul reminds us that, if we accept these societal facts, "it is absolutely impossible to say that man is free."[100]

Yet this lack of freedom is not all-encompassing. The realm of necessity exists dialectically with the realm of freedom, the domain of the spirit. If technique has stripped individuals of freedom, how can it be regained? Ellul maintains that only by looking to Jesus Christ can one fully know God, who is the only one who can liberate us. Just as God's freeing revelation is a theme throughout the Scriptures, the Gospels demonstrate that Christ was, and is, the "only free man."[101] This freedom came from his voluntary choice to follow God's will rather than his own. Christ, having "been made like us in all things," transcends the realm of necessity by choosing to *refuse* power, control, violence, and even death.[102] All of these are key characteristics of the realm of technique.

Christ's refusal was a choice, and "Choice is the most tangible expression of freedom."[103] For Ellul, the clearest example of Christ's freedom was his rejection of violence and power.[104] Power is the essential human temptation, according to Ellul. It is enticing because humans want to be in complete control of themselves and their surroundings. However, by desiring control of all things, one seeks to situate oneself in the place of God. This not only distorts and perverts the natural relationship between God and humans; it is precisely what has already taken place.[105]

100. Ibid., 34.
101. Ibid., 51.
102. Ibid.
103. Ibid.
104. Ibid., 57.
105. Ibid., 51.

By looking to Christ we can see freedom. "He is authentically and completely free in the fact that he accepts his relation with God."[106] Christ's freedom is a result of his choice to recognize who he truly is and who God truly is. It follows from this recognition that Christ refuses to worship any of the idols of the world: efficiency, money, and possessions, among others. Instead, he chooses to worship the true God and to follow God's path. Ellul writes, "Freedom is knowing God's will and doing it." [107] And, "We can destroy our freedom by not living it out."[108]

Therefore, by turning to the Word of God, humans can escape the realm of necessity and live in freedom.[109] As aforementioned, the Word of God is the living and ever-present communication of God to individuals. It is most clearly revealed in the Holy Scriptures, but it is not limited to them. It is embodied in Christ, and it continually manifests through him. Because the Word of God is something that is "heard" and experienced in a direct and existential way, when one encounters the Word of God, one "participates" in the freedom of God.[110]

It is important to emphasize that, for Ellul, the activating ingredient of freedom is not just human decision, but the free choice of God as seen in Christ. God intervened in the world by incarnating as a real and concrete symbol—but not merely a symbol—of the antithesis of necessity. By responding to Christ—the Word of God—one can begin to live freely. This sort of active relationship between humans and God mirrors Ellul's wider dialectical method.[111]

---

106. Ibid., 61.
107. Ibid., 62.
108. Ibid., 236.
109. It is helpful to recall that for Ellul, the realms of necessity and freedom exist dialectically alongside one another.
110. Ellul, *The Ethics of Freedom*, 66.
111. Ibid., 226–34.

The freedom that is acquired through Christ is not a complete freedom. It is an event that is introduced into the life of the believer through grace. This occurrence simultaneously creates a new opposing force into the world of necessity, opening up a different dialectical channel for the Christian to move within.[112] For Ellul, the freedom that comes from Christ is a concrete freedom that ultimately must be experienced to be understood. One cannot demonstrate it through empirical means alone; it can only be acquired when one openly receives the revelation of the Wholly Other in faith.[113]

Ellul's dialectical worldview is quite visible when one recognizes the apparent contradiction between his theory of universal salvation and his interpretation of the individual's freedom in Christ. Ellul maintains that all humanity has been reconciled to God in Christ, and that all are ultimately bound to be free from sin. However, it is only through accepting the fact of the incarnation that one can fully actualize the freedom that is in Christ. Ellul says that by believing Christ's message, there is an "ontic" (or, existential) change in the individual. This transformation enables one to see the world of necessity in a new light: through a framework of authentic hope and freedom. This does not mean that Christians are free from necessity; it simply means that Christians can see the world as it truly is by seeing it dialectically. Christians recognize that they live in a fallen world, an arena of power, violence, and exploitation—necessity. They concomitantly understand that they have been reconciled with God through Christ—freedom. They know that they live not statically, but in constant flux between these two spheres, and that eventually all will be reconciled with God, completely freed from necessity. These four acknowledgements correspond perfectly to the four principles of dialectic.[114]

112. Ibid., 75.
113. Ibid., 51–55, 75.

Some maintain that once Christians accept the revelation of God, they receive a new nature, one that is different from the nonbeliever's. Ellul rejects this line of thinking. Even though there is a qualitative change in the believer, there is not a "metaphysical" transformation. All humans are still conditioned by the realm of necessity and have the same essential nature. The main difference is that Christians clearly see their freedom. However, to understand true freedom, one must first comprehend necessity. Likewise, to fully grasp hope, one must clearly understand reconciliation. One might call this a new type of consciousness or a different worldview; or perhaps, even the "mind of Christ."[115]

Ellul maintains that freedom is primarily for service; that is, action, obedience, and responsibility.[116] Jesus, as the only truly free human, freely chose to reject the values of the world and to instead to follow the living God as found in the Hebrew Scriptures. Likewise, Ellul believes that recognizing one's freedom entails obeying God. Believers should therefore look to the revelation in the Scriptures—primarily to the life and teaching of Christ—as a guide for ethical behavior. This is not a privilege, but an obligation. True freedom is coupled with responsibility.[117]

Yet, Ellul admits that throughout the history of Christianity "freedom is at the heart of neither its teaching nor activity," and "the dominant note of the Church has been incontestably that of authority and the negation of liberty."[118] These are harsh but true indictments. The church has been primarily concerned with dogma, power, moralism, and its own survival. As we have seen, this is not

---

114. This is of central importance to Ellul's thought. Recall the earlier discussion of Ellul's four principles of dialectic in chapter 2.
115. Phil. 2:5-11.
116. Ellul, *The Ethics of Freedom*, 87.
117. For an insightful discussion of freedom and responsibility, see ibid., 88–92.
118. Ibid., 88–90.

authentic Christianity, according to Ellul. True Christianity entails a rejection of the values of the world—power, violence, and efficiency, among others. In contrast, it works in the world for the liberation of all.[119]

Ellul also believes that it is possible to lose the freedom found through Christ. He states, "To lose this freedom, to fail to practice it, is to render impossible the efficacious work . . . of Christ."[120] Because freedom requires responsibility and action, it ceases to exist when responsibility is shunned, apathy reigns, or deeds are not performed with the right intentions. It is the obligation of every Christian to activate their freedom through morally correct behavior.[121]

Indeed, the moral actions of the Christian are predicated on freedom. However, those who dogmatically endorse rigid moral codes and legalistic ideologies do not understand true freedom. Whenever a certain form of behavior is forced onto others, another form of necessity is created and freedom disappears. Ellul maintains that Christians should certainly follow the ethical precepts of the Scripture, but not in a legalistic or forceful manner. If they truly comprehend their freedom, then their behavior follows from this recognition in a radically liberated way. These Christians, being free from the laws of necessity, no longer need to kill, steal, lie, or engage in any type of behavior mandated by the world. They are free to choose to love God and love their neighbor. In this light, the commandments of the Scriptures are all positive and liberating—providing guidance and opportunities to exercise freedom—rather than negative and constraining. This is one reason why freedom in Christ is foundational for Ellul. Without it the

---

119. See Ellul's *Subversion of Christianity* for a full account.
120. Ellul, *The Ethics of Freedom*, 94.
121. Ibid., 187.

revelation of God's Word is reduced to nothing more than lifeless rules and regulations.[122]

Ellul's theology illuminates a realm of freedom to counter the realm of necessity. This is a clear and broad example of his dialectical worldview. And within the realm of the spirit, we find his worldview mirrored again and again: a God who is Wholly Other, yet active and living; freedom that exists alongside alienation; and salvation—like dialectic—that ultimately ends in, and offers, reconciliation.[123]

In the next chapter, we will turn to a description and analysis of the negative pole of Ellul's dialectic: the realm of necessity, that is, technique. This is a sphere that—in a superficial sense—we all know very well, but that few have stepped back to reflect upon objectively. As we will see, Ellul calls us to become familiar with the many forms, characteristics, and entailments of technique. This knowledge is imperative, as our very well-being may depend on it.

---

122. Ellul writes, "On the basis of liberation, the law becomes . . . a source of spring and action, an incentive to discovery, invention, and expression. As the life of the Living One, it promotes life," *The Ethics of Freedom*, 149.
123. Ellul, *Humiliation of the Word*, 237–41.

4

Technique, Necessity, and Consequences

We live in a world saturated in technology. Indeed, we are determined—psychologically and physiologically—by it. However, many people do not stop to reflect on technology, and continue to put their faith in it. The field of philosophy that questions and challenges the technological milieu is known as the philosophy of technology.

The Philosophy of Technology

Just as philosophers of science analyze the axioms and assumptions underlying the world of science, philosophers of technology challenge the tacit beliefs and presuppositions underlying the technosphere. The philosophy of technology deals primarily with such ethical and political questions as the following: How is technology changing human consciousness? Is technological progress value free? Is technology an ideology? What is the relationship between technological progress and war? What is the relationship between technology and our present ecological problems? [1] But raising these questions is not commonplace. Very few thinkers have had the courage to ask these monumental questions. These handful of theorists make up the intellectual framework upon which the field of philosophy of technology rests.

In 1995, the first academic journal devoted to the philosophy of technology was published under the title *Techne: Research in Philosophy and Technology*, edited by Joseph C. Pitt at Virginia Technical University. In the first issue, Carl Mitcham states that the three main philosophers of technology were Jacques Ellul, Lewis Mumford, and Martin Heidegger.[2] Very little intellectual work can be found on Mumford's philosophy and social theory. A great deal of scholarship has been published on Heidegger's philosophy of technology, and a substantial amount of scholarship exists on the work of Ellul, but most of it concerns his theology in isolation from his philosophy of technology. In this chapter I will briefly introduce the reader to Ellul's philosophy of technology. First, I will sketch out some of the common theories dominating this field.[3]

In the twentieth century, a handful of philosophers began to wonder critically and reflectively about the implications of modern technology. There is by no means a consensus among these thinkers concerning technology, but there are two distinctive approaches to the issue: continental and analytic.[4] Within the continental

1. See Val Dusek, *Philosophy of Technology: An Introduction* (Oxford: Blackwell, 2006), chapters 1–2.
2. Carl Mitcham, "Notes Toward a Philosophy of Meta-Technology," *Techne: Research in Philosophy and Technology* 1, nos. 1–2 (1995): 3–5.
3. A helpful introduction to common theories in the philosophy of technology can be found in Andrew Feenberg, *Questioning Technology* (London: Routledge, 2000), chapter 1.
4. Analytic philosophy and continental philosophy are two distinct philosophical approaches and areas of interest. This distinction does not refer to specific geographic regions, which the title "continental" might imply. Analytic philosophers tend to emphasize philosophical issues which can be analyzed and evaluated through a strictly empirical methodology. Continental

discussion, the approach has generally been an overall critique of technology as a deterministic phenomenon. The first two continental philosophers of the twentieth century to bring technology into the realm of philosophical discussion were Martin Heidegger, with his "Die Frage nach der Technik" ("The Question Concerning Technology," 1954), and Jacques Ellul, in his *La Technique ou l'enjeu du siècle* (*The Technological Society*, 1954). Though Heidegger and Ellul approached technology from different angles and drew different conclusions, it is fair to say that both viewed technology as very problematic and as having negative deterministic effects on humans and nature. In fact, almost the entire continental approach to technology shares the same cautious, skeptical mood. This can be seen in Herbert Marcuse's *One Dimensional Man: Studies in the Ideology of Advanced Industrial Society* (1964), Jürgen Habermas's *Technology and Science as Ideology* (1968), and Jean-François Lyotard's *The Postmodern Condition* (1978), among others.[5]

In contrast to the continental tradition, the analytic approach tends to discuss particular technologies, rather than the technological phenomenon as a whole.[6] In its focus on one form of technology, such as artificial intelligence or biotechnology, the analytic approach draws out both the positive and the negative effects of each form considered. Conversely, the continental tradition tries to deal with the nature of technology as a whole and its larger effects on human life and society. Thus, it can be said that much of the continental tradition engages in the critique of aspects of modern societies, rather

philosophers tend to approach philosophical issues through a phenomenological (purely descriptive) or existential methodology.

5. See Carl Mitcham, *Thinking through Technology* (Chicago: University of Chicago Press, 2004).

6. This distinction between analytic and continental approaches in the philosophy of technology does not assume that all analytic approaches are by philosophers who themselves are within the analytic tradition.

than engaged in specific philosophical concerns such as epistemology and ethics.[7]

However, there are certainly some areas where these two types of concerns cross over, as we shall see in the following exploration of theories within the philosophy of technology. Within both the analytic and the continental approaches, the five main theories are optimistic determinism, instrumentalism, postmodernism, neo-Luddism, and substantivism.[8]

Optimistic Determinism

In optimistic-deterministic theories of technology, we generally find a confidence rooted in the idea of progress.[9] Here, technology is seen as a great success that is both autonomous and neutral. That is, technology advances side by side with the advance of humanity throughout history. Technology is neither good nor evil, in that it simply serves the natural end toward which humanity is progressing. Furthermore, this theory is quite supportive of technological advances, believing that they merely fulfill natural needs. The optimistic-determinist view is best seen in the work of R. Buckminster Fuller.[10] Fuller's writings on technology are marked by what historian William Kuhns calls a sincere "hope in man, science, and technology."[11] It is interesting to note that one of Ellul's critiques

7. For a helpful discussion of the difference between analytic and continental philosophy of technology, see Dusek, *Philosophy of Technology*, chapters 3–4.
8. For a discussion of these categories, except neo-Luddism, see Feenberg, *Questioning Technology;* for a brief but excellent discussion of neo-Luddism, see Rudi Volti, *Society and Technological Change* (New York: Worth, 2000).
9. There are, however, technological determinists who are pessimistic as well. See Bruce Bimber, "Three Faces of Technological Determinism," in *Does Technology Drive History?*, ed. Merrit Roe Smith and Leo Marx (Cambridge, MA: MIT), 79–100.
10. See R. Buckminster Fuller, *No More Secondhand God and Other Writings* (New York: Doubleday, 1971); and R. Buckminster Fuller, *Utopia or Oblivion: The Prospects for Humanity* (Zurich: Lars Muller, 1998).

of modern theology is that it is naively deterministic. He believes that a good example of this can be found in the work of Pierre Teilhard de Chardin. For Ellul, Teilhard de Chardin represents one who holds an overly optimistic view of technological development.[12]

Instrumentalism

In instrumentalism, technology is not seen as determined, but is viewed as humanly controlled. This view combines a liberal faith in progress with a belief that technology is completely under control. Herein, technology is simply a neutral instrument that is used to better our living conditions and our world. It is safe to say that the dominant view today is that of the instrumentalist. In fact, Andrew Feenberg writes that the instrumentalist view is "a kind of spontaneous product of our civilization, assumed unreflectively by most people."[13] As we will see, thinkers like Ellul believe this worldview to be especially pernicious. According to Ellul, it is necessary continually to challenge and question technology, rather than simply allow any and all technological progress to continue.[14]

11. William Kuhns, *The Post-Industrial Prophets: Interpretations of Technology* (San Francisco: Harper & Row, 1973).
12. Jacques Ellul, *The Political Illusion*, trans. Konrad Kellen (New York: Vintage, 1967), 214. For Pierre Teilhard de Chardin's optimistic view of technology, see his claim that technology and science are pushing humans toward greater knowledge of ourselves and the world in *The Heart of Matter* (New York: Harcourt & Brace, 1978), 36-38.
13. Andrew Feenberg, "What Is Philosophy of Technology?" (transcript of lecture, University of Tokyo, June 2003), 5, http://www.sfu.ca/~andrewf/komaba.htm.
14. Jacques Ellul, *Propaganda: The Formation of Men's Attitudes*, trans. Konrad Kellen (New York: Vintage, 1962), xxi.

Postmodernism

There are many postmodernist responses within the philosophy of technology. These are generally marked by a view of technology as ideology or technology as power. Therefore, it is humanly controlled (not autonomous); however, it is value laden. Technology is seen as a social structure in much the same way as institutions are, in that it is an extension of larger power struggles. Thus, technology clearly has political implications, such as the bureaucratization of society and the ever-growing increase of military conflict. The postmodern approach within the philosophy of technology is best seen in the work of Jean-François Lyotard and Michel Foucault.[15]

Ellul agrees with thinkers like Lyotard and Foucault for the most part. However, unlike these postmodern thinkers, Ellul is convinced that the solution to our technological predicament lies in the spiritual realm rather than strictly in the political sphere.[16]

Neo-Luddism

In the neo-Luddite view, technology is humanly controlled, value laden, and must be done away with for the survival of humanity and the environment. There are generally two types of neo-Luddites: primitivists and environmentalists. Primitivists, sometimes called anarcho-primitivists, promote a return to a simpler way of life—often,

15. See Jean-François Lyotard's *The Postmodern Condition: A Report on Knowledge,* trans. Geoff Bennington and Brian Massumi (Minneapolis: University of Minnesota Press, 1978); Michel Foucault, *Power/Knowledge: Selected Interviews and Other Writings, 1972–1977,* ed. Colin Gordon (New York: Vintage, 1972); and Ian Hamilton Grant, "Postmodernism and Science and Technology," in *The Routledge Critical Dictionary of Postmodern Thought,* ed. Stuart Sim (New York: Routledge, 1999), 65–77.
16. For Ellul's critique of political solutions to technological problems, see Ellul, *The Political Illusion.* For Ellul's spiritual solution, see Jacques Ellul, *Anarchy and Christianity,* trans. Geoffrey W. Bromiley (Grand Rapids: Eerdmans, 1991); and Ellul, *Hope in Time of Abandonment,* trans. C. Edward Hopkin (New York: Seabury, 1972).

one that strictly limits the use of modern technologies such as computers, microwaves, and automobiles. According to many primitivists, with the rise of industrialization and technology came the rise in socioeconomic class stratification and alienation. Therefore, the solution is to deindustrialize and simplify society. On the other hand, environmentalists often attack new technological developments because they view technology as an entity that sucks the earth dry of its natural resources. The work of the prominent primitivist philosopher John Zerzan is a good example of the primitivist movement, and Carolyn Merchant's work is a good example of an environmentalist's critique of technology.[17] It should be noted, however, that primitivists and environmentalists are not necessarily easily classifiable. Each has their own criticisms and approaches to technology, which are often unique.

Ellul is quite sympathetic to primitivists and environmentalists. In fact, John Zerzan's writings on anarchism are greatly influenced by Ellul, and one often finds references to Ellul sprinkled throughout Zerzan's work.[18]

Substantivism

In substantivism, technology is seen as autonomous and value laden. In other words, technology has an automatic and unilinear character that tends toward the domination of people and the environment. Technology moves forward in a deterministic manner; however, its advancement is only making things worse. In this view, the

---

17. See John Zerzan and Alice Carnes, eds., *Questioning Technology: Tool, Toy, or Tyrant* (Philadelphia: New Society Publishers, 2001); John Zerzan, *Future Primitive and Other Essays* (New York: Autonomedia, 1994); and Carolyn Merchant, *The Death of Nature: Women, Ecology, and the Scientific Revolution* (New York: HarperOne, 1990).
18. See John Zerzan, *Running on Emptiness: The Pathology of Civilization* (Los Angeles: Feral House, 2008).

"substance" of technology is the drive for efficiency, calculability, and control.[19]Furthermore, substantivists argue that the spread of technology confuses means and ends, and leads to greater exploitation and alienation. It is in the work of both Siegfried Giedion and Friedrich Juenger that helpful examples of substantivism can be found.[20] However, it is most suitable to note that Jacques Ellul was himself a substantivist theorist. This will become clear as we discuss Ellul's theory of technique—the central theme of his work.

The Concept of Technique

It is self-evident that we live in a society saturated in technology. Ellul calls modern societies (both East and West) "technological societies," that is, societies dominated by various forms of technology, as well as by a technological mindset. Ellul employs the term *technique* to refer to both. According to Ellul, technique encompasses specific technologies such as cars, computers, and cellular phones, as well as an overly rationalistic, calculating worldview preoccupied with efficiency and productivity.[21] This is the realm of necessity, as opposed to the realm of freedom.

Ellul primarily defines technique in two ways. First he states that technique is "the totality of methods rationally arrived at and having absolute efficiency (for a given stage of development) in *every* field of human activity."[22] Second, technique is a general reference to the specific technological phenomenon found in modern, Western societies.[23] Technique is both an abstract method and a concrete

---

19. Feenberg, *Questioning Technology*, 3.
20. See Siegfried Giedion, *Mechanization Takes Command: A Contribution to Anonymous History* (New York: Norton, 1975); Friedrich Georg Juenger, *Die Perfektion der Technik* (Frankfurt: Vitorio Klostermann, 1946).
21. Jacques Ellul, *The Technological Society*, trans. John Wilkinson (New York: Vintage, 1964), 4–5.
22. Ibid., xxv.

phenomenon. In order to fully understand what Ellul means by technique, we need to analyze its forms and entailments.

Technique as Tools

According to Ellul, technique began with machines. In ancient civilizations, humans desired to create technologies that would efficiently aid them in their work. In fact, archeological and historical evidence demonstrate that primitive societies used a variety of hunting, fishing, and food-gathering techniques. These techniques employed various forms of technology that were inextricably tied to the desired outcomes of the ancients. They rationally calculated which technologies (tools) would be most efficient and used them. These tools would then be superseded by new methods and tools that proved more efficient as society evolved. These tools would eventually become machines. Like their predecessors, these machines existed for various forms of food gathering, as well as military engagement.[24]

Ellul argues that the ancients believed their tools and machines to be somewhat divine in nature because of their helpfulness. He states, "Our modern worship of technique derives from man's ancestral worship of the mysterious and marvelous character of his own handiwork."[25] Whether we agree with this claim or not, it is clear that an overwhelming percentage of society today seems to worship the newest forms of technology. This can be seen every holiday season in the United States. Millions upon millions of individuals scurry about, desperately trying to obtain the latest cellular phone, video game, or computer.

23. Ibid.
24. Ibid., 23–26.
25. Ibid., 24.

These technologies are nothing more than human-made tools that, to many, seem quite impressive. The fact that we are often so enamored with these technologies rests in part on the fact that we are ignorant of the internal workings of these tools. In general, we do not know how the latest phone can engage in multiple activities at once. We do not know how computers are programmed. We are unaware of the complex mechanisms that lie beneath the newest cars. These technologies amaze us. This amazement, in turn, becomes a type of worship.[26]

It is important to remember that, for Ellul, these technologies are one component of technique.[27] We cannot escape this component of technique. We are forced to live in and with various technologies. However, there is more to technique than technology; for instance, one of the other important components of the world of technique is science.

Technique as Science

Many believe that science came prior to technique. This is not the case, according to Ellul.[28] It is necessary to remember that when Ellul discusses technique, he is often referring to a *method* that strives above all else for *efficiency*. A rational method was a prerequisite for science and for tools. As with tools, science has become technique. In other words, science as a discipline is no longer concerned with abstract or theoretical formulations in themselves.[29] Rather, science is

26. Ibid.
27. Ibid., 3.
28. Ibid., 7.
29. Hegel's s systematic philosophy was an excellent example of abstract science rather than concrete, applied science. According to Ellul, abstract science aims at synthesizing various facts and viewpoints, while concrete science aims at efficiency and productivity (Ellul, *The Technological Society*, 9).

largely *applied science* in modern societies. Ellul states that because of this, it is clear that technique has taken over the scientific realm and transformed it into a realm of its own.[30]

Ellul refers to modern science as "technical activity."[31] This activity requires large numbers of scientists who work together toward a specific end. This end is usually funded by a large corporation or government in order to arrive at specific, predetermined goals that correspond to their agendas. For this reason, Ellul considers science to be ideology.[32]

Technique as Consciousness and Ideology

Machines and science are concrete examples of technique. Technique is also abstract and theoretical. According to Ellul, the modern mindset is dominated by technique. This is a mindset that strives toward the goals of technique: efficiency and productivity. These goals are aimed toward regardless of cost. Concomitantly, human value is measured in terms of these goals. If one individual is less productive than another, then the less productive individual is a priori less valuable. The same can be said for nonhuman animals and the earth's landscapes and vegetation.[33]

This modern consciousness arose in the eighteenth century. According to Ellul, after the rise of Descartes's method and philosophy, more people in the Western world embraced an overly rationalistic and rigid mindset. [34] Incredible scientific achievements followed, but at great cost.[35] Ellul believes that Marx was the first

30. Ibid.
31. Ibid.
32. Ibid., 11.
33. Ibid., 72–74.
34. Ellul explains, "The principles established by Descartes were applied and resulted not only in a philosophy but in an intellectual technique. . . . This systematization, unification, and clarification was applied to everything—it resulted not only in the establishment of budgetary

to point out the dark underbelly of the industrial world. Yet most people today still continue to be guided by a worldview that cherishes efficiency and productivity above all else. Because of this, we have a new system of values, created for us by technique; it is impossible to separate one's consciousness from one's value system. Ellul states, "In Western society, it is technique that has struck us as the determining element in the creation of . . . values."[36] This value system is purely utilitarian; it always strives for the greatest good for the greatest number of people. Ellul believes that this is a corrupt ethical system, however. Utilitarianism is not concerned with truth or falsehood, but with *quantity*. The greatest good and the greatest number of people are the guiding principles of utilitarianism. Quantification becomes the determining factor of the value system of technique. No one seems to question utilitarianism. In fact, it is not uncommon to hear political leaders (of all parties) appeal to utilitarian principles. In Ellul's view, this is further evidence that technique is not true consciousness, but false consciousness: ideology.[37]

Like Marx and Habermas, Ellul argues that technique is an inherited belief system that simply reinforces the values and goals of technique itself.[38] The only possibility of fighting this pernicious ideology is to continually question and challenge it in its various

rules and in fiscal organization, but in the systematization of weights and measures and the planning of roads," (Ellul, *The Technological Society*, 43).

35. Ellul states, "Until the eighteenth century, technique was, purely and simply, a practical matter. In the eighteenth century, people began to think about the technologies: they compared and tried to rationalize their application, which completely changed their perspective. A technology was no longer merely a practice; it was no longer merely an operation. Now, technology passed through a rational intervention and it had a completely different object; its object was efficiency," (Jacques Ellul, *Perspectives on Our Age: Jacques Ellul Speaks on His Life and His Work*, trans. Joachim Neugroschel [Toronto: Canadian Broadcasting Company, 1981], 36).

36. Ibid., 33.

37. Jacques Ellul, *The Technological Bluff*, trans. Geoffrey W. Bromiley (Grand Rapids: Eerdmans, 1990), 178.

38. For an insightful discussion of technique as ideology, see Jürgen Habermas, "Technology and Science as Ideology," in *Toward a Rational Society*, trans. J. Shapiro (Boston: Beacon, 1971).

forms. This, however, is not enough to escape this false consciousness. It can only be overcome when one recognizes the dialectical nature of reality: that is, the realm of freedom and the spirit that counterbalances the realm of necessity.[39]

Technique as Total Environment

According to Ellul, technique has infiltrated nearly every sphere of human existence: technology, politics, military, economics, education, and religion, to name a few. Thus, technique has become the total environment of necessity. Ellul writes, "Having become a *universum* of means and media, technology (technique) is in fact the environment of man. These mediations are so generalized, extended, multiplied, that they have come to make up a new universe; we have witnessed the emergence of the 'technological environment.'"[40] This environment continues to shape our consciousness and our relationships to others and the earth. It also situates us in a world dominated by machines, applied science, and the desire for efficiency and quantification. The environment of technique also has other characteristics, some of which are not so obvious.

Characteristics of Technique

For Ellul there are two primary "obvious" characteristics of technique in the modern world: rationality and artificiality, which are two dialectical poles.[41] Rationality is the static pole of technique; artificiality is the pole in flux. Both qualities require the other for

---

39. See Jacques Ellul, "On Dialectic," in *Jacques Ellul: Interpretive Essays*, ed. Clifford G. Christians and Jay M. Van Hook (Urbana: University of Illinois Press, 1981).
40. Ellul, *The Technological Bluff*, 38.
41. Ellul, *The Technological Society*, 78–79.

its continued existence and progress. Of the two, rationality is the primary motivating factor of technique. Ellul states, "In technique, whatever its aspect or the domain in which it is applied, a rational process is present which tends to bring mechanics to bear on all that is spontaneous or irrational."[42] This rationality is best seen in the systematization and specialization of labor and education. In both fields, highly specialized types of knowledge are taught and acquired. Fields of study and professions almost never rely on integral or comprehensive knowledge; instead, areas of expertise are reductionistic and one-sided. Ellul believes that this condenses individuals to one-dimensional beings and robs them of personal creativity. Furthermore, this causes individuals to see themselves, others, and the world in a "logical dimension alone," where all is physical, practical, and nonspiritual.[43] This dimension creates a lens of efficiency through which all beings are judged. Technique thus creates a society in which efficiency is the motivating factor as well as the determiner of value, opening the door for exploitation of the environment and humans as "resources."

Rationality also manifests itself in a concrete form: artificiality. As the second obvious characteristic of technique, artificiality is a "plastic" and malleable feature of technique. The world we inhabit today is primarily artificial, according to Ellul. This is the logical and necessary consequence of rationality. The artificial is always more efficient and predictable than the natural world, and thus it is necessitated in a system governed by technique. Examples of artificiality are found in the modern living and working structures in which we dwell. Ellul believes that this artificial system is a pernicious threat to the natural world. He writes, "The world that is being created by the accumulation of technical means is an artificial world

42. Ibid.
43. Ibid.

and hence radically different than the natural world. It destroys, eliminates, or subordinates the natural world, and does not allow this world to restore itself or even to enter into a symbiotic relationship with it."[44] The artificial realm follows directives and imperatives that are antithetical to the natural world. For this reason, the two cannot work side by side in a mutually beneficial manner. Ellul argues that the artificial is destroying the natural environment, and in the near future there will be no nature at all: "When we succeed in producing artificial *aurora boreales*, night will disappear and perpetual day will reign over the planet."[45] Like the aurora borealis, the artificial can be stunningly mesmerizing, and it often invokes a sense of awe. However, we must not lose sight of the simple and clear fact that the two worlds are deeply opposed to each other.[46]

In addition to the two primary characteristics of technique, there are also important secondary qualities that Ellul believes must be apprehended. It is helpful to think of these as laws that technique must follow. The first is automatism. According to Ellul, once technique takes over the consciousness of a society, the free agency of individuals is radically diminished. No longer can one choose which course of action to take; technique has chosen already. Technique always decides according to the most effectual and productive means available. Humans can only submit to the most efficient path, the one that technique has already decided upon. Ellul explains,

> There is no personal choice, in respect to magnitude, between say 3 and 4; 4 is greater than 3; this is a fact which has no personal reference. No one can change it or assert the contrary or personally escape it. Similarly, there is no choice between two technical methods. One of them asserts

---

44. Ibid., 79.
45. Ibid.
46. For Ellul, the development of the artificial necessarily leads to the destruction of the natural (ibid., 77–79).

itself inescapably: its results are calculated, measured, obvious, and indisputable.[47]

This is a clear example of the automatism of technique. Likewise, if a factory worker decides to accomplish her task in a manner that is not the prescribed standard, but is less efficient, she will likely lose her job. Or, if an office worker requests to use an outdated and less efficient computer, rather than the latest version, he will likely find himself unemployed. Technique dictates that the most efficient means are automatically employed.[48]

Automatism also slowly eliminates nearly all less efficient means. In addition, more technical activities are combined and added to other technical activities, which in turn create more efficient and productive human action. For example, one can e-mail while jogging and listening to the latest news all at the same time. Further, one can do all of these things on a home treadmill, removing the need to travel to the gym. Once the individual gets into the habit of engaging in all of these activities at once, he or she is not likely to stop this practice. Thus the automatism of technique continues to determine the course of action for the individual. Ellul is skeptical about escaping from the grasp of technique's automatism.[49]

As we can see, Ellul believes that technique is advancing and nothing stands in its way. It truly is a realm governed by necessity. Rationality robs us of our creativity, the artificial destroys the natural, and automatism radically restricts our free will.[50]

Another secondary characteristic of technique is self-augmentation. Ellul argues that technique will continue to evolve and progress without human intervention. He states, "Modern men

47. Ibid., 80.
48. Ibid., 82.
49. Ibid., 85.
50. Ibid., 86.

are so enthusiastic about technique, so assured of its superiority, so immersed in the technical milieu, that without exception they are oriented toward technical progress."[51] Here we see the blind worship and adoration of technique and anything technological. Because of this uncritical attitude toward technique, humans continue to subscribe to its dictates and laws. This is one element of technique's self-augmentation or autonomy.[52]

As technique grows and seeps into every aspect of society, more and more techniques rely on each other and become interdependent. One invention or technological creation always engenders others, and so on. Ellul believes that this progression is necessary and inevitable. He argues, "A technical discovery has repercussions and entails progress in several branches of technique and not merely one. Moreover, techniques combine with one another, and the more given techniques there are to be combined, the more combinations are possible."[53] A clear example of the autonomous entailments of other techniques is found in the internal combustion engine. These engines were first used to power farm equipment in the early nineteenth century. Soon they were used for locomotives, ships, and automobiles. Ellul's point is that one technology always creates—directly or indirectly—other related technologies. Furthermore, Ellul believes that techniques always create technical problems that can only be resolved by using another technique.[54]

---

51. Ibid.
52. Ibid., 89.
53. Ibid., 91.
54. One of the most contentious aspects of Ellul's philosophy of technology is his claim that technique is autonomous. This assertion has been discussed in length by Langdon Winner in *Autonomous Technology: Technics-Out-of Control as a Theme in Political Thought* (Cambridge, MA: MIT, 1977). Winner argues that technical autonomy is best exemplified in modern politics. Herein, technological problems are always discussed in terms of technological solutions. In turn, this creates an autonomous technological realm. Winner's examples and arguments are quite convincing and Ellul would surely agree. Winner is sympathetic to Ellul's work, but disagrees with Ellul's belief that humans have forfeited their freedom to technique. Winner is more optimistic in this respect. In his essay "The Enduring Dilemma of Autonomous

Thus the relationship between technique and its successes and failures is always circular and interdependent. Ellul calls this the "closed world of technique."[55] This leads us to the final secondary characteristic of technique: monism.

According to Ellul, all technical phenomena constitute a closed system. The world of technique is one that is highly complex and multifaceted. Each technique in this system is related to and dependent upon many other techniques. One cannot exist by itself. This milieu has clear boundaries that separate it from the natural world, but if anything from the natural world merges with technique, it can no longer return to its natural state. "Technique modifies whatever it touches, but it is itself untouchable."[56] The monism of technique will continue to expand as more aspects of the natural world intersect with it. Thus technique grows in form and content and creates a thoroughgoing unity. This unity, according to Ellul, despite its seemingly diverse components, retains its essence: the desire for efficiency.[57]

Consequences of Technique

According to Ellul, the consequences of technique are ambivalent. In other words, there are always two sides of technique's development: positive and negative. Ellul recognizes that technique has brought good to humankind, but he also emphasizes the evils that necessarily follow technique. Ellul believes that it if we are to be realistic about

Technique," *Bulletin of Science, Technology, and Society* 15, nos. 2–3 (1995), 62–72, Winner argues that humans have not entirely lost their freedom to technique, but can use it to overcome the problems created by technique. As we will see, Ellul does not share this optimism.

55. Ellul, *The Technological Society*, 93.
56. Ibid., 94.
57. Ibid., 21, 72, 74, 110.

technique, then we need to analyze and discuss its harmful entailments rather than simply ignoring them.

Ambivalence

The clearest embodied, concrete form of technique is technology. Many argue that technology is not harmful in and of itself, but that it depends on how the technology is used. From this standpoint, technology is seen as neutral. Ellul argues that this view is simplistic and naïve.[58]

As Ellul has demonstrated, technique is not neutral. It follows its own path and serves its own purpose. It does not stop for moral considerations; it is directed by efficiency, productivity, and its own well-being. Once a technology has been created, it will be used if it adds to the efficiency of technique. If it is not efficient, then it will be rejected. There is no clearer example of this than in the world of computers.[59]

Ellul maintains that humans have been conditioned by technique to embrace its values and goals. Thus, society cannot view it objectively.[60] The technological universe "makes determinations that are not dependent on us and that dictate a certain use."[61] If we do make choices as to what technologies we utilize, they are usually small and insignificant. In general, we must all use certain forms of technology simply in order to survive.

As to the question of the intrinsic good or evil of technology, Ellul maintains that it is not *inherently* one or the other. He firmly believes that the question is overly simplistic. Ellul says that instead

---

58. See ibid., 97.
59. See Ellul, *The Technological Bluff*, 262–70.
60. Ellul, *The Technological Society*, 37.
61. Ibid.

of concerning ourselves with these sorts of moralistic questions, we should first try to objectively—even though this is impossible—analyze the entailments of technique. By doing this, we will be able to recognize the true ambivalence of technique. Ellul does maintain, however, that even though it is ambivalent, there are always more harmful outcomes from technique than beneficial. Since we have been programmed to only view technological progress in a positive manner, Ellul gives four guiding propositions to aid us in seeing it for what it truly is.[62]

The first guiding proposition is, "All technical progress has its price."[63] According to Ellul, with all technological advancement, there are always setbacks. One clear example of this is the aesthetic of major US cities. Many of these cities are lined with strip malls and freeways. To be sure, these make shopping and travel more efficient, but they also are eyesores.[64] Ellul says, "Everywhere technique creates ugliness. This is the price we have to pay."[65]

Another example is the increase in pollution and health problems with the centralization of cities and living arrangements, not to mention noise nuisances and a rise in crime. These aspects of the city certainly existed to a certain degree in ancient cities, but Ellul reminds us that they still exist today—in a much more pronounced manner.

The price of technological progress is seen in what Ellul calls the "game of substitutions."[66] For example, mechanized farming has largely replaced traditional forms of agriculture. The mechanized method is more efficient in terms of production, but it requires far

---

62. These four guiding propositions are found in ibid., 39–45, and Ellul, *The Technological Bluff*, 35–73.
63. Ellul, *The Technological Bluff*, 40.
64. Herbert Marcuse also makes this case in *One-Dimensional Man: Studies in the Ideology of Advanced Industrial Society* (Boston: Beacon, 1964), chapter 1.
65. Ellul, *The Technological Bluff*, 40.
66. Ibid., 41.

more natural resources than traditional farming. So, while modern agriculture provides us with more food, it exploits and harms the earth to a much greater degree.[67]

Another example of substitution is found by looking to the success of Wal-Mart. Small businesses in rural towns across the United States have been monumentally affected by the behemoth retailer. Goods that were once sold at local hardware stores, pharmacies, and grocery markets have been substituted with the massive "one-stop shop." While goods are offered at a lower price at Wal-Mart, the effects on the local community are often devastating.[68]

Ellul argues that there is also substitution of seasonal rhythms with the pulse of the machine. We are no longer conditioned by the rising and setting of the sun or by the seasons of the year. Instead, we are programmed to follow the ever-increasing speed of technologies—most often the computer. This inevitably leads to loss of physical and mental rest, and to what Ellul calls a loss of "vital force": strength that comes from our connection to the natural world.[69] In turn, Ellul argues that although humans may be living longer than ever before, they are also more fragile and vulnerable than ever.[70]

In addition to this loss of health, there is the loss of individual choice. Technological progress dictates that planning always be done in regard to the larger population rather than the individual. The more technique and technologies dominate the earth, the more of these utilitarian functional constraints are imposed.[71] This reduces the free actions of the individual. As we will see in our discussion of

---

67. Ibid., 149–59.
68. This fact has been well documented (see, e.g., Anthony Bianco, *Wal-Mart: The Bully of Bentonville* [New York: Crown Business, 2007]).
69. Ellul, *The Technological Bluff*, 43.
70. Ibid.
71. Ibid., 45.

propaganda, Ellul believes that anything that strips the individual of freedom entails a loss of personal growth.[72]

Ellul believes that the restriction of human freedom is ever increasing and corresponds to the proliferation of technological progress.[73] We must remember that Ellul is not saying that technological advancement is not beneficial. He is simply pointing out that it always has a cost, and that the price is the loss of the earth's well-being and individual freedom.[74]

Ellul's second guiding proposition regarding the ambivalence of technological progress is that it always "raises more and greater problems than it solves."[75] Every advancement in technology is created to solve a particular problem. Usually that problem has to do with efficiency, but not always. This is why every few months, or sooner, we see new computers, phones, cars, and other forms of technology emerging. Each new form solves some "problem" of its technological predecessor. This process, however, is not limited to the technological realm. As we saw when discussing various forms of technique, this movement is applied to all spheres of society: political, educational, military, and so on. The important aspect to remember—even though most people fail to recognize it—is that nearly all of the problems solved by technique were originally caused by it. For example, Marx saw clearly that capitalism was not the sole cause of class division and exploitation. Capitalism was a response to technological development. It was the "solution" to the problem of centralized mechanization. However, capitalism ended up causing far more harm than technologies of the nineteenth century.[76]

---

72. Jacques Ellul bemoans the loss of personal freedom through nearly all of his work, but especially in *Propaganda* and in *Violence: Reflections from a Christian Perspective,* trans. Cecilia Gaul Kings (New York: Seabury, 1969).
73. Ellul, *The Technological Bluff*, 45.
74. Ibid.
75. Ibid., 47.

Another example is found in our present ecological dilemma. What is its cause? According to Ellul, its cause is technique and unrestricted technological development.[77] In the eighteenth century and afterward, populations began to increase. Cities began to develop into massive urban centers. In response, factory production of food and other necessities began to arise. This caused the flow of goods to the masses to be more efficient than ever before. However, this also had negative effects. The factories produced considerable contamination and contributed to the rapid development of various other health problems. Ellul explains, "Wholesale pollution, nuisances, the production of new chemical elements that do not exist in nature, the final exhaustion . . . of natural resources, the great threat to our water, the destruction of our countryside, the wasting of tillable soil. . . . They are all the result of frenzied growth, the unrestricted application of technique."[78] Clearly, a pernicious snowball effect occurs when the application of technique is perpetually used as the solution to the very problems it creates.

The third proposition that Ellul states regarding technological advancement is, "The harmful effects of technical progress are inseparable from its beneficial effects."[79] This notion is closely related to Ellul's previous (second) proposition. Ellul maintains that those who look at technology in a simple bifurcated way as "good" or "bad," and those who argue that it is neutral, are both naïve. Once

76. See Karl Marx, "Economic and Philosophical Manuscripts," in *Marx's Concept of Man*, ed. Erich Fromm (New York: Continuum, 2004), 73–151.

77. As an integral thinker, Ellul reminds us that we should not look at specific ecological problems without regarding the whole. He says: "There is a tendency to divide up the danger, for example, water pollution, or the ultimate exhaustion of copper. This is a technocratic mistake. We must look at the ecological question in its entirety, with all the same interactions and implications, without reductionism. We then see that the problem raised is a thousand times more vast and complex than any of those raised in the 19th and 20th centuries," *The Technological Bluff*, 51.

78. Ibid., 50–51.

79. Ibid., 54.

one carefully analyzes technology, one will understand that while there are beneficial aspects, there are *always* concomitant negative entailments.[80]

Examples of this proposition are everywhere. Automobiles, for instance, have made travel faster and more comfortable than in previous eras; however, they guzzle fossil fuels, pollute the air, and kill thousands of people every day. Likewise, e-mail has reduced our reliance on paper and is delivered instantly, but has drastically reduced the personal aspect of written interaction (unlike handwriting, every typed e-mail looks the same), and it has created an immense reliance on computers. These concurrently positive and negative entailments of technology are undeniable.[81]

Similarly, as technology proliferates, it offers us more and more choices: products, travel options, types of media, and so on. But all these decisions add considerable complexity and even confusion to daily life. They also congest our lives with sounds, images, and information, dragging the individual further into the world of technique and its problems. The phenomenon of congestion, which is an inseparable effect of technique's unfettered growth, results in more individuals unable to adapt to modern society.[82] This is a natural result of the complexity of technique—a complexity that is often praised! Ellul maintains that humans are not naturally meant to live in a world congested with technology. This has devastating effects on our minds, our relationships, and our general well-being.[83] Certainly, the rate of mental illness, addiction, and suicide are on the rise.[84] Ellul

---

80. Ibid.
81. A helpful discussion of the positive and negative entailments of technique is found in Steven E. Jones, *Against Technology: From the Luddites to Neo-Luddism* (London: Routledge, 2006).
82. Ellul, *The Technological Bluff*, 58.
83. This is also argued quite persuasively in Zerzan, *Future Primitive*.
84. For information on the increase of mental illness see, Tyger Latham, "Mental Illness on the Rise in the US: New Government Data Suggests that 1 in 5 Adults Suffer from Mental Illness" in *Psychology Today*, May 18th, 2011. http://www.psychologytoday.com/blog/therapy-matters/

attributes all of these ailments to the technological milieu in which most of the world is forced to dwell. Every beneficiary of technology is concomitantly its victim.[85]

Ellul's fourth and final proposition is that technological progress "has a great number of unforeseen effects."[86] This seems to be an obvious statement, but unfortunately, for many it is not. Unpredictability has always been one of the entailments of technique. Ellul explains that all technological progress has three kinds of results: the desired, the predicted, and the unpredicted.[87] When technicians create new technology, they seek clear and precise results. They may be aware of various alternate outcomes to that which they are seeking, but inevitably there will be unforeseen effects or accidents. While the unpredicted results are seemingly problematic, they are actually helpful to technique. Without these complications, technique would not be able to strive toward more efficiency; the undesired outcome is merely the "error" of the trial-and-error process.[88]

On a related note, Paul Virilio has argued that the proliferation of technology has created a new collective anxiety rooted in the unknown, unintended consequences of technology. He calls this the "society of the accident."[89] Virilio, who was greatly influenced by

---

201105/mental-illness-the-rise-in-the-us (accessed, May, 5, 2014). On the rise of suicide, see a discussion of the findings of the Centers for Disease Prevention and Control, by Tara Parker-Pope, "Suicide Rates Rise Sharply" in the New York Times, May 2nd, 2013. http://www.nytimes.com/2013/05/03/health/suicide-rate-rises-sharply-in-us.html?_r=0 (accessed May 10, 2014). For evidence of an increase in alcoholism see, Frank Newport, "U.S. Drinking Rate Edges up Slightly to a 25-Year High," in www.gallup.com, July 3th, 2010. http://www.gallup.com/poll/141656/Drinking-Rate-Edges-Slightly-Year-High.aspx (accessed, May 11th, 2014).

85. Ellul, *The Technological Bluff*, 60.
86. Ibid.
87. Ibid., 68–72.
88. The trial-and-error process of technique adds to its self-augmenting process (Ellul, *The Technological Society*, 85–94).
89. Paul Virilio, *The Original Accident*, trans. Julie Rose (London: Polity, 2005), 9.

Ellul, maintains that modern technology has "invented" new and unique accidents.[90] For example, on a regular basis we hear of airline disasters, automobile collisions, and other freak technological catastrophes. Humans are aware of these threats, and they live in a constant state of anxiety because of these technological risks. Furthermore, they are always on the lookout for accidents, and when they see one—which is a regular occurrence, thanks to mass media—they are simultaneously captivated, awestruck, and sickened with anxiety.

Virilio argues that the culprit behind our "society of accidents" is *speed*. He calls himself a "dromologue"—one who studies the phenomena of acceleration.[91] Virilio has persuasively maintained, through many books, that the love, pursuit, and unquestioned devotion to speed is the central fault of the modern world. Like Ellul, he says that technological accidents are "absolute and essential" to the furthering of science and technology.[92] Without accidents, new, more efficient technologies cannot be created.[93]

This speaks to the necessity of technique. This realm we inhabit, thanks to technique, is a realm of absolute and complete necessity. Technological disasters and accidents must happen; it cannot be otherwise. There is no way to opt out of seeing or being part of one or more unforeseen technological occurrences.[94]

At this point, we should note that there are two crucially important aspects of Ellul's four propositions. The first is that Ellul reminds

---

90. For Virilio and Ellul, a fundamental and determining factor in modern societies is technological accidents (Virilio, *The Original Accident*; Ellul, *The Technological Bluff*). For those who find Ellul's analysis of technique intriguing, I recommend three of Paul Virilio's books: *The Lost Dimension*, trans. Daniel Moshenberg (New York: Semiotext(e), 1991); *The Aesthetics of Disappearance*, trans. Philip Beitchman (New York: Semiotext(e), 1991); and *The Information Bomb*, trans. Chris Turner (New York: Verso, 2000)
91. Virilio, *The Original Accident*, 11.
92. Ibid.
93. Ellul, *The Technological Bluff*, 54.
94. See Ellul, *The Technological Society*, 300–18.

us that technological progress always has a dark side. In his characteristically dialectical way, he describes it this way: "There is no progress that is ever definitive, no progress that is only progress, no progress without a shadow."[95] The industrial revolution of the nineteenth century had a shadow, which Marx saw clearly. Likewise, military progress of the twentieth century clearly had its dark side. Ellul's emphasis on the ambivalence of technological progress is essentially a Socratic appeal to reflection and examination, a wake-up call to the high costs of technological development.[96]

The second key aspect of Ellul's guiding propositions is that all progress necessarily entails unforeseen consequences. We can never predict exactly what its effects will be. These can take the form of "accidents" as Virilio described them, or, as Ellul pointed out, the consequences can be the exploitation and destruction of the earth.[97] There are also many other radical consequences, including the emphasis on instrumental reason and the rise of propaganda, which will be discussed later.

Some apologists of technology might argue that unfettered technological progress is necessary for the advancement of freedom and democracy. As we will see, this attitude is mistaken. Technique always entails a greater loss of freedom, personal growth, diversity, and truth than it can ever create. Still, many fail to see technique's shadow. Ellul says, "We refuse to see what real technical progress is. We refuse to see its real consequences and the way in which it calls into question all that we are. We refuse to pay the price that technique exacts."[98]

Ellul outlines the three primary reasons that people dismiss or remain ignorant of technique's dark side. First, Ellul maintains that

95. Ellul, *The Technological Bluff*, 71.
96. See David W. Gill, "Jacques Ellul: The Prophet as Theologian," *Themelios* 7, no. 1 (1981): 4–14.
97. Ellul, *The Technological Bluff*, 60–64.
98. Ibid., 72.

the benefits of technological progress are often immediate, whereas the costs are not. The negative effects are usually long-term or are only seen in retrospect.[99] Second, many are unaware of the shadow of technique because usually only a small percentage of individuals pay its high price. For example, consider the amount of land in the world that is uninhabitable because of pollution. Compared to livable areas, this might seem insignificant; however, this in no way diminishes the fact that human lives and precious land are being destroyed everyday by technological progress.[100]

The third reason many remain ignorant to the price of technique is propaganda. Ellul maintains that there can be no technological progress without the consent of the masses. This consent is created by mass psychological manipulation.[101] The forms, characteristics, and entailments of propaganda will be presented at a later point. For now, it is important to understand that ignorance of technique is a fundamental attribute of the realm of necessity. This lack of understanding has a massive price. We should never blindly accept technology as simply good or evil. It is always ambivalent.

Double Feedback

Related to the ambivalence of technological progress is *double feedback*. We should recall that technique is a total, comprehensive system. It has infiltrated every aspect of human life. For every step forward technology takes, there is always feedback.[102] There is positive feedback, which brings more efficiency and progress to the process of technique. There is also negative feedback, which usually

99. Ibid., 72–75.
100. Ibid., 73.
101. This is one of the central arguments found in Ellul's *Propaganda*.
102. Ellul has a very different understanding of feedback than that found in contemporary systems theory.

includes unforeseen consequences. Combined, these comprise the double feedback of technique. According to Ellul, double feedback is a regulator that balances the process of technique while moving it forward. He explains, "The one tends to check the acceleration of technique in every direction; the other tends to increase it." Both reactions are beyond human control. They are necessary and unpredictable consequences of technological progress.[103]

What are the origins of double feedback? Positive feedback, according to Ellul, arises from "the relation between politics and technique and science and technique." Negative feedback comes from "the relationship between technique and the economy."[104] Technique has proven very successful in the realm of politics. Whether on the right or left, technique always moves toward unification—in political parties, ideologies, and collective action. Unification is always a goal of technique, because the more unity, the more efficient technique will be. This was foreshadowed in our previous discussion of the automatism of technique.[105]

The more centralized the political system becomes, the more efficient it will be. For Ellul, politics is essentially motivated by a desire for power and control.[106] Unification and centralization are necessary if there is to be control. Fundamentally, unification is a movement toward simplification. This increases the concentration of power and enables an efficient progress of state control.

One of the necessary factors for the unification of politics is the manipulation of the mass media. By utilizing the media, the state works toward creating a homogenized consciousness that in turn supports its own goals and those of technique. The state cannot

---

103. Ellul, *The Technological Bluff*, 101.
104. Ibid., 101–2.
105. Ellul, *The Technological Society*, 79–85.
106. This is a key aspect in Ellul's thought that should always be recalled when studying Ellul's philosophy or theology.

advocate or support true diversity. This would be inefficient. It must eliminate all dissimilar thoughts and ideas, and with them, individual freedom in political decisions.[107]

The state cannot have control if it is powerless. Technique gives power to the state because technique is legitimate in itself. It is legitimate, because it is required to solve problems efficiently. All crises in the modern world are solved by technique—be they military, political, economic, and so on. Therefore, technique is legitimized by the simple fact that it is utilized.

Technique is often understood as a kind of scientific power that does not need to be defended or rationalized. It is implicitly accepted and agreed upon. Why? Because it always employs the most efficient means. Ellul writes, "Power affirms itself scientifically. Science validates it because it can do nothing without power. For the public, science is the great goddess which it cannot question and which validates those who serve it."[108] Science acts as positive feedback for technique. Both theoretical and applied sciences require technique for their advancement, and technique requires science for progress.[109] It is a reciprocal relationship that enhances both.

In addition to the positive feedback of science, there is also negative feedback. Ellul maintains that the force of negative feedback is primarily found in various economic systems. Technique requires natural resources and capital to further itself. These requirements continue to grow at an alarming pace, but resources cannot keep up with technique's demands. This inevitably leads to the monopolization of massive amounts of capital—natural and

---

107. Ellul defends these claims in *The Political Illusion* and *Propaganda*. For these reasons, among others, Ellul endorses anarchism.
108. Ellul, *The Technological Bluff*, 103.
109. Concerning the positive feedback of science, Ellul says, "All real scientific progress, in biology, chemistry, physics, astronomy, physics, and microphysics (and, more relatively, medicine), depends solely on technical equipment," ibid., 103–4.

artificial—by technique. This monopolization strips the market of capital and imposes unnecessary financial stresses on it. This in turn forces the financial system to limit technique. Ellul explains, "The system works as follows. Technique makes economic growth possible. But it demands such enormous funding by the economy that the economy reacts by putting a brake on it by forcing it to make choices."[110] Imposing restrictions on technique only makes it develop at a slightly slower rate. Technique will still continue to progress, but now it has to take into account what forms of development will aid its further unfettered growth. It will then place all of its available resources into these forms.[111]

Some might argue that technique causes economic growth in all sectors of society equally. Ellul maintains that this is false. He explains that technique is not concerned with democracy or the equal distribution of wealth. It is only concerned with its own progress.

Technique always causes a loop of double feedback. It is difficult to say with any precision what the degrees or limits to this feedback are. The important issue to understand is that the phenomenon of feedback is global, and many of its effects are unknown at the present time.[112]

The Ethical Side Effects of the Realm of Necessity

Now that we have looked at the characteristics of technique, we will turn to its moral side effects.[113] One of the first side effects of

110. Ibid., 105.
111. Ibid., 100–4.
112. Ibid.
113. For Ellul, there are concrete and abstract side effects of technique. The concrete include ambivalence, double feedback, accidents, and the like. The abstract side effects include a distortion of ethics (Ellul, *The Technological Society*, 97, 134).

technique, according to Ellul is the creation of a new "technical morality."[114]

Technical Morality and Systematic Ordering

Ellul believes that technique has its own value system and moral imperatives. Technique is completely unmoved by traditional moral issues. Only those issues that concern technique are considered legitimate. The first aspect of this new moral system is that it eliminates all moral issues that do not relate to progress, efficiency, or production. The only issues that are seen as moral are those that might hinder technique's methods and goals. Technique moves along blindly, eliminating all moral concerns that do not affect it. That which promotes more techniques is moral, and that which hinders technique is immoral (or irrelevant). Progress becomes the primary guiding ethical principle of technique.[115]

The second aspect of technical morality is what Ellul calls systematic "ordering."[116] This refers to the increasing stress on the systematization of human thought and behavior. *Order* is of tremendous importance in the technological milieu. Without it, technique cannot develop efficiently. Thus order has become a goal and a value of millions of individuals. Systematic ordering is necessary today and individuals are indoctrinated from a very young age that they should live an efficient, productive, and orderly life. This in turn does away with spontaneity and creativity (two essential aspects of human life), according to Ellul.[117]

114. Ibid., 97.
115. Ibid., 1–7.
116. Ibid., 110.
117. Ibid., 102–3.

Instrumental Value and the Problem of End and Means

Related to the first two characteristics of technical morality is a worldview that sees individuals as having instrumental rather than intrinsic value. This is an extremely disturbing trend, but is one that follows necessarily from technique.

Instrumental value is also known as extrinsic value. This moral worldview maintains that human value or worth is contingent upon one's efficiency, productivity, and the extent to which the individual is a praised member of his or her society. According to those who hold this view, human worth is not intrinsic or innate in any sense; value or worth are projected from humans onto others and the world in general.[118]

According to Ellul, the instrumentalist's ethical stance now dominates the Western world. Furthermore, people and the earth only have worth when they mirror the values of technique—namely, efficiency and productivity. Those who do their jobs efficiently are the ones respected and valued. Those who are inefficient are often marginalized.[119] A clear example of this can be seen in the way the elderly and the disabled are treated in the United States. Often they are seen as being less productive members of society, and because of this, they are viewed as somehow inferior or even invisible.[120]

The antithetical ethical position, and the one maintained by Ellul, is that all humans have intrinsic value. Ellul believes that we have worth a priori, and that we should respect and treat others in accordance with this recognition. He illustrates this point in a short essay titled "The End and the Means." In it, Ellul demonstrates that humans have become the means of technique. No longer do humans

---

118. For a discussion of instrumental and intrinsic value, see Holmes, *Basic Moral Philosophy* (Belmont, CA: Wadsworth, 2003).
119. Ellul, *The Technological Society*, 398–402.
120. Ibid.

control technique, but because of the characteristics of technique, humans must follow the autonomous progress of the system. This in turn creates a world where we are used, and use others, for the sake of technique's goals. Intrinsic human value is no longer recognized, and all are viewed as having only extrinsic value.[121]

Ellul maintains that this modern problem (that of justifying the means by the end) is radically different than it was in ancient and classical civilizations. Modern technology has transformed the problem into an all-encompassing issue from which no one in the modern world can escape. This is not an abstract, philosophical problem. The issue of end and means is a concrete, lived reality. Ellul argues that there are three main facts that characterize the problem of end and means in contemporary industrial society.[122]

The first fact is that "everything has become a 'means,'" and "there is no longer an 'end.'"[123] In other words, humans and technique work harmoniously toward an end, but this end is not clearly stated or unambiguously described. Rather, the end is discussed in abstract and vague terms. Verbiage such as "progress" or "humanity" or "the greater good" are employed by politicians, economists, and military officials. But these words, according to Ellul, are empty. He explains,

> No longer is it a sort of game, giving an abstract response to an abstract question, but it is a concrete question of one's attitude to life. The error of our makers of economic and political systems is that they play a game which consists in giving an abstract answer to a concrete question! . . . Thus *man*, who used to be the end of this whole humanist system of means, *man*, who is still proclaimed as an "end" in political speeches, has in reality himself become the "means" of the very means which ought to serve him: as, for instance, in economics or the state.[124]

---

121. Ellul, "The End and the Means," in *The Presence of the Kingdom*, trans. Olive Wynon (London: SCM, 1951), 49–78.
122. These facts are discussed primarily in Ellul, "The End and the Means." However, they are also referred to in Ellul's *The Technological Society*.
123. Ellul, *The Presence of the Kingdom*, 62.

Ellul believes that modern men and women have become blind to this fact. In fact, many today use the same abstract arguments used by politicians and other leaders in order to rationalize their own behavior and existence. Ellul sums up this first aspect of the problem by stating, "Fully persuaded that we are procuring the happiness of man, we turn him into an instrument of these modern gods, which are our 'means.'"[125]

The second fact that characterizes this pressing problem is that technical means have become more important than the truth. For Ellul, truth is defined as an accurate description of reality. Due to technique, a correct analysis of the world is of secondary importance. Of primary importance is the search for better means. A clear example of this can be found in modern science.

> Science has had to become more and more effective for technical purposes and now science is only significant in terms of technology. Its whole direction is applied science. It is at the service of means. It has become a means for the creation of a more perfect means; and the abstraction called "science," to which homage is always paid, has replaced our search for Truth.[126]

An example of what Ellul is describing can be seen clearly in university philosophy departments across the United States. More philosophy programs, in order to receive government (and private) funding are combining with cognitive science and computer programming departments. This radically changes the intent, methods, and goals of a traditional philosophy department. Philosophers must now demonstrate how philosophy has practical, efficient effects in the modern development of technology.[127]

124. Ibid., 63.
125. Ibid.
126. Ibid., 64.
127. Philosophy departments at U. C. Davis and U. C. Berkeley presently do extensive work with cognitive science and applied computer science. This is clearly seen in many of their faculty's

Philosophy at one time was the search for the true, the good, and the beautiful (Plato) and that which brought tranquility of mind (the Stoics and Epicureans). It was carried out in dialogue (the Socratic method), through which the truth surfaced.[128] Now, philosophy is often understood as the search for what is useful and efficient in the applied sciences and is often carried out in lecture classes "efficiently" enrolled by the hundreds.[129]

The third fact of the problem of end and means is that—for the most part—people do not question the means to the end. This is a great danger, according to Ellul. Modern men and women have become pacified and no longer challenge and critique the modern means and end of technique. They simply buy into abstract phrases that give the appearance of definition, but in reality they are submitting to its will. Thus, the ends become universally accepted and implicit. For instance, people generally agree that "the greatest good" or "happiness" or "progress" is the end of humankind, but these empty words signify nothing clear or concrete. In reality, the means create more means, and this creates a self-augmenting, vicious cycle of means. Ellul believes that this harsh fact could possibly be challenged if individuals could muster the courage to question the means and the illusory end.[130]

Ellul's ethical convictions here bear a similarity to those of Immanuel Kant. According to Kant, individuals have intrinsic value. This is due to the fact that everyone participates in the moral law, which Kant believes to be universal. Because of this participation, all

research into artificial intelligence. See, e.g., Hubert Dreyfus, ed., *Husserl, Intentionality, and Cognitive Science* (Cambridge, MA: MIT, 1993); and John Searle, *Minds, Brains, and Science* (Cambridge, MA: Harvard University Press, 1986). (These were required texts when I was a graduate student at the Graduate Theological Union and U. C. Berkeley in 2003–2004.)

128. See Roochnik, *Retrieving the Ancients: An Introduction to Greek Philosophy* (Boston: Wiley-Blackwell, 2004).
129. See Marcuse, *One-Dimensional Man*, chapter 7 for a discussion of "efficient" philosophy.
130. Ellul, "The End and The Means," 73.

humanity has equal worth, regardless of how they behave. There is no doubt that some behave better than others, but this does not mean that their worth is contingent upon their moral acts.[131]

Kant argues in his ethical treatise, *Fundamental Principles of the Metaphysics of Morals*, that due to the intrinsic value that humans have, ethical behavior should be motivated out of duty and respect for this value. For this reason, humans should treat all people equally, regardless of status, power, or intellect. Kant formulates three imperatives that he believes should guide moral action. These are well-known, so we will only briefly survey them, rather than going into depth.[132]

First, Kant argues that humans should "only act on that maxim whereby thou canst at the same time will that it become a universal law."[133] In other words, humans ought to ask themselves the following question: "What behavior would I want to be legally mandated?" Found in many religions and philosophies, this guiding ethical principle seems to be one of the most universally accepted ideas. It is simply a reformulation of the Golden Rule or the ethic of reciprocity. Kant believes that by following this first formulation of his categorical imperative, we respect the autonomy of the individual. This autonomy is of the utmost importance. For Kant, the essence of a human being is freedom, and this freedom should be respected. By refusing to act toward others the way one would want to be acted upon, one disrespects and ultimately discounts the autonomy of others.[134]

Ellul does not agree completely with Kant's insistence that we should follow the principle of universalizability, but he does share

---

131. See Immanuel Kant, *Fundamental Principles of the Metaphysics of Morals*, trans. T. K. Abbott (New York: Prometheus, 1987).
132. Kant, *Fundamental Principles*, 29–51.
133. Ibid., 29.
134. Ibid., 29–35.

with Kant a deep respect and reverence for the autonomy of the individual.[135] Ellul believes that technique destroys the freedom of the individual while providing the illusion of autonomy. In our present technological society freedom is being stripped away, and Ellul argues that this is our greatest threat.

Kant's second formulation of the categorical imperative is, "Treat humanity, whether in thine own person or in that of the other, in every case as an end withal, and never as a means only."[136] Here, Kant argues that individuals should never be seen as mere tools or instruments, but as they truly are, in themselves. As we have seen, Ellul observes that technique uses all humans (and the earth) as a means to an end. Technique makes no distinction between intrinsic and extrinsic human value; it sees only through one lens: efficiency. This breaks down the ability of humans to treat others as ends, despite Kant's call for us to do so. Locked into the will of technique, humans have no choice but to use others for their own benefit and for the benefit of technique. For example, in order to become successful today, one must be able to use the Internet competently. If one refuses to use the Internet, one will most likely be refused employment. But, if one uses the Internet, then one is participating in the burning of fossil fuels (plastics and metals used in manufacturing the computer) and in the exploitation of workers who assemble a great deal of computer technologies. Thus, technique entails the use of humans and the earth as means rather than ends. It seems impossible to escape from this pernicious cycle, which epitomizes the very warning Kant offers.

Kant's third formulation of the categorical imperative is as follows: "Work toward a kingdom of ends."[137] Here Kant is reinterpreting

---

135. Jacques Ellul, *The Ethics of Freedom*, trans. Geoffrey W. Bromiley (Grand Rapids: Eerdmans, 1972), 239.
136. Kant, *Fundamental Principles*, 36.
137. Ibid., 44.

the notion of the "kingdom of God" found in the New Testament. Kant argues that humans ought to do everything in their power to bring about a global community that treats all of its inhabitants with complete respect and dignity. Ellul would agree with this sentiment, but he argues that in order to truly bring about a kingdom of ends, technique needs to be questioned, challenged, and limited. Ellul realizes, however, that this is a monumental task.

While Ellul is critical of Kant at various points,[138] there are resemblances between the two thinkers that cannot be denied. First, both maintain that the freedom of the individual is of primary importance. Second, both believe that one of the greatest problems of ethics is the failure to recognize that people (and other beings in the natural world) have intrinsic value and should be treated as ends rather than means. Furthermore, Ellul and Kant recognize that modern society forces people into treating others as means, and that it is increasingly difficult to break away from this trend.[139]

Other Philosophers of Technology: Marcuse and Heidegger

Now that we have discussed Ellul's critique of technique and his similarities to Kant, we turn to two additional central figures within the philosophy of technology: Herbert Marcuse and Martin Heidegger. Ellul's work will become clearer when we compare his thought to their well-known analyses.

138. See Ellul, *The Ethics of Freedom*, 239, 245.
139. See Ellul, "The End and the Means."

Marcuse on Technology: One-Dimensional Man

Just before World War II, several members of the renowned Frankfurt School took asylum in the United States.[140] Included among these intellectual giants were Theodore Adorno, Max Horkheimer, and Herbert Marcuse. Perhaps more than the other members of the Frankfurt School, Marcuse (1898–1979) acutely perceived the dangers of technology. According to his view, technology is now completely integrated into all modes of scientific, political, and social life. This has created a highly complex, bureaucratized, rationalized, administered society. Furthermore, this technical world alienates modern humans and robs them of creativity, individuality, and true autonomy.[141]

The most pernicious effect of the technological system, according to Marcuse, is that it forces modern humans to think in a "one-dimensional" mode. In other words, multidimensional, integrative, dialectical thinking is stripped away from the individual. Human reason is squeezed into narrow categories of overgeneralizations, oversimplifications, and bifurcations. Furthermore, with academia's rising emphasis on symbolic logic and purely pragmatic reason, our cognitive capacities for creativity and imagination are dismissed as useless and outdated—unless, that is, we create and imagine within singular dimensions that aid the progress of the technological system. Only this kind of "creativity" proves efficient enough to be embraced by the technical worldview; all the while, it is simply a one-dimensional, technological rationality.[142]

---

140. The Frankfurt School refers to a school of philosophy associated with thinkers such as Jürgen Habermas, Erich Fromm, and Walter Benjamin, among others. Most within the Frankfurt School were greatly influenced by Kant, Hegel, Marx, and Freud and sought to expand and extend the work of these thinkers. Ellul's philosophy, in many ways, parallels the work of the Frankfurt School, especially in his dialectical worldview and his criticism of instrumental rationality and positivism. For more on the Frankfurt School, see Rolf Wiggershaus, *The Frankfurt School: Its History, Theories, and Political Significance* (Cambridge, MA: MIT, 1994).

141. Marcuse, *One-Dimensional Man.*

But this "reason" (which Marcuse refers to as rationality) is a false reason. It is a "logic" created by science and technology. It only supports the techno-political milieu and the further integration of individuals into that very structure. Conversely, true reason—found in classical (Socratic) logic, rather than in modern, formal logic—involves the power of negation. By engaging in a constant questioning or negation of what was encountered in the world, this dialectic forced a continual advancing of reason toward objective truths.[143]

In contrast, the false reason of the modern Western world is a logic that fails to engage in negation. Marcuse observes that the ability to question and view an issue, event, or concept from a spectrum of angles has been lost. This is the case because the technological system forces individuals to think in one-dimensional categories in order to survive. In fact, even if people believe that they are actually reasoning in a truly dialectical fashion, they are usually only thinking in narrow categories that have been created for them. Marcuse gives a clear example of this:

> A man who travels by automobile to a distant place chooses his routes from the highway maps. Towns, lakes, and mountains appear as obstacles to be bypassed. The countryside is shaped and organized by the highway: what one finds en route is a byproduct or annex of the highway. Numerous signs and posters *tell the traveler what to do and think*; they even request his attention to the beauties of nature or the hallmarks of history. *Others have done the thinking for him*. . . . Giant advertisements tell him when to stop and find the pause that refreshes. And all this is indeed for his benefit, safety, and comfort; he receives what he wants. Business, technics, human needs and nature are welded together into one rational and expedient mechanism. He will fare best who follows its directions, subordinating his spontaneity to the anonymous wisdom which ordered everything for him.[144]

142. Ibid., 16–18.
143. Ibid., 11.

Because we are presented with such limited options, "rationality" within the technological machine robs us of the freedom to choose as creative individuals. However, since we are given a preset, foreordained domain of concepts within which we can think and live, we *believe* we are truly free. Perhaps the clearest example of this—mirroring Marcuse's map imagery—is found in the countless prefabricated tract homes that exist in the suburbs of many cities throughout the U.S. One must struggle to identify the actual differences between these houses. When one does, it is clear that any diversity is quite superficial, such as a slightly different shade of paint or small variations among window shades. However, the significant point of this example is that those who live or exist within these houses are often fully convinced that they freely chose their homes. In actuality, the "choices" being made are nothing but selections between limited options that have been predetermined by technological rationality.[145]

We now live in a world designed with a preestablished artificial harmony. It is simple, palatable, comfortable—but misguided and erroneous. Within this system, our creativity is stripped because the individual no longer thinks outside the predesignated categories of thought. Freedom, concomitantly, is taken away due to a neglect of possibilities that are limited, disguised, and hidden by the technological worldview, world, and products.[146]

The most pressing goal in our present day, according to Marcuse, is to bring about liberation. As technology and industrialization continue to envelop every facet of society, individuals are forced to submit to a one-dimensional, technological rationality that restricts and changes human thought and possibilities. Thus, the liberation of

144. Herbert Marcuse, *Technology, War and Fascism*, vol. 1 of *Collected Papers of Herbert Marcuse,* ed. Douglas Kellner (New York: Routledge, 1998), 47.

145. Marcuse discusses the myth of freedom/choice in *One Dimensional Man*, 6.

146. See ibid., 42–52; Ellul, *The Technological Society*, 137–39.

humanity must be restored. Marcuse does not offer specific solutions to our current predicament, but he does discuss various possibilities.[147]

For example, Marcuse continually uses the word *project* to describe the task of dealing with the problems arising from our techno-industrial system.[148] Most likely, Marcuse picked up this terminology from his contemporaries—specifically, the existentialists who employed it. Sartre, for instance, used the word *project* to refer to the continual chore that individuals bear: to imaginatively and resourcefully create themselves.[149] This creation is never finished and must be done in a way that is true (authentic) to one's own desires and goals. In the same way, it is clear that Marcuse sees our current technological milieu as one in need of constant and creative responses. This immediately eliminates the possibility of quick, one-step solutions. As such, those who simply reply that God is the answer, or that technology's problems will be solved by creating new technology, have not fully grasped the problematic depths of technology. For Marcuse, there is no one answer; *we must commit to a continuous and creative struggle with technology*.[150]

Unlike Ellul, Marcuse does not believe that technology is autonomous and beyond the control of humans. Rather, technology is controlled by the elite and powerful within society. They have no concern for the well-being of humanity, only for personal economic gain and for the absolute control of the masses. For this reason, Marcuse argues that the power must be taken from the elites and given back to all people. Only when power is back in the hands of the people can technology be controlled and redirected. This will entail

147. Marcuse, *One Dimensional Man*, 7.
148. Ibid., 125, 196.
149. Jean-Paul Sartre, *Existentialism Is a Humanism*, trans. Carol Macomber (New Haven, CT: Yale University Press, 2007), 23.
150. Marcuse, *One Dimensional Man*, 256–57.

the possibility of individuals engaging in a process Marcuse calls "self-determination"—that is, creative, individual choice.[151]

Clearly, Marcuse is calling for nothing other than the *democratization of technology*. Rather than a handful of politicians and technicians creating and selling technology (via propaganda) to the public, all individuals should have a voice in this process. Marcuse does not specifically detail the way this power shift will take place. However, he does discuss the outcome of this goal.

> Freedom indeed depends largely on technical progress, on the advancement of science. But this fact easily obscures the essential precondition: in order to become vehicles of freedom, science and technology would have to change their present direction and goals. . . . Then one could speak of a technology of liberation, product of a scientific imagination free to project and design the forms of a human universe without exploitation and toil.[152]

From this it is clear that Marcuse wants to reverse the power process, and in doing so redirect technology. Together with true democracy, this new direction will creatively move away from the alienation of humanity. This reversal is required for the well-being of the earth and its inhabitants, and in order to achieve it, revolution may be necessary.[153]

For Marcuse, the project of democratizing and redirecting technology first requires a movement of the people. The earth community must come together as one, united against the corrupt political institutions that control the techno-industrial system. Marcuse refers to this movement toward liberation as "The Great Refusal." He states,

---

151. Ibid., 251.
152. Herbert Marcuse, *An Essay on Liberation* (New York: Beacon, 1969), 19.
153. See Marcuse, *One Dimensional Man*, chapter 9.

Underneath the conservative popular base is the substratum of the outcasts and outsiders, the exploited and persecuted of other races and other colors, the unemployed and the unemployable. They exist outside the democratic process; their life is the most immediate and the most real need for ending intolerable conditions and institutions. . . . When they get together and go out into the streets, without arms, without protection, in order to ask for the most primitive civil rights, they know that they face dogs, stones, and bombs, jails. . . . Their force is behind every political demonstration for the victims of law and order. The fact that they start refusing to play the game may be the fact which marks the beginning of the end of a period.[154]

Marcuse admits that this refusal may not be successful. However, he firmly maintains that this step is necessary if we are to overcome the corrupt system.[155]

Like Ellul, Marcuse was aware of the consequences of the technological society. Unlike Ellul, Marcuse's analysis of technology lacks depth due to his unfamiliarity with its origins: technique. In any case, Marcuse's "one-dimensional man" is quite similar to Ellul's analysis of technique as consciousness and ideology.

Heidegger on Technology: The Flight from Thinking

Like Marcuse, Martin Heidegger has also had a tremendous influence within the continental tradition. He has by far been the most-read philosopher of technology to date. Heidegger was acutely aware of the dangers of technology. However, his critique was more reserved than Ellul's, despite the contemporaneous publications of their work on technology.[156]

154. Ibid., 256–57.
155. Ibid.
156. Martin Heidegger's "Die Frage nach der Technik," in *Die Technik und die Kehre* (Tubingen: Neske), 5–36, and Jacque Ellul's *La Technique ou l'enjeu du siècle* (Paris: Armand Colin) were both first published in 1954.

First of all, we must understand Heidegger's definition of technology. Heidegger states, "We ask the question concerning technology when we ask what it is. Everyone knows the two statements that answer our question. One says: Technology is a means to an end. The other says: Technology is a human activity. The two definitions of technology belong together."[157] For Heidegger, these two definitions of technology, which he calls the "instrumental" and the "anthropological," should be understood not as two opposing views of technology, but as one conception of technology. However, in Heidegger's view, this definition of technology is helpful only if we understand what the essence of technology is; namely, efficiency. He explains, "Expediting is always itself directed from the beginning . . . towards driving on to the maximum yield at minimum expense."[158] Heidegger maintains that because of the essence of technology, technology itself actually orders society, rather than the opposite. He states, "The subject-object relation thus reaches, for the first time, its pure 'relational,' i.e., ordering, character in which both the subject and the object are sucked-up as standing reserves."[159] And, "Everywhere, everything is ordered to stand by, to be immediately at hand, indeed to stand there just so that it may be on call for a further ordering."[160] For Heidegger, then, a bus, for example, actually "uses" people in order to fill itself. Thus, the subject-object is "relational" and human beings are used as resources as they use certain other resources. This must be brought to light, according to Heidegger, so that we will not become enslaved by technology.[161]

---

157. Martin Heidegger, *The Question concerning Technology and Other Essays*, trans. William Lovitt (New York: Harper, 1977), 4.
158. Ibid., 15.
159. Ibid., 173.
160. Ibid., 17.
161. See Hubert Dreyfus, "Nihilism, Art, Technology, and Politics," in *The Cambridge Companion to Heidegger*, ed. Charles Guignon (Cambridge: Cambridge University Press, 1993), 289–316.

Heidegger's entire philosophical oeuvre—from his early work in *Being and Time*, first published in 1927, to his later work on technology, *The Question concerning Technology*, first published in 1954—was concerned with ontology. If one does not properly understand the essence of technology, Heidegger maintains, then one will not grasp that technology now determines our understanding of being. And through this knowledge, we can free ourselves from our practices that value efficiency, and can therefore come to a new understanding of being. Heidegger calls this new understanding the "clearing." Once the clearing opens up, then one can enter into a "free relationship" with technology.[162] However, Heidegger reminds us that the essence of technology is often not grasped, and that the individual easily becomes its slave. He gives a poignant illustration: "Hourly and daily they are chained to radio and television. Week after week the movies carry them off into uncommon, but often merely common, realms of the imagination, and give an illusion of a world that is no world."[163]

In addition to the threat of bondage to technology, according to Heidegger, we will also be in danger of becoming indifferent to true, meditative thinking, if we do not understand the essence of technology. He explains, "Then man will have denied and thrown away his own special nature—that he is a meditative being. Therefore, the issue is the saving of man's essential nature. Therefore, the issue is keeping meditative thinking alive."[164] For Heidegger, meditative thinking is contrasted with "calculated" thinking and with "thoughtlessness." Both of the latter types of thinking go hand in hand with enslavement to technology. The calculated thinker has been taught by technology how to think. When one thinks in a

---

162. Heidegger, *The Question concerning Technology*, 3, 6, 44.
163. Martin Heidegger, *Discourse on Thinking*, trans. John M. Anderson and E. Hans Freund (New York: Harper, 1966), 48.
164. Ibid., 56.

calculated way, one thinks in a narrow, cold, and mathematical manner. No matter what the question or problem, the best solution is nearly always the most efficient one for this type of thinker.[165] More importantly, one who has lost the ability to think meditatively has lost his or her essential nature as a human being.[166]

Thoughtlessness is the uncritical state of mind in which we are spoon-fed information.[167] Heidegger says, "Let us not fool ourselves. All of us, including those who think professionally, as it were, are often enough thought-poor; we all are far too easily thought-less."[168] Both calculated thinking and thoughtlessness are the result of technology, and they drive humans to what Heidegger calls a "flight from thinking"; in other words, nonmeditative thinking: "Man today will even flatly deny this flight from thinking. He will assert the opposite. He will say—and quite rightly—that there were at no time such far-reaching plans, so many inquiries in so many areas, research carried on as passionately as today."[169] Although calculated thinking and thoughtlessness are sometimes considered legitimate forms of thinking by Heidegger, they are not "true" forms of thinking. True thinking requires reflection, openness to various types of thinking other than one's own, and also openness to mystery. Heidegger explains, "Meditative thinking demands of us not to cling one-sidedly to a single idea, nor to run down a one-track course of ideas. Meditative thinking demands of us that we engage ourselves with what at first sight does not go together at all."[170] Only when we open up to a meditative type of thinking will we be able to grasp the essence of technology. This grasp will come by way of "being open

165. Heidegger, *The Question concerning Technology*, 135, 172.
166. Dreyfus, "Nihilism, Art, Technology, Politics."
167. Heidegger, *Discourse on Thinking*, 45.
168. Ibid.
169. Ibid., 45.
170. Ibid., 53.

to the mystery"—that is, the mystery that lies in technology.[171] A free relationship to technology will thus be possible. Heidegger states,

> Our relation to technology will become wonderfully simple and relaxed. We let technical devices enter our daily life, and at the same time leave them outside, that is, let them alone, as things which are nothing absolute but remain dependent upon something higher. . . . We can use technical devices, and yet with proper use also keep ourselves free of them, that we may let go of them at any time. We can use technical devices as they ought to be used, and also let them alone as something which does not affect our inner and real core.[172]

For Heidegger, it is obvious that a free relationship with technology is a possibility, as long as technology is approached in thoughtfulness and with "releasement." Heidegger does not deny the autonomous nature of technology, nor does he deny the "essence" of technology: efficiency. In this light, Heidegger can be seen as a substantivist who is at least somewhat optimistic.[173]

Ellul, as we have seen, would reject Heidegger's notion of a "free relationship" with technology. For Ellul, technique has infiltrated every aspect of our society, including specific technological devices. Thus, it is impossible to "let go" of technology "at any time," as Heidegger believes. Modern society is dependent on cars, computers, and cellular telephones. If one were to refuse to use such things, one would have a very difficult time maintaining a job, going to college or even obtaining food, for that matter. According to Ellul, it is an illusion to think that technology does not dominate us. In this light, Heidegger's view of technology can be seen as idealistic and naive.[174]

---

171. See Heidegger, *The Question concerning Technology*, 110; Dreyfus, "Nihilism, Art, Technology, Politics."
172. Heidegger, *Discourse on Thinking*, 54.
173. See Feenberg, *Questioning Technology*, 151, 182–85.
174. Ellul, *The Technological Bluff*, 73.

We have now discussed Ellul's philosophy of technology: his concept of technique, its characteristics, and entailments. We also discussed the forms of necessity that are created by technique, as well as its ethical consequences. Finally, we related Ellul's worldview to two other philosophers of technology: Marcuse and Heidegger.[175]

In the next chapter, we will address two fundamental spheres within the realm of necessity: propaganda and politics. As we will see, these are inextricably linked with the growth and domination of technique.[176]

---

175. A good anthology on the philosophy of technology, which includes writings by Ellul, Marcuse, and Heidegger, is Robert Scharff and Val Dusek, eds., *The Philosophy of Technology: The Technological Condition* (Oxford: Wiley-Blackwell, 2003).
176. For the linkage of technique to politics and propaganda, see Ellul, *The Technological Society*, 233–39, 369–75.

5

Propaganda and Politics

Ellul's book *Propaganda: The Formation of Men's Attitudes*, is an analysis of propaganda in modern Western societies. This work was the second in his trilogy, the first being *The Technological Society*, which primarily discusses the forms and characteristics of technique. The third was *The Political Illusion*, an analysis and critique of the machinations of modern political systems. A vital feature of this trilogy is that the first book describes technique (the realm of necessity), while the second and third books describe two realms that are entailments of technique. The spheres of propaganda and politics are separate but interdependent domains of technique.[1]

---

1. The trilogy is discussed in Jacques Ellul and Patrick Troude-Chastenet, *Jacques Ellul on Politics, Technology, and Christianity* (Eugene, OR: Wipf & Stock, 1995), 14.

Propaganda

The analysis of propaganda remains one Ellul's most overlooked intellectual achievements. Ellul systematically described propaganda and its characteristics in order to awaken the public to its nefarious consequences. But at the current date, there are few readily available scholarly works on Ellul's book *Propaganda*, other than a handful of journal articles, book reviews, and dissertations.[2] Unfortunately, this leaves Ellul scholars with an incomplete understanding of his work, much like the common ignorance of his dialectical worldview.[3]

One of the most pernicious aspects of modern capitalist society is propaganda. It is found on the internet, television, radio, billboards, magazines, newspapers, textbooks, religious tracts, political pamphlets, and in many other areas of society. Many people, however, never stop to question propaganda. Perhaps they believe that it is not harmful or that it is a necessary evil. Even more likely, perhaps they do not recognize it as part of reality that can and should be critiqued and challenged. Ellul believed that propaganda was a cancerous component of modern life that robbed individuals of their freedom. In *Propaganda*, published in 1962, he presented one of its first sociological analyses. Here, Ellul discussed at length the characteristics of modern propaganda, and also its ethical implications. He outlines the methods used to entangle individuals into the sphere of necessity. These methods include limiting options in decisions, omitting information, and the use of psychological

2. One of the few books that delve into Ellul's views on propaganda is Randal Marlin, *Propaganda and the Ethics of Persuasion* (New York: Broadview, 2002).

3. For a brief overview of Jacques Ellul's book, *Propaganda: The Formation of Men's Attitudes,* trans. Konrad Kellen (New York: Vintage, 1962), see Jacob Van Vleet, "A Theoretical Approach to Mass Psychological Manipulation: Jacques Ellul's Analysis of Modern Propaganda," in *Censored 2012: Sourcebook for the Media Revolution,* ed. Mickey Huff (New York: Seven Stories, 2011), 313–24.

manipulation. These entanglements and their relationship to technique and necessity will now be discussed.

According to Ellul, propaganda is necessarily linked to technological development and the technological mindset, that is, technique. As we have seen, technique includes specific technologies such as computers, cars, and phones, and it also includes a mindset that sees the world through the lens of progress, efficiency, and instrumental value. Additionally, technique is necessarily linked to the state. Propaganda only exists in a symbiotic relationship with technique and the state. As we will see, Ellul argues convincingly that technological and political "progress" cannot take place without propaganda.

Defining Propaganda

The closest Ellul comes to defining propaganda is in the following statement, which he refers to as only a "partial" definition: "Propaganda is a set of methods employed by an organized group that wants to bring about the active or passive participation in its actions of a mass of individuals, psychologically unified through psychological manipulations and incorporated into an organization."[4] Ellul maintains that in its broadest sense, propaganda usually (but not necessarily) involves one or more of the four following components.[5] First, there is *psychological action*, in which the propagandist seeks to manipulate and modify public opinion using psychological means. In

---

4. Ellul, *Propaganda*, 61.
5. Ellul is primarily a sociologist, so his work is often descriptive rather than definitional. This will be evident in my description of propaganda's four realms. Those who are looking for clear-cut, simple definitions will not find them in Ellul's work. It is helpful to think of Ellul as a phenomenologist similar to Hegel. Ellul often works to describe a large system of thought—including all of its components, corollaries, and entailments. This manner or scholarship fits hand in hand with Ellul's dialectical worldview; it covers broad areas of what is being observed without dismissing them.

other words, appeals to fear, pity, guilt, sexual desire, and the like are employed in order to unconsciously sway the audience. This can be clearly seen in visual advertisements that display scantily clad men and women in provocative sexual positions—even when the commodities being sold have nothing to do with sex. One can also observe this psychological manipulation in political and military campaigns that rely on fear. Clearly, there are many other examples all around us, reminding us that psychological action appeals to the irrational and unconscious with very effective results.[6]

Second, propaganda often involves what Ellul calls *psychological warfare*. Here, the propagandist tries to "break down" the public's self-confidence in their own decision-making abilities. In other words, the propagandist tries to convey that its message supersedes the knowledge of the individual and the public. Often a group of people working for a corporation or institution, the propagandists seeks to win the trust of the masses, to the extent that we stop trusting ourselves. This creates a society where people become ever more dependent upon the media and other social institutions. People cease to think critically and analytically about the messages they are receiving, and they simply allow the propagandist to spoon-feed them the "truth."[7]

Third, Ellul points out that propaganda often involves *reeducation or brainwashing*. This can be seen clearly when sources of public information are limited, textbooks are edited, and certain political websites are banned or shut down in order to further a dominant ideology.[8]

Finally, in its broadest sense, propaganda commonly employs *public relations*. Institutions and corporations are always concerned with

6. Ellul, *Propaganda*, xiii.
7. Ibid.
8. Ibid., 28–29, 193–202.

their relationship to the public and the public's perception of them. Thus, these entities often rely on a group of public relation experts to "sell" their product or service. According to Ellul, this will always include a restriction of the truth and a misrepresentation of the institution in order that it might appear more palatable to the masses. Furthermore, public relation technicians often use manipulatory means to sway the public.[9]

The key to understanding these four domains of propaganda is to recognize that each of them is a *method*. The first two employ psychological methods and the last two employ a method of limiting or manipulation of information. All four, according to Ellul, are based on the propagandist's knowledge of modern psychology and sociology. He states, "The propagandist builds his techniques on the basis of the knowledge of man, his tendencies, his desires, his needs, his psychic mechanisms, his conditioning—and as much on social psychology as on depth psychology."[10] Public relation technicians, advertisers, and marketers use these basic procedures and principles to achieve a calculated outcome. Propaganda, therefore, has become a highly specialized technique that is generally not discussed in the public realm. Furthermore, propaganda, even though it is all around us, is in many ways invisible. This is so because many propagandists are skilled in camouflaging their message with music, graphics, political rhetoric, and a myriad of other cultural spheres.[11]

It is vital that we recognize that modern propaganda is not simply a "trick" or a "gimmick," as many people suppose. Rather, propaganda is incredibly complex and multifaceted. It is created by experts who specialize in psychological, sociological, and cultural knowledge. The average person is usually completely unaware of the propagandists'

9. Ibid., 225, 283, 287.
10. Ibid., 4.
11. Ibid., 33–38.

involved techniques and methods.[12] For this reason we should analyze what Ellul and others have written about propaganda. By doing so, we will become more aware of our surroundings, enabling us to think for ourselves and become authentic, engaged members of a democratic society.

External Characteristics of Propaganda

According to Ellul, modern propaganda is aimed at both the individual and the masses concomitantly. This is the first specific external characteristic of propaganda. The propagandist always creates his or her message for the crowd, but also for the individuals that make up the crowd. In other words, individuals are only recognized insofar as they are related to the masses. Knowledge of average likes, dislikes, and emotional responses are used in order to address the specific person within society.

For example, consider a solitary woman watching a political debate on television. She knows that she is alone, but she is also aware that she is part of a large group. The televised debate is not aimed at the individual or at a sector of society. Yet, using emotional appeals and selective information, the speakers manage to "communicate" to the audience as both individual and crowd.[13] This is significant for one main reason: the individual is not seen as a unique being that has value. Rather, the individual is an abstraction of the greater whole. Specific personal eccentricities and idiosyncrasies are not taken into account. Nontraditional groups of people are not considered; only the average person—the mean—is recognized and validated.[14]

12. Ibid., 4–6.
13. Ibid., 6–9.
14. Ibid.

This is clearly a type of marginalization. The person who does not have the average tastes or predispositions is considered weird, different, or even an extremist. Thus, the people who fall into this category are pushed to the margins of the discussion (political, religious, ethical, etc.) and more often than not, ignored.[15]

In addition, this abstraction of the average person unconsciously motivates people to think in certain preordained categories. Even those on the margins find themselves entering into dialogue using the discourse and categories of thought determined by the propagandist, lest they be labeled as crazy or abnormal. This is incredibly effective. Many people simply want acceptance from others and will do whatever is necessary in order to feel accepted. Thus, nontraditional ideas and the people who hold them are becoming increasingly rare. People cease to think for themselves and begin to concern themselves only with what they are instructed to think about. Propaganda, in aiming at the "average" individual, creates a one-dimensional society where increasing numbers of people are thinking the thoughts of others—the propagandists.[16]

The second external characteristic of modern propaganda is that is must be *total*.[17] In other words, propagandists—if they want to truly be effective—must use all forms of media. Propaganda must use all available means in order to spread its message as fast as possible. After all, propaganda is driven by a desire for efficiency and effectiveness. This is so, because, according to Ellul, totality is a necessary entailment of technique. If efficiency is to be accomplished, the propagandist must use all of the means available for this end.[18]

15. Ibid., 137, 148, 171.
16. Ibid., 6–9, 105–6.
17. Ibid., 9.
18. Ibid., 9–17.

Ellul calls this the "organized myth" of propaganda.[19] In all forms of media, the same messages are being systematically conveyed, infiltrating every aspect of the individual's life and creating a narrative that is based on partial or distorted truths. Ellul describes this organized myth: "Through the myth it creates, propaganda imposes a complete range of intuitive knowledge, susceptible of only one interpretation, unique and one-sided, and precluding any divergence. This myth becomes so powerful that it invades every area of consciousness, leaving no faculty or motivation intact."[20] According to Ellul, propaganda is always one-sided and only conveys its message in one direction—toward the masses. There is no dialectical or dialogical relationship between the propagandist and the individual. Propaganda excludes all contradictory viewpoints and opinions. Thus, it must be total, and it must dominate every aspect of the human's psychological and social life. It is no longer simply a technique; propaganda is totalitarian in its very being.[21]

We see this clearly in our political system as conveyed to us by the media. We are told that there are only two legitimate options: Republicans and Democrats. Nearly everywhere we look—television, newspaper, Internet, magazines—only these two groups are represented. Of course, we occasionally hear about other options. However, in the same breath that they are mentioned, we are virtually always told that endorsing one of these "nontraditional" parties is only for extremists or kooks, or that voting for them will do nothing but take away votes from one of the "real" parties. The media establishment only provides its audience with limited options, ensuring a calculated outcome while providing the appearance of free choice (voting).[22]

19. Ibid., 11.
20. Ibid.
21. Ibid., 6–9.
22. Ibid., 60n61.

The all-encompassing nature of technique entails the totalizing nature of propaganda in the realm of necessity. Later, we will see that both of these factors produce what Ellul calls the ubiquitous political illusion.[23]

The third external characteristic of propaganda is *continuity and duration*.[24] According to Ellul, propagandists do much to keep up appearances and perpetuate the organized myth. This entails repetition ad nauseam and the constant appropriation of new means. Any new form of technology that develops and is used widely must immediately be usurped. The new form is, in turn, used for the duration, until a newer form of technology replaces the old. This cycle is unceasing. Ellul states, "Propaganda must be continuous and lasting—continuous in that it does not leave any gaps, but must fill the citizen's whole day and all his days."[25] This method is necessary in order to keep the individual's point of reference within the circle of myth. After all, if there were any holes in this system, they might expose the individual to a form of thinking that does not cohere with the propagandist's narrative. This constant flow of information creates a total environment that is self-referential and self-justifying. Born into this realm, and numbed by it, the individual submits to propaganda's power, uses its language, thinks in its categories, and engages in its game.

The fourth external characteristic to which Ellul refers is the *organization* of propaganda. By this, he means the necessary and concrete linkage between propaganda and other institutions in modern capitalist, technological societies. Propaganda is always directly and indirectly related to political, military, educational, healthcare, and other institutions. These establishments provide

23. Jacques Ellul, *The Political Illusion*, trans. Konrad Kellen (New York: Vintage, 1967).
24. Ellul, *Propaganda*, 17.
25. Ibid.

propaganda with a concrete referent; their relationship to propaganda demonstrates to the individual that the myth he or she has accepted has a true basis—an illusion of legitimate ground for the propagandist's narrative. However, simply because propaganda refers to actual institutions in society, this does not necessarily mean that these are legitimate, truthful, or altruistic.[26]

The fifth external characteristic of propaganda is *orthopraxy*. For Ellul, this is perhaps the most important ethical entailment of modern propaganda. The primary aim of the contemporary propagandist is to provoke action. Of course, the propagandist wants to manipulate individual's ideas and beliefs. This manipulation, however, is only a means to an end: action that serves capitalism and technique. Ellul describes propaganda's orthopraxy in this way: "It is no longer to change adherence to a doctrine, but to make the individual cling irrationally to a process of action. It is no longer to transform an opinion, but to arouse an active and mythical belief."[27] This fact is evidenced in the immense deal of advertising we encounter daily. For the most part, advertisers do not care about the religious or political affiliations of the consumers. Advertisers do not care what its audience believes, as long as they are enticed to consume or purchase a particular product. The same is true in political campaigns. For example, politicians do not seem to be concerned with changing how the public perceives them (unless it affects how people vote). Politicians are concerned primarily with obtaining the vote—the action of the masses. This is why politicians do not use intellectual persuasion. Instead they rely on irrational, emotional appeals. If politicians were to engage in intellectual dialogue—which is, in its pure form, a dialectical process—with the public, this would be extremely time-consuming and inefficient. The politician is instead

26. Ibid., 20–24.
27. Ibid.

concerned with quick and efficient action on the part of the individual.[28]

Here we should recall the fourth external characteristic of propaganda: organization. Propaganda only has meaning when it brings about the convergence of the individual's actions with a particular institution. This locks the individual into a dependent relationship with various institutions, while at the same time integrating the individual into a society whose thoughts and actions have been prescribed and determined by these institutions. According to Ellul, this circular and self-referential system makes it nearly impossible to reverse the effects of propaganda.[29]

Enticing and locking the individual into the system requires what Ellul calls "pre-propaganda."[30] He distinguishes this from "active propaganda" (which we have been discussing). Ellul maintains that the goal of pre-propaganda is to prepare individuals to act. He states, "Pre-propaganda does not have a precise ideological objective; it has nothing to do with an opinion, an idea or a doctrine. It proceeds by psychological manipulations, by character modifications, by the creation of certain feelings or stereotypes useful when the time comes."[31] In other words, in order to prepare one for orthopraxy, one must be conditioned beforehand. One needs to think in certain categories and truly believe that one's actions are necessary and efficacious. Pre-propaganda involves two methods according to Ellul: *conditioned reflex* and *myth*.[32]

Propagandists first try to condition reflexes through training the individual from a very young age. They train people to respond to certain signs, symbols, words, and authority figures. By doing this,

28. Ibid., 25.
29. Ibid., 20–24.
30. Ibid., 30. Ellul also refers to pre-propaganda as "sub-propaganda."
31. Ibid., 31.
32. Ibid., 28–30, 31–32.

the propagandist can predict with accuracy the given response.[33] An example of conditioned reflex is found in the symbol of the US flag. From a young age, those of us who grew up in the United States have been programmed to unquestioningly respect and honor the flag. Reciting the Pledge of Allegiance in grammar school, singing the "Star-Spangled Banner" at sporting events with hand on heart, and watching presidential debates take place with the flag in the background all add to this pre-propaganda. As a symbol, the flag evokes in many a deep sense of pride and patriotism. Furthermore, if anyone disrespects or damages the flag, then he or she is often assumed to be disrespecting the United States and all of its good qualities. This is an excellent example of a conditioned reflex shared by most Americans.[34]

The second method of pre-propaganda is myth. According to Ellul, propagandists create myths, narratives and images that shape the individual's consciousness. Myths help to create a worldview that is rarely questioned. Some examples include a blind faith in the superiority of one's country, political system, race, rituals, and customs. This faith creates individuals who never stop to question the common beliefs with which they were raised. Instead, they simply assume that their worldview is legitimate and beneficial. This, in turn, creates a firm foundation of pre-propaganda that prepares the individual to further participate in the technological system.

Internal Characteristics of Propaganda

Consisting of the general tendencies and goals of the propagandists, Ellul's internal characteristics of propaganda are made up of the

---

33. Ibid., 28–29.
34. Ellul does not mention these examples, but he does discuss propaganda in the United States at length (ibid., 244, 247, 255, 273).

specific knowledge and methods employed by propagandists. The first internal characteristic is psychological knowledge. In other words, the propagandist must be familiar with the psychological impulses, desires, and motivations of the individual. The propagandist relies heavily on psychology.[35]

Furthermore, in order for propaganda to be effective, it must connect itself to the basic motivations of humans. The first of these motivating factors are external bodily needs, such as food, shelter, clothing and protection. Exploited by the propagandist to achieve his or her goals, these needs are explicitly and implicitly appealed to in order to manipulate the masses.[36]

Additionally, humans have certain universal internal motivations: fear, sexual desire, and longing for acceptance, among many others. As with the external needs, the propagandist exploits his or her knowledge of these internal propensities to further the agenda at hand. Indeed, it would be impossible for propaganda to be effective if the most basic psychological terrain of humanity was not exploited.[37]

The second basic internal characteristic of propaganda is its knowledge of and its appeals to societal impulses, currents, and ideologies. This requires an acute awareness of particular social inclinations and motivations of the constituents of a given society. It is the job of the propagandist to mirror this social knowledge in his or her work.[38]

There are two essential forms of this societal knowledge. The first consists of presuppositions regarding one's society. By this, Ellul means "a collection of feelings, beliefs, and images by which one

---

35. Ellul is aware of various types of psychological theories, but he also argues that the basic structures and motivations of individuals are, in general, quite similar. Furthermore, depending on the goal of the propagandist, he or she will choose to use whichever psychological theory proves itself most useful (ibid., 4–6, 33–38, 241).
36. Ibid., 37.
37. Ibid., 38.
38. Ibid., 15, 62–72.

unconsciously judges events."[39] These collective presuppositions, which are both created by and consist of pre-propaganda, provide the propagandist with knowledge of the social milieu. Propagandists must utilize and build upon the collective presuppositions of the West.[40] If propaganda did not do this, then no one would take it seriously.

One of the best examples of a collective presupposition is the belief in unending progress. Without question, the majority of people in modern societies today firmly believe that science, technology, and humans are evolving—and that this is all undoubtedly good. Advertisers use this presupposition endlessly in marketing new products. Politicians use this assumption in arguing for change. Educators use this belief to argue for new pedagogical techniques. Ellul explains, "a person listens to a particular propaganda because it reflects his deepest convictions without expressing them directly."[41] The propagandist knows this and uses this societal knowledge to manipulate the thoughts and behavior of the individual.[42]

In addition to appealing to societal presuppositions, the propagandist must also have knowledge of current events and must be ready to appeal to these. This is the third basic internal characteristic of propaganda. According to Ellul, most people do not have a deep knowledge of history. Instead, the majority of individuals live within a worldview dominated by present events only (or events in the immediate past). Knowing this, propaganda relies heavily on appealing to the latest scientific findings, social trends, and products.

39. Ibid., 39.
40. At one point, Ellul argues that the four great collective presuppositions of the modern world are the following: one, the aim of life is happiness; two, human nature is essentially good; three, the myth of progress; four, everything in reality is physical. There are also many other presuppositions that propagandists build on: the myths of youth, the hero, true love, and money, among others (see ibid., 35–38).
41. Ibid., 41.
42. Ibid., 4–6.

The propagandist rarely refers to ancient history or historical figures to persuade the public. Rather, he uses popular culture, celebrities, and the latest fashions to manipulate the masses. These current images are symbols of the new—of progress and innovation. By utilizing current events, the propagandist taps into the tacit assumptions of society.[43]

Propaganda and Truth

Of those who stop to reflect on propaganda, many assume it is simply the dissemination of lies. Believing that they are quite capable of discerning truth from falsehood, these people assume they can recognize propaganda and easily dismiss it. Ellul points out that this is a dangerous position to maintain for two reasons. First, propagandists often use a combination of true and false statements in their appeals. (In fact, for Ellul, this is the most effective type of propaganda.) Second, propagandists often rely on true statements in their appeals, while leaving out other relevant and factual information. This creates the illusion of objectivity, when in fact it is a one-sided presentation of the issue at hand. Both of these methods contradict the notion that propaganda simply consists of lies.[44]

Ellul is not a relativist when it comes to truth. He believes that truth should be defined as the accurate description of reality.[45] However, when institutions and their propagandists begin to manipulate the masses through the constant use of corporate media, truth becomes hard to decipher. Ellul recognizes this, and maintains that as institutions have presented their false and distorted descriptions of reality, these filtered descriptions have become "truth" to millions.

43. Ibid., 43–48.
44. Ibid., 52–61.
45. Ibid., 52.

This is quite similar to Michel Foucault's reflections on truth. In his essay entitled "Truth and Power," Foucault writes,

> Each society has its regime of truth, its general politics of truth: that is, the type of discourse which it accepts and makes function as true; the mechanisms and instances which enable one to distinguish true and false statements, the means by which each is sanctioned; the techniques and procedures accorded value in the acquisition of truth; the status of those who are charged with saying what counts as true.[46]

Here Foucault argues that those in power determine what is true. He wants to challenge systems of power and exhort individuals to discover truth without relying exclusively on media, government, educational, and other institutions. With Foucault, Ellul argues that we need to stand up against the institutions that create and ordain a "regime of truth." In order to do this, we need to distinguish between overarching categories of propaganda.[47]

Types of Propaganda: Political and Sociological

According to Ellul, there are two primary categories of propaganda in modern societies. The first and clearest form is political.[48] This type of propaganda is concerned with achieving two goals. The first, and most important, is to inspire people to place their faith in the political system and in politicians. A political regime cannot function if the majority of people do not support it. For this reason, politicians hire public relations firms and spend millions of dollars on advertising in order to propagandize the masses. An additional goal of political propaganda is to make military acts of war acceptable to the public.

---

46. Michel Foucault, *Power/Knowledge: Selected Interviews and Other Writings, 1972–1977*, ed. Colin Gordon (New York: Vintage, 1972), 131.
47. Ellul, *Propaganda*, 61.
48. Ibid., 62.

As we will see, Ellul believes that in societies governed by technique, the military is inextricably tied to economic systems; and in order for a country to be economically stable, it must always be at war or be preparing for war. For this reason, political propaganda has become ubiquitous.

The second type of propaganda is what Ellul refers to as social or "sociological."[49] For Ellul, this is a form of propaganda that aims to influence society's "style of life."[50] This propaganda appeals to and reinforces common societal assumptions. Examples in the United States include the conviction that forty hours constitute a work week; that more money equals a better job; that traditional gender roles should be followed; and that democracy is better than other political systems. All of these deeply held convictions are nothing more than ideologies, according to Ellul.[51] These ideologies lead individuals to believe that their society—including their government, educational, and economic systems—offers the best way of life. It follows from this form of reasoning that other societies and cultures are inadequate at best and evil at worst. We see a clear example of this when people refer in a pejorative manner to those who are acting "un-American" or "anti-Christian." These terms expose the underlying ideology of the speaker.

Of course, there are many other types of societal assumptions appealed to in social propaganda. These include ideologies concerning the free market, private property, and individual status, among others. These, along with the aforementioned examples, all serve one primary purpose: to integrate the individual into the system of necessity; that is to say, technique. Once this occurs, the system can continue to develop, grow, and dominate.[52]

49. Ibid.
50. Ibid.
51. Ellul's understanding of ideology is quite similar to Marx's definition. For Marx, ideology is false consciousness, or an illegitimate (groundless) belief system (Ellul, *Propaganda*, 104–8).

The State and Propaganda

The modern state—whether socialist, communist, or capitalist—is inextricably linked to technology, the military, and propaganda. In fact, propaganda is needed once the population of the state numbers in the millions. Large populations are united by mass transportation, and corporate media links the constituents of a society with its leaders. Politicians and those in charge of large institutions must pay careful and constant attention to the masses. In order to maintain leadership and control, these commanders must precisely choose what to communicate with the people. Through various forms of media, the authorities of both the media and the state present the public with a selective collection of information. In doing so, the state manipulates and shapes the opinion of the masses. The state cannot give the people full and complete information—this would invoke distrust. Rather, it decides what is in its best interest: technological progress, economic growth, and public obeisance and compliance.[53]

The question arises, then: If the state is so concerned with the public's opinion, isn't this an example of true democracy? According to Ellul, no; this does not imply an authentic democracy. Democracy is based on two basic principles: a rational public, and a fully informed public. Ellul argues that, due to constant manipulation of the public through propaganda, more and more people think and act in irrational ways. Furthermore, the private control of the mass media and the limiting and distortion of information has left the public far from fully informed. This results in a modern society that is largely undemocratic. There is an illusion of democracy, but in reality it does

52. Ibid., 106–8.
53. Ibid., 40, 49, 64.

not exist. More will be said concerning democracy and the state later on.[54]

The state also needs propaganda in order to secure its military. Individuals are called upon and enticed to fight for the state in order to secure it. The state must necessarily use propaganda in order to convince individuals to fight and die for its own subsistence. If the state truly and fully released all information—from real motivations to likely effects—about a particular war in which it was engaging, very few people would choose to fight for it. So the state uses psychological appeals such as appeals to patriotism, fear, freedom, and security in order to maintain its military.[55]

It should be noted that the military is always a necessary component of the modern state, according to Ellul. Modern motivations for war include securing natural resources and establishing centers of control worldwide. Because of these, the state will always be at war in some capacity. Meanwhile, traditional motives for war—protection of one's family or property—no longer exist. These have been replaced with what is in the state's best interest. Ellul believes that this causes the modern individual to "live in a permanent atmosphere of war."[56]

This leads us to question the relationship between technique, propaganda, and the state. It should be clear that all three, according to Ellul, are interdependent. In order for this connection to become clearer, it is necessary to turn to the third book of Ellul's trilogy, an insightful sociological description and damning critique of the political dimension in the realm of necessity: *The Political Illusion*.

54. Ibid., 16, 235–42.
55. Ibid., 60, 190.
56. Ibid., 142.

Politics

The political dimension, in Ellul's view, is entirely the domain of the state. Ellul maintains that as a consequence of technique, the state has become a totalizing phenomenon in the modern era, with complete centralization and total organization in its hands, owing to technique. Both of these inevitabilities are guided by technique's infiltration into the public sector, largely due to propaganda. The outcome of this infiltration is what Ellul calls the "politization" or political saturation of society.[57]

Ellul defines politics in the following manner:

> The term political must be taken here in its precise and restricted sense, i.e. with relation to the state and not to just any power, or just any social activity. Max Weber's definition is both classic and excellent: "Politics is the leadership by a political body called the state, or any influence exerted in that direction." I also agree with Weber that the state can be defined sociologically only by its specific means, which is force.[58]

Here we see that politics for Ellul comes down to control by the state. Furthermore, the state uses force to direct society. Like technique, the state must work for its own progress and for it alone. It is not concerned with the well-being of all its constituents, only with those who benefit the state.

According to Ellul, in the modern era, politization is total. In every sector of society, political values, judgments, and consequences affect every individual. Ellul explains,

> The state is the great ordainer, the great organizer, the center upon which all voices of all people converge and from which all reasonable, balanced, impartial—i.e., just—solutions emerge. If by chance we find this not so, we are profoundly scandalized, so filled are we with this

---

57. Ellul, *The Political Illusion*, vii–viii, 8–9.
58. Ibid., 15–16.

image of the state's perfection. In our current consciousness no other center of decision in our social body can exist.[59]

Here we see another characteristic of the politization of society: like technique, it is a type of consciousness. This consciousness is informed by the values of technique and is furthered by various types of propaganda. It has changed human consciousness and has become a central judge and decision maker for nearly all we do. Politics, therefore, has been reduced to ideology: a false consciousness.[60]

Ellul maintains that because of the various types of propaganda that surround us, we believe the "myth" of the state. This mirrors the title of his book: *The Political Illusion*. But what is the myth? What specifically is the illusion? *It is the false belief that the state equals freedom.* This erroneous assumption has been foisted upon us by technique through the agency of propaganda. We center our lives on this conviction, thinking that we are offered freedom with the political and consumerist choices we are given. But, according to Ellul, this is the inversion of reality.[61]

The Necessary and the Ephemeral

Ellul insists that the political realm is a "fusion of two contradictory elements: the necessary and the ephemeral."[62] Here we see Ellul's dialectical methodology, once again, in practice. Ellul believes that these two opposing factors expose vital aspects of politics. Primarily, they show that politics leads to an ever-greater loss of individual

59. Ibid., 13.
60. Ellul explains, "What used to be a utopian view of society, with the state playing the role of the brain, not only has been ideologically accepted in the present time but also has been profoundly integrated into the depths of our consciousness," ibid., 12.
61. Ibid., 129–31, 165.
62. Ibid., 29.

freedom, and they reveal that political involvement is ultimately futile.[63]

The first element involved in the political realm, *the necessary*, is characterized by a loss of possibility or freedom.[64] This is seen clearly in the limiting of political choices and the restriction of information, both of which are a prevalent consequence of technique's desire for efficiency or efficacy. Ellul explains,

> From the moment efficacy becomes the criterion of political action, new limitations restrict all decisions. This is exactly what is happening today. Even with the best intentions, no one nowadays could select any other political criterion than efficacy. Already democracy's game rests entirely on success. . . . Yet the choice of efficiency, if not dictated in advance or unanimous, is, at the given moment under the prevailing circumstances, not a free choice at all.[65]

For this reason, we see that the realm of the political is the realm of the necessary. It follows the rules that have been set for it by technique.[66] It is a reality that is determined beforehand and thus limits human freedom.

The necessary's counterpole, the *ephemeral*, exists at the other end of the political arena. According to Ellul, the ephemeral is "perhaps the most tragic sign and characteristic of our day."[67] The ephemeral, in Ellul's work, refers to a state of existence where individuals believe that their political decisions are concrete and lasting, but in fact they

---

63. To act within the political realm, with an unquestioning reliance on the state, is futile according to Ellul. This is because the state is simply a product of technique. Furthermore, the state espouses the same primary values of technique: efficiency and productivity. As long as these are our fundamental guiding moral principles, then our political decisions truly are futile (ibid., 30).

64. As we have seen, the loss of possibility or freedom is central to Ellul's critique of the realm of necessity and technique in general (Jacques Ellul, *The Technological Society*, trans. John Wilkinson [New York: Vintage, 1964], 115; *The Political Illusion*, 61).

65. Ellul, *The Political Illusion*, 35–36.

66. Once again, we see the inextricable relationship between technique, propaganda, and politics. We should keep in mind, however, that for Ellul, there are always contradictory spheres of society that act as counterbalances (Ellul, *The Technological Society*, 245–47).

67. Ellul, *The Political Illusion*, 49.

are illusory. It also describes a society where individuals have lost all sense of historical consciousness: a society that focuses only on the immediate events of the day.[68]

On the one hand, these characteristics mirror Ellul's description of the necessary; they point out the fact that political choices are already predetermined, so no individual decision really has any firm affect. On the other hand, the ephemeral specifically relates to the mass media. Ellul spends a great deal of time critiquing corporate media, arguing that it has created mass ignorance.[69]

By consuming meaningless, unrelated information via the media, one ceases to think for oneself. Furthermore, without historical knowledge, the framework needed for recognizing and discovering truth vanishes. Together with his description of the necessary and its lack of freedom, Ellul's description of the ephemeral demonstrates the sad futility of our political actions.[70]

Autonomy and Violence

Ellul argues that, like technique, the political realm—the state—has become autonomous. No longer are politics a matter of choice or freedom; they are now a matter of power and efficiency. Ellul says, "The autonomy of political affairs is essentially the result of . . . force."[71] The very existence of the state is dependent on, and inseparable from, its own use of force and violence. In contrast, the state's laws do not permit the people to use this kind of violence or power. In fact, Ellul calls the modern state a "monopoly" of power and violence.[72]

68. Ibid., 50.
69. Ibid., 58–61.
70. Ibid.
71. Ibid., 71.
72. Ibid., 68.

Examples of this monopoly are ubiquitous. For instance, it is unacceptable for a labor union or for activists to use violent means, but the state certainly can. Similarly, it is against the state's laws for individuals to kill others, but the state itself can execute murderers. According to Ellul, no state or political party is truly "legitimate"; that is, they all require and make use of violence in order to maintain themselves.[73] It would be difficult to find a counterexample to refute Ellul's claim. The use of violence and force is an inescapable reality of the modern political sphere.

Some argue that the state is not a product of violence, but a result of law and order. Ellul counters this claim by pointing out the fact that nearly every modern state breaks its own laws concerning torture, violence, and war, when its own well-being is in danger. This hypocrisy demonstrates that the rule of political law is no longer an overarching guiding ethical principle. The only laws that the state actually follows are the laws of technique: efficiency, power, control, and so on.[74]

The state is not only governed by technique; it also mirrors technique in its autonomy and monopoly of violence.[75] Ellul argues that the individual no longer has any role in politics, other than to support the predetermined rules and regulations of the state. Therefore, there are really no substantive differences in political parties. All of the dominant parties, especially the main two on the right and the left, always support the decisions and goals of technique and of the state. Because of this, "the entire political enterprise is *de facto* autonomous."[76]

---

73. Ibid., 74.
74. Ibid., 76.
75. Ibid., 79.
76. Ibid., 80. Echoing Ellul's prophetic pronouncement, David W. Gill writes, "Politics is increasingly autonomous today. It is an illusion to cling to the idea that politics is subject to moral values or religion, or that the Church or the University are an important counterbalance.

One result of the autonomy of the state is that it disintegrates authentic values and morality. Ellul maintains that the larger the state grows, the more power it has, and the more it becomes the arbiter of justice and truth. However, the state has no concern with what is truly good or virtuous. Its ultimate concerns, as pointed out earlier, are with its own survival and with the values of technique. This means that whatever is opposed to the state it is seen as a priori evil, and whatever supports the state, good.[77]

In order for the state to continue with its autonomy, it must have the consent of public opinion. This is where propaganda comes in. In our previous discussion of propaganda, we saw clearly how public opinion is manipulated and perverted. This is a necessary entailment of the political realm. The state *must* make use of propaganda for its own survival. This is another crucial fact that supports the autonomous nature of the political sphere.[78]

Some might ask the following: If the state determines what is just and true, and if the state must use propaganda, then isn't it a totalitarian entity? Ellul answers yes. Any political system guided by technique—whether democratic or fascist—will be totalitarian in practice. Herein, the best interest of the people is not of primary concern; only the best interest of the ruling powers of the state ultimately matters. For these reasons, Ellul maintains that the political sphere is constituted by illusions. These illusions come in the form of values, of truth, of the state's intentions, and most glaringly in the form of propaganda.[79]

If the political realm is an illusion, what is the solution? If involvement in politics leads to a loss of freedom, how can we regain

Machiavelli's efficiency is the law of politics and the state" (*The Word of God in the Ethics of Jacques Ellul*, 130).

77. Ellul, *The Political Illusion*, 68–70, 91–92.
78. Ibid., 66, 72, 77, 97, 104–8.
79. Ibid., 238–39.

freedom and still make a concrete impact on society? Ellul's clearest answers come out of his theology. It is important to remember that the two tracks of Ellul's work, the sociological/philosophical and the theological, are necessarily interdependent. We cannot find the answers to the aforementioned questions within the realm of necessity; for solutions we need to turn to the realm of the spirit.

Summary of Ellul's Philosophy of Technology

At the outset of this work, Ellul's dialectical methodology and worldview were presented. We then detailed, analyzed, and discussed the three central themes of Ellul's sociology and philosophy: technique, propaganda, and politics. How are these matters related specifically to his theory of dialectic? Broadly speaking, Ellul asserts that there are two contradictory realms of reality: technique (necessity) and the spirit (freedom). Technique is the sphere of determinism and ultimately, death; propaganda and politics exist within this realm. Conversely, the realm of the spirit is one of liberty and life.

The domain of technique—including propaganda and politics—is comprised of all four aspects of dialectic itself. First, technique always includes a permanent process of change. This is illustrated in the fact that technique is continually evolving and progressing toward more efficiency. Second, technique contains contradictory elements that can never be synthesized. For example, technique envelops the human sphere and is constantly changing, but ultimately humans exist as contraries to technique. Their essence is not efficiency, like that of technique, but something qualitatively different, and thus they remain fundamentally unsynthesizable aspects within technique. Third, technique includes noncontradictory elements that can be synthesized. The realm of the artificial falls into this category. It is noncontradictory to technique, and technique continues to synthesize the artificial further into itself. Finally, technique's ultimate goal is to reconcile all of nature and humanity into itself. This may happen to a large extent, but in the end, according to Ellul, this is impossible.

As we have seen, Ellul argues that the realm of the spirit—the domain of Christ—is the only place that can offer to reconcile and redeem all of reality. In this realm, history is moving toward the final goal of salvation for all, humans and the earth included. In order to further understand the realm of the spirit—the dialectical counterpart to technique (and necessity)—we must now detail and analyze three additional central components of Ellul's theology; namely, the role of hope in the life of the Christian, nonviolence, and Christian anarchism.

6

———

Hope, NonViolence, and Christian Anarchism

As we have seen, Ellul views Christians as living in two realms, those of necessity and freedom. Christians cannot separate themselves from technique; they must live within its bonds and continually strive against it. That is, Christians are called to "break the fatality" that dominates the world.[1] For Ellul, this call does not imply that Christians ought to proselytize or to engage in apologetics. Rather, the true calling of a Christian is a "mission of which the natural man can have no idea."[2] In other words, those who are ignorant of the realm of the spirit cannot possibly understand their mission.

1. Jacques Ellul, *The Presence of the Kingdom*, trans. Olive Wyon (London: SCM, 1951), 2.
2. Ibid., 3.

The Role of the Christian

God has sent Christians into the world of necessity to fulfill three primary functions, which correspond to three statements from Jesus.[3] The first is, "You are the salt of the earth."[4] According to Ellul, this phrase refers to the fact that Christians are to be the "visible sign" of the covenant God has made in Christ.[5] In their speech, relationships, and actions, Christians should represent the freedom that has been made possible through Christ. This is freedom from the concerns (efficiency, productivity, materialism, etc.) and from the methods (violence, power, etc.) of those who live according to the laws of technique. Christians can offer the world preservation and an end to bland, inescapable necessity; in this way, they are the "salt of the earth."[6]

Second, Ellul says that Christians are called "to be the light of the world."[7] According to Ellul, light is necessary in order to see reality as it is. Christians are to expose the diabolical nature of technique and its entailments. This means questioning, challenging, and speaking out concerning the hopeless condition of the modern world. By revealing the underbelly of the realm of necessity, Christians can help others to see clearly.

Finally, Ellul reminds Christians that they are "like sheep among wolves."[8] Christians are like their master, Christ, who sacrificed himself for the sake of the world—the "Lamb" of God. The sphere of necessity is dominated by "wolves": those who want power and freely use violent means. Ellul encourages Christians to view themselves not

---

3. Ibid., 2–5.
4. Matt. 5:13.
5. Ellul, *Presence of the Kingdom*, 3.
6. Ibid., 1–2.
7. Matt. 5:14.
8. Matt. 10:16.

as wolves but as lambs, and to understand that this means they may have to sacrifice themselves just as Christ did.[9]

These three exhortations are Ellul's reminders that Christians are to be living signs of the good news of Christ. In fact, Ellul maintains that the message of Christ is betrayed when a Christian does not express it in these ways. There are various mistaken "solutions" that lead Christians astray from these three duties.[10] The first is to place faith in the virtues of humanity. Ellul reminds us that because of technique, the realm of necessity is thoroughly corrupting. It is no longer possible to believe in the goodness of others or the justice of democracy. Even the best human intentions or the noblest laws will never solve the problems that technique has created.

Another mistaken solution is to forcefully push Christian morality onto the non-Christian world. Many do not understand the role of technique and the harm that it is causing, nor do they understand that they are in the realm of necessity without freedom. Yet, in a misguided attempt to correct societal problems, some Christians try to force nonbelievers to act in Christian ways. Ellul explains, "People who take this line aim at having a kind of Christian conception of things: they want to have 'good' institutions, 'good' morals; they want to know what is 'the good' in every situation, and thus to gloss over the actual situation of our present world."[11] Even when well-intentioned, these Christians are nothing more than ideologues who are trying to cover up the demonic world of technique with virtuous behavior. This will never work as more than a temporary, incomplete solution. The realm of necessity follows its own moral codes, corrupting everyone who comes in to contact with it.

9. Ellul, *Presence of the Kingdom*, 10–11.
10. Ibid., 12–17.
11. Ibid., 14–15.

Ellul maintains that both of these misguided attempts "are trying to make tolerable the situation in which the world puts us."[12] However, the world is dominated by technique and necessarily entails exploitation and alienation. These issues can never be solved by appealing to the virtues of humankind or by moralizing nonbelievers.[13] If Christians really want to make a difference in the world, the first thing they should do is to change their view of sin. Christians are forced into a paradoxical situation, living within a dialectic of sin and grace. On the one hand, they are sinners; on the other, they are forgiven. They cannot escape sin, but they are told to refuse it. Within this constant tension, Christians find themselves in a very agonizing situation.[14]

According to Ellul, Christians must find ways to live within this dialectic while at the same time rejecting the means of technique. If one accepts the methods of technique, this will only entrench one more deeply into its world. One must embrace the message and methods of Christ instead. This is the foundation of a truly Christian ethic. But creating a Christian moral system, in Ellul's view, is very problematic. He explains, "It is evident that neither a theological decision, nor an intellectual argument, even if it be based on Christian revelation, will enable us to know the Christian ethic. At heart, this is a fight of faith: individual and in the presence of God."[15] Ellul believes that a Christian ethic cannot be a list of virtues or a system of guidelines for behavior. Rather, it is an "attitude, adopted according to the measure of faith of each person."[16] In other words, there is no single ethical system to apply to all Christians. Instead, one's ethic relies on the individual him or herself.

12. Ellul, *Presence of the Kingdom*, 15.
13. Ibid.
14. Ibid., 21.
15. Ibid., 20.
16. Ibid., 21.

However, Ellul is not a moral relativist. He even describes various aspects and characteristics of correct Christian life. In doing so, he believes that he can point Christians in the right direction without succumbing to a rigid list of moral precepts. He admits that his depiction is by no means complete or universal: "We can never make a complete and valid description of the ethical demands of God, any more than we can reach its heart."[17]

With this in mind, Ellul maintains that there are two dominant characteristics of a Christian ethic.[18] The first is that it is always *temporary*. There are always ethical variables that change with the situation at hand. Because of this, a Christian ethic must have guidelines, but no hard and fast rules. Its rules must be continually reformed and revised in the light of God's ongoing revelation. A Christian must be flexible and receptive to his or her surroundings in order to make the right decisions.[19]

The second characteristic is that a Christian ethic is always *apologetic*. Ellul does not mean that Christians should be rationally defending their beliefs and moral behavior. Apologetics, for Ellul, is a lifestyle and an attitude. It is living out the faith rather than fighting for it or defending it. According to Ellul, a Christian ethic is something that must be adopted with heart and mind, and put into practice. Christ's three statements can be starting points for this active faith.[20]

These two characteristics still leave us with the question: What constitutes Christian ethics? Ellul refuses to present a systematic description of right and wrong behavior, instead describing various attributes of the authentic Christian life. It is clear, however, that Ellul believes that some types of behavior are more correct than others

17. Ibid., 20.
18. Ibid., 21.
19. Ibid.
20. Ibid., 22–23.

and that Christians have certain responsibilities that non-Christians do not have. These duties include embodying hope, resisting power, and practicing nonviolence.[21]

Hope

Because technique only exists in the category of necessity, the path of technique is a determined one that ends in death: the death of the word, the death of the Church, and the death of those governed by technique. This predicament is shared by most (if not all) of the Western world. However, Ellul does not remain pessimistic. For Ellul, the free God has given us the option of liberty in Jesus Christ. This is, indeed, the only way to break free from the bonds of necessity.

It is here that Ellul's dialectic comes into full swing. Modern industrial societies are governed by technique and are therefore destined to the category of necessity. However, through the freedom and loving revelation of God in Christ, the individual can break free from technique and live in freedom and gratitude. However, even more fundamental than freedom, Ellul believes that it is hope that must be understood and emphasized in our world of technique.[22]

For Ellul, freedom is an ethical expression of one who hopes. Moreover, "Hope is the relation with God of the person liberated by God."[23] Ellul explains,

> Hope is the act itself of freedom. If I were without exception caught in the toils of predetermination, of fixation and fatalism, I could not hope.

21. These duties are discussed in Jacques Ellul's *Hope in Time of Abandonment*, trans. C. Edward Hopkin (New York: Seabury, 1972); *Violence: Reflections from a Christian Perspective*, trans. Cecilia Gaul Kings (New York: Seabury, 1969); and *Anarchy and Christianity*, trans. Geoffrey W. Bromiley (Grand Rapids: Eerdmans, 1991).
22. Ellul, *Hope in Time of Abandonment*, 213.
23. Ibid., 239.

That would be unthinkable intellectually, psychically, and spiritually. Hope is the extraordinary moment in which man, abandoned by God, presses (God willing) his demand upon God by the one act of freedom possible to man. All other acts of freedom are actually derivative of man's emancipation by God.[24]

However, it should be realized that hope does not come about by a sheer act of the will. Hope is a gift of grace from the Wholly Other. It is not something that can be worked up or intellectually decided upon.[25]

Because it relies on the present moment, hope cannot be systematized or be made into a theology or even a philosophy (such as that of Ernst Bloch).[26] It is in these structures that hope becomes a technique, when in fact it is a free gift of the living and free God—a gift that cannot be neatly packaged or systematized. Ellul explains, "Actually, to want to produce a theology or a philosophy of hope is to transform hope into the opposite of what it is."[27]

Ellul has acknowledged the limitations of his own discussion of hope.[28] However, we must recall that his is not a systematic theology, but rather a description of the foundations, causes, and expressions of hope.[29] This is precisely why Ellul never gives an explicit definition of hope. Ellul explains,

In spite of all intellectual precautions [hope] is bound to be objectified, that is to say, it is no longer hope. Neither can it be fixated, and consequently a discourse on it does not give an account of what it is. Nor can it be treated as a constructed, justified, and explained object placed in relation to other theological data, for anything manipulated in

---

24. Ibid., 241.
25. Ibid.
26. See Ernst Bloch, *The Principle of Hope,* volume 1, trans. Neville Plaice, Steven Plaice, and Paul Knight (Cambridge, MA: MIT, 1995).
27. Ellul, *Hope in Time of Abandonment,* 271.
28. Ellul states about his theology, "Only words . . . words which bear witness but do not give life," ibid.
29. Ibid., 282.

that way is the opposite of what hope is. . . . If there is such a thing as hope, it is so close to the truth of God that it cannot be delimited in any theology."[30]

So rather than construct a theology of hope or give definitions of hope, Ellul claims that he wants to clearly describe the expressions of Christian hope. The closest he comes to a definition is simply claiming that "hope is man's answer to God's silence."[31] For Ellul, hope comes into being only when God has become silent and has abandoned us to ourselves and our systems. God has chosen to be silent, and the only authentic response is hope. This is expressed not only in expectation and certitude, but also in a demand.[32] In this sense, hope is "blasphemous" in that is refuses the decision of God's silence.[33]

For biblical support of this view, Ellul is fond of Job and Ecclesiastes.[34] In both of these books we find a hope against hope, an active protest against the silence of God.[35] Hope, a free gift of a free God, is also a protest against and for God in the age of abandonment, where technique has touched everything, including our language, and thus has aided in silencing God.[36]

Ellul's dialectical worldview is utterly evident in his understanding of hope: reality is based on and contains contradictions. Furthermore,

---

30. Ibid., 175.
31. Ibid., 176.
32. Ibid., 177.
33. Ibid., 180–81.
34. It is important to note that Ellul also draws heavily from the work of Andre Neher, especially *The Exile of the Word: From the Silence of the Bible to the Silence of Auschwitz*, trans. David Maisel (Philadelphia: Jewish Publication Society, 1981).
35. Ellul, *Hope in Time of Abandonment*, 181. Also, consider Kierkegaard on God's silence: "Father in heaven! Thou dost speak to man in many ways; Thou to whom alone belongeth wisdom and understanding yet desirest thyself to be understood by man. Even when Thou are silent, still Thou speakest to him. . . . [I]n time of silence when man remains alone, abandoned, when he does not hear Thy voice . . . this silence is Thy word to man." In Perry LeFevre, ed., *The Prayers of Kierkegaard* (Chicago, University of Chicago Press, 1956), 76.
36. Ellul, *Hope In Time of Abandonment*, 181.

it must be remembered that Ellul seeks not to form a systematic theology—he is against the notion that a systematic theology can correctly represent the free God.[37]

Hope as a Passion for the Impossible and as Perseverance

Our technological world, along with the artificiality and rationality that now dominate almost every aspect of our society, do not offer us hope. As a matter of fact, the technological society is the antithesis of authentic hope. Within technique, there is only the possible and the not possible: only that which works and that which does not work. True hope has no place within the world of possibilities alone. If it did, then it would not be hope; it would be a confidence in calculations and odds. It would be a faith in the visual, quantifiable category of existence. True hope, on the other hand, is quite different. "Hope is a passion for the impossible. It makes no sense, has no place, no reason for existence, except in the situation in which nothing else is actually possible . . . thus it never expresses itself through a concurrence of means, but through the absence of means."[38] Authentic hope must exist in the impossible, in that which is not predictable or forecasted. Therefore, it cannot be subjected to the mere realm of possibilities and eventualities. Hope must exist in the unknowable freedom of God. According to Ellul, this hope usually manifests itself in three human ways: perseverance, prayer, and realism. He describes these three expressions of hope in order to substantiate his understanding of it.[39]

The first and most fundamental expression of hope is waiting. The person who hopes perseveres and waits in spite of the necessity

37. Ibid., 101–2.
38. Ibid., 197.
39. Ibid., 258–82.

and decay caused by the technological milieu. It is a paradoxical but intentional stance that cannot be rationally justified. Ellul explains, "Perseverance is truly an absurd attitude in the eyes of men, but it is the gauge of those who 'inherit the kingdom' (Heb. 6:12)."[40]

Also, perseverance does not need an assurance of success in order to keep going. True perseverance denies all the "success criteria" of action, which would exist within the category of the possible. Rather, perseverance presses on in order to experience the impossible, "the return of Jesus Christ and the establishment of his reign."[41]

Just as in the case of Job, waiting and perseverance are not rational: they are not means to an end. Rather, they are the expression of the living gift of freedom that is birthed from hope by way of the Liberator.[42]

Hope as Prayer

Ellul maintains that prayer has little place in the contemporary church and life of the Christian. There are many sociological reasons for its rarity, the most important being that prayer is frequently viewed as an inefficient and impractical use of valuable time. Prayer requires silence, solitude, and reflection—all of which are scarce in our technological society. Furthermore, many have come to understand prayer simply as a means for obtaining results. According to Ellul, the efficaciousness of prayer is often heavily emphasized by those who have unconsciously adopted the mindset of technique, making prayer itself into another technique among many. This type of prayer seeks "to achieve direct results, without bothering about the truth or the

40. Ibid., 268.
41. Ibid.
42. For a discussion on God as liberator, see Ellul, *Anarchy and Christianity*, 46–55.

special will of God."[43] But even this understanding of prayer is fading away. Ellul states,

> Technology is now endowed with an efficacy in and of itself. That is even its specific characteristic. It is not uncertain or insufficient. Today it is futile to say, "God heals," since that supposes a very great doubt about the means which we are employing. . . . Under these circumstances it is superfluous to call upon God, introducing an additional order of efficacy through prayer.[44]

True prayer, however, has nothing to do with efficaciousness. For Ellul, "In prayer God invites us to live with him. . . . Prayer is nothing more than 'God with us.' It is nothing more than the self-emptying of God of which Paul speaks to the Philippians. It is the testimony of the nearness of God who comes."[45] Thus, without entering into true prayer, one can have no hope, and without hope one cannot even think of truly praying. Real prayer is the utmost expression of hope, and the praying person is a hopeful person in spite of necessity.[46]

Hope as Realism

For Ellul, hope can only live within the pessimism of the real world. The harshness of reality can only be understood and grasped through hope, which finds its foundation in a concrete realism. This is precisely what Ellul means when he states, "Hope finds its substance in realism, and the latter finds its possibility in hope."[47] This is fundamental. Without a living hope, there is absolutely no capacity to consider the actual situation.[48] He states, "Man can never stand

43. Jacques Ellul, *Prayer and Modern Man*, trans. C. Edward Hopkin (New York: Seabury, 1970), 176–77.
44. Ibid., 78–79.
45. Ibid., 48.
46. Ellul: "Prayer is the heartbeat of the spiritual person. It ought to become as natural as breathing," *Prayer and Modern Man*, vi.
47. Ibid., 275.

reality. He spends his time lying to himself, covering up the real, providing himself with illusions and rationalizations."[49] Ellul believed that Marx clearly saw this and tried to expound on it in his theory of ideology and his criticism of religion; Marx could discern and grasp the harshness of reality because he had hope. However, Marx's hope was grounded in the historical process, which, for Ellul, was insufficient.[50]

In any case, Marx is an example of one who rejected idealism and understood the world through a lens of hope, which allowed him a clearer perspective.[51] In its refusal to accept cold, hard reality, idealism distorts this reality in order to fit it into a system by which one can deceive oneself and live in a false hope. Idealism is "the worst of all traps, and represents the greatest danger for man."[52] It is no surprise, then, that Hegel's philosophy of history is the greatest deception of philosophy for Ellul. In contrast to Hegel's idealism, it is realism that accepts the cruelty of history and, only from this acceptance, can hope be birthed.

The three expressions of hope—perseverance, prayer, and realism—are also decisions. In each case, an intentional choice of the agent must take place; hope then manifests itself from these decisions. However, for Ellul—as with nearly everything—hope is always dependent on a dialectical relationship. Hope is an act of the will, and it is also a free gift of the free God. If the conscious decision is made to pray, to persevere, and to adhere to realism, then hope

48. Ibid.
49. Ibid.
50. Concerning Marx, Ellul states, "Marx's hope was deceptive and insufficient to the degree to which it was purely human, and based on the historical, and not on the only possible source of hope" *Hope in Time of Abandonment*, 275. See Jacques Ellul, *Jesus and Marx: From Gospel to Ideology*, trans. Joyce Main Hanks (Grand Rapids: Eerdmans, 1988); and Ellul, "Needed: A New Karl Marx," in *Sources and Trajectories: Eight Early Articles by Jacques Ellul That Set the Stage*, ed. and trans. Marva J. Dawn (Grand Rapids: Eerdmans, 1997), 29–48.
51. Ellul, *Hope in Time of Abandonment*, 278.
52. Ibid., 276.

will thrive. If the decision is made against these three, then hope will die. Existing in this dialectical tension, hope is always a "mysterious phenomenon" and "an expression of the Holy Spirit," which can only be lived and experienced within the relationship between the individual and the Wholly Other.[53]

False Hope: The Realm of Politics

According to Ellul, one of the greatest temptations of modern society is to put our hope in the governmental system. Almost every aspect of the Western world is now touched by the realm of the political, far more than most previous societies were. We now live, thanks to technique, in a "politicized" sphere in which there is a tendency to treat all social problems with the procedural framework of politics. Furthermore, most of these problems themselves have become political—decided or resolved by a few elected leaders. Thus, the orientation of the modern person's thoughts and energy are nearly always directed toward the government. As a result of everything being turned toward the political, individuals increasingly put their hope in the state for a solution to their concrete, everyday problems. This misled hope leads to three evils: inflation of the state's size and power, increasing dependence on the state by the individual, and the illusion that the people control the state, whereas in reality they are dependent on it.[54]

The latter is the most fundamental of the illusory aspects of politics for Ellul. Many believe that the state is commanded by the voters, when in fact they are not actually in control of the state, despite their slight influence. While the citizen genuinely believes that he or she

53. Ibid., 283.
54. Ibid., viii.

can control "the political machinery" by way of the ballot box, this is an illusion.[55]

For Ellul, the state is a complex bureaucratic web of various intermingled techniques in much the same way as our modern technological society as a whole exists. Within this bureaucracy, it is next to impossible to resolve the complicated and individual problems of our society. Thus, to place our hope in politics is to embrace a false hope.[56]

In addition to calling it a false hope, Ellul scrutinizes the political system in many ways throughout his work. Within his sociological and philosophical writings, the realm of the political is seen as a problematic technique run by technicians who propose a political solution to every social ill. In his theological work, Ellul further critiques the politization of society as a diabolical manipulation of power. For instance, he describes politics as "the acquisition of power: the means necessary for getting it, and once you have it, the means for defending yourself against the enemy and so holding on to it. But what does one use it for—for goodness and virtue? No, one uses it for power; it's an end in itself."[57] Aside from these severe observations, Ellul goes on to call politics the art of multiplying false problems, of prescribing false goals, and of manufacturing debates. The term *false* is used in reference to the fact that politics can never truly remedy actual socioeconomic trends and situations.[58]

Politics has become the only mediator between the individual and society. It remains the only option for one to try to affect or change society. Politics has an a priori legitimacy in our modern society, and when events are translated into the language of the political, they

55. Ibid., 141–42.
56. Jacques Ellul, *The Political Illusion*, trans. Konrad Kellen (New York: Vintage, 1967), 143–44.
57. Jacques Ellul, *Living Faith: Belief and Doubt in a Perilous World*, trans. Peter Heinegg (San Francisco: Harper & Row, 1983), 235.
58. Ibid., 244.

are unquestioningly assumed to be rational and comprehensible.[59] However, in Ellul's final analysis, it is in vain that the individual puts hope in the political system. It is a system and a technique, neither of which can grasp the concreteness of existential, everyday human problems.

In response to the futility and harm of politics, Ellul encourages Christians to consider the path of what he calls "Christian anarchism." In fact he devoted an entire work to the topic, entitled *Anarchy and Christianity*. Christian anarchism entails two things: an absolute rejection of violence and a refusal to put hope in any modern political system.[60] Ellul maintains that the political game "can produce no important changes in our society and we must radically refuse to take part in it. Society is far too complex. Interests and structures are far too closely integrated into one another. We cannot hope to modify them by the political path."[61] Instead, Christians should organize and create new nonhierarchical institutions at the grassroots level. In doing so, they will "denounce not merely the abuses of power but power itself."[62] For Ellul, the more the power of the state grows, and with it bureaucracy, the more Christians must reject it. Christian anarchism then is "the sole and last defense of the individual, that is, of humanity."[63] Ellul's anarchism will be explained more fully later on.

Ultimately, Ellul acknowledges that Christians may choose to take varying political paths. In whatever path is chosen, however, the most important undertaking in the life of a Christian is to maintain a radical hope in the Wholly Other through perseverance, prayer, and

---

59. For striking similarities between Ellul's view of politics and Kierkegaard's, see Howard A. Johnson, "Kierkegaard and Politics,"in *A Kierkegaard Critique*, ed. Howard A. Johnson and Niels Thulstrup (Chicago: Gateway, 1967), 74–84.
60. Ellul, *Anarchy and Christianity*, 11–15.
61. Ibid., 14.
62. Ibid., 23.
63. Ibid.

realism. Only hope expressed in these ways will nurture and sustain the Christian in our present age.[64]

Jürgen Moltmann on Hope

Very few modern theologians have written entire works on hope. Ellul, as we have seen, published his *Hope in Time of Abandonment* in 1972. Only eight years before this, Jürgen Moltmann became widely acknowledged for his best-known work, *Theology of Hope: On the Ground and the Implications of a Christian Eschatology*. In order to gain a clearer understanding of Ellul's work on hope, and the theological context in which it arose, a brief investigation of Moltmann's theology is helpful.[65]

In his work, Moltmann revived the concept of hope through a study of the eschatological orientation of Christian theology, not one of eschatology in general. According to Moltmann, the Hebrew Scriptures, as well as the New Testament, suggest that a sense of imminent expectation is central to the entirety of the canon. Thus, biblical eschatology—even though it had been thought unacceptable to the modern mind by the likes of Rudolf Bultmann—became necessary in order to understand Christian theology.[66]

Eschatology is generally defined as a doctrine of the end things. However, for Moltmann, this definition is inadequate. He states, "Eschatology means the doctrine of the Christian hope, which embraces both the object hoped for and also the hope inspired by it. From first to last, and not merely in the epilogue, Christianity is

---

64. Jacques Ellul, *The Ethics of Freedom*, trans. by Geoffrey W. Bromiley (Grand Rapids: Eerdmans, 1972), 187.

65. Jürgen Moltmann, *Theology of Hope: On the Ground and the Implications of a Christian Eschatology*, trans. James W. Leitch (San Francisco: Harper & Row, 1967).

66. See Rudolf Bultmann, *Faith and Understanding*, trans. Louise Pettibone Smith (Philadelphia: Fortress Press, 1987).

eschatology, is hope, forward looking and forward moving."[67] For Moltmann, the eschatological is not one element of Christianity; it is the medium of the Christian faith. It is that which embraces and at the same time rejects our present situation in the world. Hope both brings rest to and develops into impatience. In other words, hope is dialectical for Moltmann, and it must be understood dialectically. Moltmann finds support for this view in the symbols of the cross and the resurrection. The cross, representing death, directly contradicts the notion of resurrection. The promise of God, herein, contradicts reality. Furthermore, Jesus was fully dead upon the cross and fully rose from the dead. The message of hope in these realities is paradoxical, according to Moltmann, and it is precisely within this dialectical environment that hope grows and flourishes. Thus, the resurrection of Christ is a contradiction that births a concrete hope. Moltmann explains, "The raising of Christ is not merely a consolation to him in a life that is full of distress and doomed to die, but it is also God's contradiction of suffering and death, of humiliation and offence, and of the wickedness of evil. Hope finds in Christ not only a consolation *in* suffering, but also the protest of the divine promise *against* suffering."[68] Because of this hope, the Christian will be able to live in the world with "the answer." It is the only true Christian way of being in the world, according to Moltmann. The hope of the Christian is always linked to the promises of God. This is the specifically unique characteristic of Christianity. Other religions are all "religions of revelation, in their own way," but it is only in the Old and New Testaments that we find a "religion of Promise."[69] That is, eschatology is hope precisely because it is a promise—one that sustains and nourishes the faith of the believer. This occurs

67. Moltmann, *Theology of Hope*, 16.
68. Ibid., 21.
69. Ibid., 42–43.

because the promise is inexorably united with knowledge of four future realities: the future of Jesus Christ, righteousness, life, and the kingdom of God, which is the freedom of humanity.[70]

For Moltmann, hope is always in search of true understanding, and in fact, hope opens the door to true understanding. Thus, he alters St. Anselm's celebrated phrase to read, *Spes quaerens intellectum*, (hope seeking understanding.)[71] In other words, hope provides a way of knowing. Moreover, knowledge of the future of Jesus Christ is always present in the hope of a Christian, according to Moltmann. He states,

> The knowledge of the future which is kindled by the promise is therefore a knowledge in hope, is therefore prospective and anticipatory, but it is therefore also provisional, fragmentary, open, straining beyond itself. It knows the future in striving to bring out the tendencies and latencies of the Christ event of the crucifixion and the resurrection. . . . Thus knowledge of Christ becomes anticipatory, provisional and fragmentary knowledge of his future, namely, of what he will be.[72]

Though fragmentary, this knowledge of the future of Christ is concrete. It is illuminated in advance by the promise of the righteousness of God, the promise of life as a result of resurrection from the dead, and the promise of the kingdom of God in a new totality of Being.[73]

For Moltmann, the righteousness of God refers to the way in which, in freedom, God remains true to his promises and brings it into reality. Because righteousness means "being in order" or "being in harmony," all of creation, to some extent, partakes in the righteousness of God. The opposite of righteousness is nothingness, for where there is no order or harmony, nothing can exist. Because

70. Ibid.
71. Ibid., 36.
72. Ibid., 203.
73. Ibid., 203–5.

of the promise of future righteousness, it is through hope that one can know that there will indeed be a future harmony established. Likewise, through the resurrection of Christ, we have a promise of a new life, which we can know through hope.[74]

Thus, we can see that, for Moltmann, eschatology is both central to the Scriptures and is also a form of hope. The gospel is therefore one of hope, which is inexorably linked to the promises of God and brings a future understanding. The Christian relies on this understanding in order to cope with the modern world. "The man of hope who leaves behind the corrupt reality and launches out on to the sea of divine possibilities, thereby radically sets this reality of his at stake—staking it on the hope that the promise of God will win the day."[75]

Ellul, unlike Moltmann, is not a systematic theologian. As we have seen, Ellul does not methodically outline specific Christian doctrines. Rather, he describes, in almost a phenomenological manner, the causes and the expressions of hope: perseverance, prayer, and realism. For Ellul, hope is not based on a promise; it is rather a "mysterious phenomenon," which is also a "free gift of God." Furthermore, hope does not give a concrete knowledge of the future, as it does in Moltmann's work. In contrast, Ellul views hope as a "protest" before the silence we encounter in the world; it cannot be justified or explained as an object placed in relation to other theological data. In fact, if one treats hope as an object, this "is the opposite of hope."[76] Thus to produce a theology or a philosophy of hope is to transform hope into that which it is not: an object. In a word, to insert hope into any type of system is a form of reductionism. However, hope is so important in the modern world, according to Ellul, that anything

---

74. Ibid., 79, 86.
75. Ibid., 227.
76. Ellul, *Hope in Time of Abandonment*, 175.

that sparks the conversation regarding hope is to be encouraged—including Moltmann's contribution.

As we have seen, hope is of critical importance to Ellul. Another vital aspect of Ellul's theology is his insistence on the practice of nonviolence, to which we will now turn.

Nonviolence

Ellul's work on violence is doggedly persuasive, and even more relevant today than when it was composed. In his book *Violence: Reflections from a Christian Perspective*, we find a thoughtful, detailed, and insightful approach to the problem of violence and war in the modern era. Ellul, as a historian of institutions, shows that within the Christian tradition there have been three main responses to the question of violence and war: compromise, nonviolence, and affirmation of violence.

Three Primary Responses

Because violence has primarily been a tool of the state or other powerful institutions, it is from these entities that we find the greatest bloodshed and destruction. Ellul argues that Christians have been predisposed to support these institutions because various scriptural passages explicitly endorse the divine right of the state. Christians, being aware of Jesus's teaching to forgive one's enemies and to pray for one's persecutors, and being aware of the state's divine legitimacy, have often felt forced into accepting a compromise between the gospel and the state. This response to violence is indeed the case for many Christians today. Many still believe that the state has been ordained by God, and at the same time, they try to remain faithful to the nonviolent teachings of Jesus.[77]

Ellul maintains that in the Middle Ages, theologians created three distinctions that would further this position of compromise. The first was a distinction between the nature of the state and the nature of humanity. According to this distinction, since the state has been ordained by God, it is justified in acting violently. Humanity, on the other hand, must follow the teachings of Jesus, and must never act violently, except when it is fighting for the state.[78]

There was also a distinction between violence and force. Some argued that the state never acted "violently," but only "forcefully." Violence, from this perspective, was only a product of the individual. When a person surrendered to his or her passions, this was violence. When the state went to war or punished criminals, this was force.[79]

The final distinction that furthered compromise concerned how the throne was acquired. If the throne was understood to be seized with the help of God, then the state had God's blessing to act in war. If the throne was supposedly gained without God's aid, then the state did not have the blessing of God.[80]

These three distinctions, needless to say, were very problematic. Ellul reminds us that each one contains built-in assumptions about the nature of humanity, God, the state, and justice. Furthermore, each distinction maintains in its own way that violence is acceptable and that a compromise between the state and the gospel is possible.[81] Eventually, these distinctions evolved into just war theory—the most persuasive illustration of compromise in response to violence. This

---

77. Ellul's primary works on nonviolence are *Violence* and *Anarchy and Christianity*.
78. Ellul, *Violence*, 3.
79. Ibid., 3–4.
80. Ibid., 4.
81. Vernard Eller develops this thought in *Christian Anarchism: Jesus' Primacy over the Powers* (Eugene, OR: Wipf & Stock, 1999).

theory is still highly influential today, especially within the Roman Catholic tradition. Following the teachings of Augustine and Aquinas, just war can be summarized by the following seven conditions:

1. The cause fought for must be just.
2. The purpose of the warring power must remain just while hostilities go on.
3. War must be a last resort, all peaceful means having been exhausted.
4. The methods employed during the war to vanquish the foe must themselves be just.
5. The benefits that war can reasonably be expected to bring humanity must be greater than the evils provoked by the war itself.
6. Victory must be assured.
7. The peace concluded at the end of the war must be just and of such a nature as to prevent a new war.[82]

At first glance, these conditions might seem noble. However, Ellul points out that just war theory is troublesome for two primary reasons. First, he claims that the term "justice" was defined in the Middle Ages in terms of Aristotelian philosophy rather than the gospel of Christ. For Aristotle, justice was moderation or the "golden mean." In this view, justice was synonymous with virtuous behavior that avoided extreme actions. Aristotle's interpretation is essential in a study of ethics, but it certainly is quite different than the notion of justice found in the teachings of Jesus, which are of central importance to Ellul. By envisioning each of their theories of justice

82. Ellul, *Violence*, 6.

applied to war, the contrast between Jesus and Aristotle becomes clear.[83]

Second, with the rise of the military-industrial complex and atomic weapons of mass destruction, Ellul maintains that just war theory is overly simplistic. He explains, "Let us point out that these seven conditions were formulated in a day when it was possible to see a war situation with relative clarity; but the phenomena of modern war—total war as well as wars of subversion—and the extent of the battlefields rule out utterly the application of these seven criteria and render them altogether inoperative."[84] In other words, just war theory cannot be applied today because modern war is highly complex and multifaceted. There are too many unknown factors—from the enormity and far distance of wars to the intricate weapons used in them—to predict the outcome of war with any certainty. Furthermore, according to Ellul, just war theory implicitly assumes that the violence of the state is acceptable, as discussed earlier.[85]

The position toward violence that Ellul calls "compromise" is exemplified by those who accept and advocate just war theory. The compromise is between the gospel and violence, and Ellul is highly critical of those who engage in it. Ellul reminds us, however, that there have always been Christian traditions that refused to compromise and instead endorsed nonviolence.[86]

Ellul believes the nonviolent advocates in Christianity are the most faithful to the life and teachings of Christ. In the Gospels, Christ refuses to retaliate against his enemies and accusers, instead instructing his followers to "turn the other cheek" and "love your

83. For a helpful discussion of just war theory, see Charles Guthrie and Michael Quinlan, *Just War: The Just War Tradition* (New York: Walker, 2007); for an insightful presentation of Aristotle's ethics, see Robert L. Holmes, *Basic Moral Philosophy* (Belmont, CA: Wadsworth, 2003).
84. Ellul, *Violence*, 6.
85. Concerning modern war, Ellul says, "Present-day long-distance weapons, which permit the collective destruction of a far-off enemy, rule out love," *Violence*, 7.
86. Ibid., 8–9.

enemy."[87] Ellul maintains that nonviolence was the "official position" of the church until the fourth century. Ellul refers to Lactantius's *Divine Institutes* and various writings of Tertullian and Clement of Alexandria to verify this claim. These church fathers state that military service and violence against one's neighbor are contrary to the teachings of Christ.

Furthermore, Ellul asserts that the church's policy against military service was abandoned during the reign of Constantine. Both Constantine and Augustine, who followed him, radically changed the face of Christianity. Both claimed that Christians were required to take up arms to defend the earthly city of God. This was a turning point in Christianity—one from nonviolence to acceptance of violence.[88]

Since the fourth century, most people within the Christian tradition have endorsed the use of violence. By doing so, they follow in the steps of Constantine and Augustine, rather than the steps of Christ and their first Christian heirs. However, many Christians today do not know about the nonviolent history of the church; they remain ignorant of the stance of the early church fathers, let alone of most religious history. Yet Ellul reminds us that there has always been a strong and resilient vein of nonviolent proponents within Christianity. Clement of Alexandria, Francis of Assisi, the Quakers, and various smaller Roman Catholic, Orthodox, and Protestant groups have all advocated nonviolence in the face of power over the span of Christian history.[89]

---

87. Matthew 5–7.
88. Ellul, *Violence*, 16–17.
89. Throughout Ellul's work, he makes many claims about Christian individuals and sects who embraced nonviolence. He does not provide evidence for these claims; however, it is common knowledge that groups such as the Quakers and individuals such as St. Francis espoused nonviolence. For a helpful study of nonviolence in Christianity, including all those who Ellul mentions, see Michael G. Long, ed., *Christian Peace and Non-Violence: A Documentary History*

In addition to those who endorsed compromise and those who advocated nonviolence, there have also been those within Christianity who unreservedly supported the use of violence. According to Ellul, one of the first groups to do this was the anchorites, a small group of hermits living on the outskirts of Alexandria in the third and fourth centuries. The anchorites viewed violence as a "purifying" power, and proclaimed to physically carry out "the stern judgment of God."[90] They focused on passages of Scripture that seemed to justify violence, such as the narrative of Jesus chasing the moneylenders from the temple.[91] In the Reformation era, figures such as Thomas Müntzer carried on this tradition by unreservedly endorsing the use of violence.[92] Müntzer taught that the poor and marginalized have a God-given duty to take up arms against their oppressors, but this ended tragically for Müntzer and his followers in the well-known Peasant's War of 1524.[93] While not as defensible as compromise or nonviolence, the affirmation of violence is still quite active today. In fact, it is often concealed within an unquestioned ideology that fuses Christianity with patriotism, nationalism, and military support.

Of these three Christian positions—compromise, nonviolence, violence—Ellul contends that the only stance that coheres with the life and teachings of Jesus is nonviolence. The nonviolent position embraces the spirit of Jesus: a spirit of the refusal of power. Technique, on the other hand, always embraces power and might.

(New York: Orbis, 2011). Ellul also admires nonviolent activists such as Gandhi, though he is critical of Gandhi's later reliance on the state (*Anarchy and Christianity*, 12, 100).

90. Ellul, *Violence*, 17.

91. Matt. 21:12.

92. See Thomas Müntzer, *Revelation and Revolution: Basic Writings of Thomas Münzter*, ed. Michael G. Baylor (Bethlehem, PA: Lehigh University Press, 1993).

93. Müntzer is considered by many to be one of the "fathers" of liberation theology. Ellul is highly critical of liberation theology because of its many adherents who endorse the use of violence. See Ellul's *Jesus and Marx*.

The life of the Spirit entails saying no to all systems of power. According to Ellul, it is only when we do this that we will be true followers of Christ.[94]

Presuppositions

Ellul admits that violence is a temptation for many Christians in the modern world. The embrace or acceptance of violence, however, is based on ideological presuppositions that need to be brought to light. According to Ellul, one of the first assumptions that leads to accepting violence is the erroneous contemporary belief that wealth and happiness depend on the accumulation of material goods.[95] "The passionate concern to consume," Ellul writes,

> and to possess goods in abundance is a modern phenomenon. Let no one say that it was perhaps because of their ignorance or apathy or stupidity that people did not conceive of life in those terms. Let no one say that it was because they had no other choice and that they compensated for their material poverty by "sublimations." No; they had a different conception, a different ideal of life.[96]

Ellul maintains that in the modern world, we have been brainwashed to accept the myth that happiness requires material gain. In ancient societies, this was not the case. Yet, today this assumption is so deep-seated that many equate injustice with lack of material wealth. This in turn leads to violence. Ellul explains, "To the ideal of high consumption and the downgrading of spiritual values corresponds a conception of injustice that centers exclusively on the problem of consumption; and equality in consumption cannot be achieved except by violence."[97] This is a stunning passage. Ellul argues that

94. Ellul, *Violence,* 174–75.
95. Ibid., 36.
96. Ibid., 36–37.

because of our erroneous understanding of wealth and happiness, we inevitably end up engaging in violence. According to Ellul, consumption of material goods has become the "number one objective" amongst Christians and non-Christians alike in the Western world.[98] Based on the belief that our belongings bring us happiness, peace, and solidarity, our consumption has become an unquestioned way of life and even an addiction. In response, Ellul warns that ideologically driven mass consumption will always lead to violence and suffering. This hardship arises not only in war, but also in substandard labor conditions and wages for those making the products we consume.

Another ideological presupposition that encourages the temptation to violence is the belief that those living in the modern world are superior to those who came before. This is the assumption that human evolution, combined with developments of science and technology, has made those living in the twentieth century wiser than their predecessors. Ellul maintains that while most people today believe this lie, we have not actually evolved to be wiser. By submitting to the "spirit of power"—that is, technique—modern humans have actually become more irrational and less independent than before. For Ellul, wisdom is not equated with scientific know-how or technological advances. Wisdom is knowledge of "the whole." What is the whole? It is reality as it truly exists: dialectically.[99]

The assumption that we are superior to our ancestors also leads to the domination and destruction of the earth. According to Ellul, when humans believe they are wiser than previous generations, they act without humility and empathy for the earth, which entails treating it violently. We view past reverence of nature as primitive,

97. Ibid., 37.
98. Ibid.
99. Ibid., 40–42.

superstitious, and ultimately unnecessary today. Ellul believes that the destruction of the earth can only be prevented if humans adopt a spirit of compassion and humility. In reality, most have embraced technique and its spirit of pride and arrogance. This attitude, like the myth of consumption, will only lead to more violence.[100]

It is important to understand that when Ellul discusses violence, he is not always referring to violence against humans; he also includes violence toward the earth. For Ellul, violence is any act of destruction that removes freedom. This means that violence can be directed at all life—humans, animals, and nature—all of which are robbed of their freedom at the hand of technique.[101]

Ellul is quite critical of Christians who accept violence and war as a means to an end. He writes, "Christians who participate in violence are generally of a distressingly simplistic cast of mind. Invariably, they judge socio-political problems on the basis of stereotyped formulas which take no account of reality. Indeed, the appeal to violence indicates incapacity to grasp the actual problems and incapacity to act."[102] Incapacity for Ellul is the inability to solve fundamental problems of the modern world. This incapacity comes from two sources. First, it comes from a limited and narrow view of reality, a view that cannot see the whole, but only the parts. Second, incapacity follows one who is unfamiliar with history. Ellul maintains that if individuals could see reality as it truly is, as an interconnected whole, and if they understood the history of humanity, then they would understand that violence and war only cause greater suffering. Ellul is primarily speaking to Christians, but his advice and his arguments pertain to nearly everyone.[103]

100. Ibid., 43.
101. Ibid., 42–43.
102. Ibid., 60.
103. Ibid., 60–64.

In some cases, Ellul is sympathetic to those who use violence to further their cause. For example, he refers to oppressed and marginalized groups such as African American slaves and to the workers' strikes of the nineteenth century. He states, "The oppressed have no other way of protesting their human right to live." Moreover, he explains, "To be on the side of the oppressed and at the same time have to tell them that their explosions of violence are futile and will bring no change—this is the most thankless position anyone can take."[104] While he does not advocate advising exploited groups to stop responding to oppression with violence, Ellul disagrees with their "explosions of violence" because this approach is futile. Instead, he advocates the nonviolent resistance of individuals like Martin Luther King and Jesus, whenever possible.[105]

What Ellul is primarily opposed to is Christians advocating violence and war. He understands that those who are not Christians may adopt this path, but for those who are followers of Christ, violence is unequivocally unacceptable. When a Christian advocates violence, he or she is embracing the spirit of technique: power. This fundamentally perverts the spirit of Christianity, changing it into a system of domination and control rather than a life of freedom and grace.[106]

Theological Consequences

Ellul maintains that there are several theological consequences that follow from Christians embracing the path of violence. First, when

104. Ibid., 69.
105. Though Ellul endorses the actions of King and Jesus, he also believes that nonviolence is "vulnerable" and may lead to unpredictable outcomes. In any case, nonviolence is always preferred to violence (ibid., 69).
106. Ellul states, "We have been called and redeemed by the Prince of Peace, but we easily follow the gods of war" (ibid., 27).

Christians embrace violence, they always consider their own theology after the fact. This entails a reformulation of one's theology to rationalize violence—for instance, "God let it happen, so it must have been God's will." For Ellul, this pseudojustification is a perversion of the essential message of Christ, and it always occurs in bad faith.

Another consequence is that violence distorts the reconciliation of Christ with the world. For Ellul, reconciliation is central to the life and message of Christ, so it should therefore be central to Christians. When Christians support violence, they cannot concurrently support reconciliation. After all, violence leads to death and separation rather than life and reconciliation. Ellul states, "The Bible speaks of the reconciliation of the wicked to God, and of loving your enemies . . . but precisely that aspect of God's work is excluded [from a violent act]."[107] Furthermore, those who advocate violence "deny that all men are reconciled in Christ; they deny that reconciliation; if it means anything, means reconciliation with the enemy and with everyone else."[108] Ellul maintains that to adopt violence is to reject the incarnation and the Trinity. Both of these core Christian beliefs, according to Ellul, speak of the reconciliation of God to humanity. In love, God desires to become reunited with all humans. For this reason, God manifested in Christ as a concrete symbol of the act of reconciliation. Ellul believes that this is perhaps the most central message of Christianity and that it must always be considered before any act of violence is considered.[109]

107. Ibid., 72–73.
108. Ibid., 73.
109. Ibid.

Christian Realism

Ellul endorses what he calls "Christian realism" in the face of violence. This was briefly discussed in the earlier section on hope, but it also pertains to Ellul's views on violence. Ellul argues that we cannot simply look to the Scriptures for evidence that condemns violence. Indeed, for every passage condemning violence, there is a passage condoning it. Instead, the convincing evidence against the use of violence is found only through adopting a "realistic" view of our modern world. Ellul says, "Realism is the necessary basis for Christian thinking on society."[110]

Most Christians today, according to Ellul, are ideologues, not realists. By realism, Ellul means two things: seeing reality as it is in a dialectical way, and knowing clearly what one is doing.[111] The first aspect of realism discourages emotional, knee-jerk reactions and encourages thoughtful analysis before action is taken. It avoids stereotypes and black-and-white viewpoints, and instead recognizes the dialectical whole. Ellul believes that if Christians truly understand the nature of reality and reflect before acting, then violence will be avoided. The second aspect requires awareness of the motivations behind one's actions, and careful consideration of the consequences of those actions. Together, these two aspects of realism mean that "we must use our heads and try to see with clarity."[112]

According to Ellul, Christian realism always leads to a humble and compassionate view of others and the world. Once one truly sees reality in its complex and multifaceted beauty, and once one fully understands one's reconciliation with God, humility and compassion will necessarily follow. Christian realism also allows one to clearly understand the nature of violence. Ellul maintains that violence is

110. Ibid., 81.
111. Ibid., 82.
112. Ibid., 82–83.

primarily a tool of the state, as mentioned earlier. Furthermore, violence exists out of "necessity" for the state's survival. Only through violence can the state maintain power and retain control. For these reasons, Ellul asserts that Christians should be hesitant to support the state.[113]

In addition to being a product of the state, violence is a result of economic and class systems. In free-market systems such as late capitalism, for instance, violence—whether subtle or overt—commonly occurs against the economically disadvantaged. Following Marx, Ellul maintains that this type of laissez-faire economy leads to a "survival of the fittest" view of society.[114] This view cannot be further from the early Christian worldview and from the teachings of Jesus. This view also leads to the alienation and marginalization of countless millions. "The system of free competition," Ellul writes, "is a form of violence that must absolutely be condemned."[115]

Despite this, many Christians today believe that late capitalism is sanctioned by God. According to their thought, a "free" market implies more individual freedom and thus is superior to other economic systems. In contrast, Ellul argues that capitalism strips people of their freedom, making them slaves to productivity, commodities, and private ownership. Furthermore, it necessarily takes advantage of underprivileged people in the name of freedom. At the same time, while Ellul is certainly more sympathetic toward forms of Christian communism and socialism than toward capitalism, it would be a mistake to think that he is endorsing these political systems.[116] Ultimately, Ellul endorses Christian anarchism over and

---

113. See Ellul, *Anarchy and Christianity*, 11–16.
114. Ellul, *Violence*, 86.
115. Ibid., 86.
116. See ibid., 32.

against any other economic or political systems. This will be explained in further detail at a later point.[117]

Violence is not only a product of economic systems; it is also an entailment of class structures. Christian realism sees this fact clearly. According to Ellul, as soon as hierarchies of classes develop, violence will soon follow because it is a natural reaction to class inequality and exploitation. Ellul asks, "How can anyone suppose that the lower class—the workers, employees, peasants—will unprotestingly accept the dominance of the upper class—bourgeoisie, capitalist, bureaucratic, technocratic or whatever?"[118] Class divisions always cause violence, whether it is violence against the lower classes, or a reaction of violence toward the upper classes. Ellul maintains that the most heinous type of violence stemming from class hierarchy is "psychological or spiritual, as when the superior makes use of morality and even Christianity to inculcate submission and a servile attitude."[119] This is the greatest form of violence, because it takes away human freedom while at the same time turning Christianity into a false moral ideology. Ellul is opposed to all ideologies, or "isms" as he calls them, especially those that pervert the original Christian message.

Yet, for Ellul, the cause of violence goes far beyond capitalism and class structures. Violence is a universal, "natural condition"; it is "of the order of necessity."[120] We must note that Ellul does not say that violence *is* necessity, but that it is *of the order of necessity*. In other words, violence belongs in and is fostered by the realm of necessity: technique. The dominance of technique has caused

---

117. Concerning economic systems, Ellul says, "Whereas our economic systems tend to condemn the poor, God's economic justice allows for the possibility to start again with a clean slate," *Betrayal of the West*, ed. Matthew J. O'Connell (New York: Seabury, 1978), 8.
118. *Violence*, 87.
119. Ibid.
120. Ibid.

humans to cease to live as independent, free agents; rather, they live according to the spirit and morality of technique. As a utilitarian system, technique views humans merely as means to an end, its own further development. Furthermore, technique's essence is efficiency, and violence is always a more efficient and immediate solution than nonviolence. According to Ellul, in the realm of technique, violence is "like the order of digestion or gravitation"; it is a natural entailment.[121]

Let us be clear: Ellul is not saying that violence is a basic and defining element of human nature, as some philosophers have argued. He is saying that violence is a fundamental expression of technique. This is precisely why Ellul refers to violence as being part of the "order of necessity." Ellul expands upon violence and its place within technique in his distinctions between five "laws of violence."[122]

Five Laws of Violence

Technique not only births and fosters violence; it creates an order of violence. After violence has been initiated, it follows certain "laws" of necessity.[123] The first law is *continuity*. Using historical examples and data, Ellul maintains that once violence is used, it is always used again. Because violence is always more immediately practical and efficient than reflection and dialogue, it appears much simpler and appealing to the masses, bringing clear and often instant results.[124] But this illusion of simplicity is misleading. Though violence is often referred to as a momentary expedient, it always begets more violence.

---

121. Ibid., 91.
122. Ibid., 93–108.
123. The five laws are found in ibid., 93–108.
124. Ellul also says of violence, "It simplifies relations with the other completely by denying that the other exists. And once you have repudiated the other, you cannot adopt a new attitude—cannot, for example, start rational dialogue with him," ibid., 94.

Ellul says, "The fact is once violence is loosed, those who use it cannot get away from it."[125]

The second law violence follows is *reciprocity*. Ellul believes that the use of violence will always lead to a reciprocal use of violence. He quotes Matt. 26:52 to support his claim: "All who take the sword will perish by the sword" (RSV). Ellul interprets this passage as evidence that violence can never be good or moral and that it is always countered with more violence. He explains, "The man who . . . uses violence should remember that he is entering into a reciprocal kind of relation capable of being renewed indefinitely."[126]

Thirdly, violence follows the law of *sameness*. Ellul maintains that violence in any form—spiritual, psychological, economic, physical—is identical with all other forms of violence. This may sound like an overgeneralization, but Ellul points out that all forms of violence have the same results: they destroy the capacity to freely further our personal development.[127] For example, Ellul refers to propaganda as "intellectual terrorism" and "psychological violence" because it causes individuals to live in constant fear, which in turn destroys their ability to grow spiritually and intellectually. Likewise, physical violence destroys lives; this also ends or limits the possibility of personal development. Thus, Ellul argues that there is no reason to distinguish between greater and lesser violence. In the final analysis, all violence is essentially the same.[128]

The fourth law of violence is that *nothing* good can come of violence. Like those who distinguish between just and unjust violence, there are those who maintain that violence, though it is wrong, can end in true freedom, justice, or democracy. Ellul denies

125. Ibid., 95.
126. Ibid., 96.
127. Ibid., 97.
128. Ellul states, "The psychological violence all countries employ is the worst violence of all, because it lays hold of the whole man, and, without his knowing, it gelds him," ibid., 98.

these claims, arguing that no result of violence is ever truly virtuous. "Whenever a violent movement has seized power, it has made violence the law of power. The only thing that has changed is the person who exercises violence."[129] Echoing the third law of violence (sameness), Ellul argues that there are no exceptions when it comes to violence's harmful outcomes. In other words, there is no such thing as a "just" or "peaceful" outcome from violence. If this were the case, then violence could be seen as honorable under certain circumstances or as a legitimate means to an end in other conditions. Ellul maintains that this view is impossible from a truly Christian perspective. The authentic Christian's response to violence cannot be to rationalize it; he or she must unequivocally reject the use of violence in all its forms.[130]

Those who excuse the use of violence are following its fifth law. This law states that those who support violence must always *justify* violence to others and themselves.[131] Ellul maintains that there are endless apologists for violence, but their arguments are always fallacious. Any valid argument for the use of violence presupposes its absolute necessity for justice. This assumption is simply false. Furthermore, the continual need to justify violence speaks of the implicit human knowledge that it is inherently unjust.

Because violence exists according to the order of necessity, it will always be with us, and it will always follow these five laws. However, Ellul asserts that if we recognize this, we can begin to overcome violence by consciously engaging in nonviolent resistance. This opposition may not change the realm of technique, but it will change the individuals involved, bringing them some freedom from necessity.[132]

129. Ibid., 101.
130. Ibid., 174–75.
131. Ibid., 103.
132. Ibid., 108.

Idealism

Christian realism requires both nonviolent engagement and awareness of the antecedents and entailments of violence. It also requires rejection of what Ellul refers to as "idealism." As discussed earlier in relation to Kant and Hegel, Ellul is opposed to all forms of idealism, philosophical or otherwise. For Ellul, idealism is ideologically driven; it is never realistically motivated.

There are four primary types of idealism related to violence.[133] The first is *revolutionary idealism*. According to Ellul, this form views violence as "liberating" and as "purifying."[134] Those who embrace this idealism believe such notions as "violence is beneficial surgery," and "it liberates man from false rules imposed on him."[135] Ellul says that revolutionary idealism appeals to intellectuals and "professors of philosophy."[136] Surely, examples of revolution are often romanticized—from liberation theology, to Che Guevara, to other subversive uprisings. However, even when the intentions behind revolutionary idealism are noble, those who truly understand the laws of violence cannot continue to view it in this idealistic manner.

Second, there is *generous idealism*, which sees violence as a prerequisite for reconciliation. Ellul insists that this stance originated with Marx, who prophesied that the proletariat would eventually violently overthrow the bourgeoisie. Afterward, humans would become reunited with each other, with the fruits of their labor, and with nature. However, bearing in mind Ellul's first law of violence—the law of continuity—we remember that violence can

133. Ellul discusses the four types of idealism in ibid., 115–25.
134. Ibid., 116.
135. Ibid.
136. Ibid.

never end in true reconciliation. Ellul maintains that only nonviolence can bring reconciliation, and even this is limited. True and complete reconciliation can come only through Christ, as discussed earlier.[137]

Pacifist idealism is the third form of idealism regarding violence. According to Ellul, this type is characterized by appeals to "peace" and "love" and is often popular with young and naive college students. These idealists argue against all types of conformism and moral bankruptcy, usually including violence. Though they are noble in their intentions, Ellul believes these pacifists fail to see the real problems of violence and instead simply react unreflectively to their intuitive repulsion of violence. In other words, their stance against violence is based on knee-jerk emotions rather than knowledge. If they were to truly understand the root cause of violence and its systemic nature, and if this knowledge were coupled with realism, true progress might be made. However, pacifist idealism in itself can do very little to solve the problem of violence.[138]

Fourth, there is *Christian idealism*, which assumes that every historical event is part of God's chosen plan for humanity. It follows from this line of reasoning that all scientific, technological, and military progress is evidence of God's loving involvement in the world. Even disastrous events such as the Holocaust are excused as God's "mysterious ways." According to Christian idealists, Satan has been conquered, Christ has brought total liberation, and Christians are free to involve themselves unreservedly in politics, science, technology, the military, and all other spheres of social life.[139] These

---

137. Ibid., 118–19.
138. Ibid., 119–21. Concerning pacifist idealists, Ellul says, "Sympathetic as I am to hippies, I fear that, because of their blindness as to both their true situation and significance and their relation to the world's society, they are in great danger of becoming a society of violence." Ibid., 122.
139. Jacques Ellul, *False Presence of the Kingdom*, trans. C. Edward Hopkin (New York: Seabury, 1963), 14–15.

idealists blindly believe the myth of progress and unquestioningly accept the legitimacy of technique, along with its entailments, propaganda and political illusions. Ellul maintains that Christian idealism fosters "illusions as to the reality of violence."[140] Christian idealists, unaware of technique and their subservience to it, will necessarily end up supporting violence—whether directly or indirectly. As long as one buys into the technological system, the political system, the economic system, or any other system within the realm of necessity, one will be supporting violence.[141]

Whether Christian, pacifist, generous, or revolutionary, idealism in any form fails to see reality as it is. Idealism is a type of false consciousness, an ideology that espouses violence even though it may attempt to refuse it. This occurs precisely because idealism never addresses the real, central issue at hand. According to Ellul, we should make a sincere effort to recognize idealism and reject it. In fact, he calls this our "first duty."[142]

In contrast with idealism, Christian realism recognizes that violence is a fundamental and natural constituent of the realm of necessity. It also sees clearly the divine dimension of reality: Christ. In understanding both of these facts, the Christian realist is freed from necessity and holds great responsibility.[143] According to Ellul, the more violence abounds, the greater is our duty to resist it. Ellul calls this the "fixed, immutable, and radical basis of the Christian option in relation to violence."[144]

Ellul maintains that the origin of the realm of necessity is described in the Adam and Eve myth. Adam and Eve existed in complete freedom in the world until they chose to break their relationship with

---

140. Ellul, *Violence*, 124.
141. Ibid., 122–24.
142. Ibid., 125.
143. Ibid., 127.
144. Ibid., 128.

the Divine. God gave them one commandment that did not limit their freedom, but gave them greater freedom. At this point, Adam and Eve "knew nothing of necessity, obligation, and inevitability."[145] Desiring freedom, Adam chose to break the commandment, thrusting himself into the realm of necessity.[146] As a constituent of nature, necessity guides, defines, and eventually destroys humans. Ellul maintains that by recognizing this, humans can choose to fight against necessity, albeit in temporary instances. For example, in the Hebrew Scriptures, the Jews fasted in order to resist the necessity of eating. They observed the Sabbath to resist the necessity of working. They created roles of common possession for the Levites in order to resist the necessity of private ownership.[147] According to Ellul, these examples demonstrate that with the grace of God, the order of necessity can be resisted, and true freedom can be obtained.

But Ellul asserts that, ultimately, Christ's life and teachings give us the fullest example of one not bound to the realm of necessity. In fact, Ellul argues that Christ brought a realm of freedom into the domain of necessity. This realm is one marked by all the opposite characteristics of the realm of technique. It refuses attachment to property, it refuses political engagement, it refuses to worship efficiency and power, and most importantly, it refuses to resort to violence as a means. The realm of freedom is where the true Christian exists, not bound to the commonplace cares, fears, or desires of the average person.[148]

Ellul maintains that the Christian's role is to "shatter fatalities and necessities."[149] Thus, a follower of Christ should resist all violence,

145. Ibid.
146. Ibid.
147. See Deuteronomy 18.
148. Concerning private property, Ellul says, "The truly radical element in early Christianity was its community life that resulted in economic sharing," *Jesus and Marx*, 9.
149. Ellul, *Violence*, 129.

including, "psychological manipulation, doctrinal terrorism, economic imperialism, and the venomous warfare of free competition, as well as torture, guerilla movements, and police action."[150] Christians who fail to see these types of violence are actually supporting violence. Moreover, Ellul goes as far as to assert that these Christians do not know the freedom of Christ, and they are not free themselves. They should not be condemned but should be encouraged to recognize the far-reaching tentacles of technique and the violence it requires. They are simply conformed to the world and the order of necessity, rather than to Christ and the sphere of freedom.[151]

Ellul encourages all Christians to engage in what he calls "the violence of love," which—despite its name—is the counterpath he offers in response to violence.[152] Ellul uses the classic distinction between eros and agape to argue his point, and he expands and classifies these two kinds of love in terms of the two realms: freedom/ Christ and necessity/technique. Eros is a type of love concerned with power and control. Agape is a type of love concerned with the complete giving of oneself to another; it is the authentic love of the other. Whereas eros is found primarily in the mentality of technique, agape is seen in the mentality of Christ.[153]

Following Christ's example, we should be willing to "love violently," that is, to fully give ourselves to others, without desiring power or control. This can only be done by observing three conditions.[154] First, we must reject the human means usually employed for victory in combat. In other words, the tools typically

---

150. Ibid., 130. Concerning the violence of capitalism, Ellul says, "The capitalist who, operating from his headquarters, exploits the mass of workers or colonial peoples, is just as violent as the guerrilla. . . . What he does is of the order of necessity, of estrangement from God." Ibid.
151. Ellul, ibid., 131.
152. Ibid., 160–75.
153. Ibid., 167.
154. Ibid., 165–71.

used in wars and revolutions—guns, bombs, torture—must be unequivocally rejected. When we use these means, we advocate technique and violence.[155]

Second, we must refuse to engage in any type of psychological violence whatsoever. The violence of love requires us to forgo the methods of propaganda, lying, deceit, and manipulation. Universally used by most institutions, corporations, and politicians, these methods, as innocent as they may seem, are violent in that they restrict the freedom and growth of the individual.[156]

Third, the violence of love requires faith in God. Rather than placing one's faith in technique or in other humans, one must ultimately trust God and the example of Christ. Only by doing so can we transcend the finite hope of this world and participate in the eternal hope given to us by God.[157]

Violent love is extremely difficult. It is far easier to take up arms, engage in propaganda, and to unquestioningly trust technique than to live by the three conditions just described. Certainly, to embrace nonviolence, to love one's enemy, to forgive, to cease striving for power and control—this is truly a challenge. Despite this, many view the path of nonviolence as a weak response, or as the "easy way out." Ellul reminds us that this claim is utterly naive and false. Jesus took the path of nonviolence, and in doing so he illustrated that the path of freedom is not an easy one.[158]

155. Ibid., 165.
156. Ibid., 169.
157. Ibid., 171.
158. Ibid., 174–75.

Christian Anarchism

A central component of Ellul's theological thought is his conviction that true Christianity is in essence a form of anarchism.[159] Indeed, Ellul's theology in its entirety is thoroughly Christian and radically anarchist. To truly understand Ellul's thought, then, an investigation of his interpretation of anarchism must be undertaken. We will now explore the ways in which Ellul's Christian anarchism exhibits antithetical characteristics to those of technique. As a method and lifestyle of radical freedom, we will find that it allows its adherents to escape the realm of necessity and truly commune with God and others.[160]

Before a discussion of Ellul's anarchism is undertaken, however, we must remember that there are many different types of anarchism, just as there are numerous types of communism, socialism, and capitalism. If there is one common theme between all forms of anarchism, it is a shared belief that the state is unnecessary and even harmful in respect to human development and progress. Ellul certainly agrees with these claims; we have seen so in our discussion of his books *The Political Illusion* and *Violence: Reflections From a Christian Perspective*.

Ellul succinctly states, "By anarchy I mean first the absolute rejection of violence."[161] As we know, Ellul rejects the use of any and all violent means, believing that violence, in its essence, is contrary to Scripture and to the message of Christ. Because violence is absolutely inseparable from the state, a rejection of violence goes hand in hand with a refusal of politics.[162]

---

159. Ellul, *Anarchy and Christianity*, 56–71.
160. Ellul: "Christians are called to live by the divine contrariness of Jesus who did not join the religious establishment, or the world-denying Essenes, or the politically radical Zealots." Jacques Ellul, *Reason for Being: A Meditation on Ecclesiastes*, trans. Joyce Main Hanks (Grand Rapids: Eerdmans, 1990), 110.
161. Ellul, *Christianity and Anarchism*, 11.
162. Ibid., 11–12.

This rejection of political involvement includes voting, political activism, and supporting any party whatsoever.

> Should anarchists vote? If so, should they form a party? For my part, like many anarchists, I think not. To vote is to take part in the organization of false democracy that has been set up by the middle class. No matter whether one votes for the left or the right, the situation is the same. . . . The political game can produce no important changes in our society and we must radically refuse to take part in it. . . . Those who say that global revolution is needed if we are not simply to change the government are right.[163]

Moreover, political involvement is useless because the political system is founded on technique, which has a life of its own, follows its own laws, and necessitates absolute submission. Therefore, engagement in politics can make no substantive change to the system of technique.[164]

We must remember that by its very nature technique is hierarchical, undemocratic, anti-individualistic, and exploitative. These same characteristics are exemplified by our current political system. To take part in politics—in the conventional way—is to support and further all of these negative aspects of technique. Because of this, Ellul writes, "We must unmask the ideological falsehoods of the many powers, and especially we must show that the famous theory of the rule of law which lulls democracies is a lie from beginning to end. The state does not respect its own rules. We must distrust all its offerings."[165] Ellul rejects the legitimacy of the state not only because it is an entailment of technique, but because it is deeply ideologically driven and hypocritical. At this point, Ellul sounds very similar to other anarchists, like Bakunin and Proudhon. However, there are some key differences.[166]

163. Ibid., 14–15.
164. Ellul, *The Political Illusion*, 61.
165. Ellul, *Anarchy and Christianity*, 16.

First, though Ellul believes that the anarchist struggle is apposite, he thinks that it is idealistic to assume that a truly democratic, nonhierarchical society could possibly exist. Ellul argues that this idealism rests on the mistaken assumption that humans are naturally good and that the state alone is evil. Ellul maintains that the state does play a large role in corrupting and perverting human goodness. However, many people are highly selfish and malevolent, regardless of the state. Here it is tempting to interpret Ellul through the lens of Augustinian Christianity and assume that he is referring to the doctrine of original sin. However, this is not the case. Ellul does not view the state as being the primary cause of evil and corruption. Neither does he view sin as a moral shortcoming or an unethical act. He makes it clear that sin only refers to the fractured relationship between God and humans. This can be overcome by knowledge and faith in Christ, and eventually all sin will be abolished when humanity is reconciled to God.[167]

According to Ellul, a purely anarchist society will never exist, because there will always be some individuals who seek power and domination rather than true community. Yet, Ellul does argue that people should work together to create grassroots anarchist institutions. By doing so, Ellul believes that anarchists can create a new social model based on the ideals of true democracy, mutual ownership, and community.[168] As an example, Ellul is fond of referring to the early Anarcho-Syndicalists and figures such as Guy Debord.[169]

---

166. A helpful guide to anarchism and anarchists such as Bakunin and Proudhon is Ruth Kinna's *Anarchism* (Oxford: Oneworld, 2009).
167. Ellul, *What I Believe*, trans. Geoffrey W. Bromiley (London: Marshall, Morgan, & Scott, 1989), 214–17.
168. Ellul, *Anarchy and Christianity*, 21.
169. Ibid., 3, 21; see also Kinna, *Anarchism*. Guy Debord's main work was *Society of the Spectacle* (Detroit: Black & Red, 1983), and it is interesting to note that Ellul commonly refers to politics as a "spectacle" (*The Political Illusion*, 60–61, 161, 168).

Ellul argues that these anarchist leaders and organizations are now more relevant and needed than ever. Many have lost faith in the political system, recognizing its corrupt and totalitarian nature. Furthermore, many clearly see that the state's only interest is often itself. Ellul says, "We can struggle against it [the state]. We can organize on the fringe. We can denounce not merely the abuses of power, but power itself. But only anarchy says this and wants it."[170] Clearly, Ellul is not a pessimist or a fatalist, as many describe him.[171] He is hopeful that Christians, anarchists, and Christian anarchists can resist the state and make lasting changes. This is not to say that anarchism will win the day. Technique will always ensnare, corrupt, and pervert society. But, Ellul continues to advocate hope and continual struggle against it. He says, "It [anarchy] has a bright future before it. This is why I adopt it."[172]

Traditionally, nearly every form of anarchism rejected the belief in God and in religion; as such, most anarchists are likely to be skeptical of Ellul. For instance, Bakunin and Proudhon viewed religion as a primary source of conflict and oppression. They also condemned religion for creating class divisions and social conflict. Ellul, in fact, agrees with both of these claims—but he also responds to them by making certain key distinctions.[173]

Against the traditional anarchist dismissal and criticism of religion, Ellul upholds and highlights the contrast between religion and revelation, Christendom and Christianity. As discussed earlier, Ellul believes that Christianity as a mere religion is inherently ideological,

170. Ibid., 23.
171. In his recent essay, Jeffrey Shaw claims that "Ellul offers us no way out of the predicament." And, "Ellul offers us no hope of liberating ourselves" ("Illusions of Freedom: Jacques Ellul and Thomas Merton on Propaganda," *The Ellul Forum* 47 [2011]: 20–21). This type of misinterpretation is common. It demonstrates a lack of knowledge concerning Ellul's dialectical work. One only needs to read Ellul's *Hope in Time of Abandonment* and *Anarchy and Christianity* to clearly see that he offers various hopeful solutions to the problems posed by technique.
172. Ellul, *Anarchy and Christianity*, 23.
173. Ibid., 25–27.

moralistic, and prone to war. True Christianity, based on revelation, is compassionate, forgiving, and nonviolent. While the accusations against religion are legitimate and warranted, they have nothing to do with authentic Christian faith, says Ellul.[174]

Another common criticism leveled against Christians by anarchists has been that believing in the Judeo-Christian God necessarily promotes hierarchical thinking. If God is the "Lord of creation" or the "King of kings," then this flatly contradicts true democratic thinking. These notions of God are inherently authoritarian and possibly totalitarian. Ellul argues that these images of God are mistaken and outdated. In contrast, the God presented in the Judeo-Christian Scriptures is primarily a God of love—not of power, control, and domination.[175]

Obviously, Ellul understands God as primarily a loving being. He even goes so far as to say that love is the "dominant and conditioning fact" of God's being.[176] Thus, the interpretation of God as angry, judgmental, and a moralistic "king" are clearly misled and utterly reductionistic. Ellul maintains that if a correct and complete understanding of God were accepted, the criticism made by anarchists would disappear.[177]

Yet another criticism by anarchists is that a belief in God limits human agency. This is a common metaphysical argument leveled against believers. Ellul argues that this assertion is based on a mistaken assumption, namely that God is limited to certain categories and logical constraints. However, Ellul says these limitations are human fabrications that actually do not apply to God. In fact, they lead to anthropomorphism, which is, in essence, idolatry. Ellul explains,

---

174. For a helpful discussion of Christendom and Christianity, see Jacques Ellul, *The New Demons*, trans. C. Edward Hopkin (New York: Seabury, 1975), 1–17.
175. Ellul, *Anarchy and Christianity*, 33.
176. Ibid.
177. Ibid., 33–34.

"The decisive contention of the Bible is always that we cannot know God, that we cannot make an image of him, that we cannot analyze what he is."[178] Ellul goes on to argue that ultimately humans can only say what God is not, rather than what he is.[179] Indeed, those who attack the idea of an omniscient God, saying that it is a logical contradiction, are correct. Many of the characteristics used to describe God—omniscience, omnipotence, immutability—are human creations that lead to profound misunderstandings of God.

Like Kierkegaard, Ellul maintains that one's intimate knowledge of God is ultimately subjective and incommunicable to others. Human categories of thought and language will always fall short when it comes to describing and understanding God. For these reasons, Ellul argues that when we discuss God, we must be careful not to ascribe overarching characteristics and attributes that could limit God in any way.[180]

Ellul believes that those who denounce Christianity usually do so because they have a misunderstanding of it or have experienced a corrupted form of it. He is sympathetic to these critics of Christianity, arguing that they are right in their fault-findings. The dialectical form of Christianity that Ellul advocates does not exclude nonbelievers, but includes everyone in God's grace. Primarily a being of love, not judgment—just as Christ was—God exists in sharp contrast to the ways of the state. Thus, Ellul believes that his conception of God—a subjective, but true conception—is compatible with traditional forms of anarchism.[181]

Ellul also states that, in addition to being a God of love, God is a liberator. Throughout the Hebrew and Christian Scriptures,

---

178. Ibid., 35.
179. Here, Ellul is endorsing negative theology, a hallmark of much of his theological work.
180. For a helpful discussion of religious subjectivity, see Louis B. Pojman, *The Logic of Subjectivity: Kierkegaard's Philosophy of Religion* (Tuscaloosa: University of Alabama Press, 1984).
181. Ellul defends this claim throughout *Anarchy and Christianity*, 45–85.

God continually frees individuals from slavery, from captivity, from unpleasant circumstances, from sin, and even from death. God's role as liberator is especially central for Ellul, because love is inevitably free.[182]

Liberation and God's love are always inextricably linked. One cannot fully love God if one worships an idol in God's place. True anarchism, according to Ellul, mirrors the liberation that God offers, as it tears down all idols—money, politics, technology, power—and encourages people to live in loving, communal relationships.[183]

Not only is anarchism echoed in God's liberating love; it is also demonstrated throughout the Bible. In fact, Ellul believes that the Bible is primarily a source of anarchism. The Greek word *arche* means "authority, power, source, or origin"; those who oppose hierarchical forms of power and authority are thus considered anarchists (from *an-arche*). Ellul points out that the Scriptures are essentially anarchist in character for several reasons.[184]

For example, in the Hebrew Scriptures we read about the twelve tribes of Israel. There was no centralized leader controlling these tribes, and when decisions needed to be made, there was inevitably a popular assembly.[185] Ellul argues that the sole authority for the ancient Israelites was God. Only when Samuel became a judge did the "real history of power" begin.[186] It was at this point that the Jews protested against Samuel and demanded a king in order to imitate other nations. Samuel prayed to God, and God responded, saying, "They have not rejected you, but they have rejected me from being king over them."[187] God then described how an earthly king would

---

182. Ibid., 39.
183. Ellul, *Violence,* 70.
184. Ellul, *Anarchy and Christianity*, 11.
185. Ibid., 46. Likewise, the early Christians often used the word *ecclesia,* a Greek term meaning "assembly" or "congregation."
186. Ibid., 48.
187. 1 Sam. 8:7, RSV.

bring wars, taxation, slavery, and other undesirable consequences to the people of Israel. Samuel then tried to explain this to the people, but they still demanded to have a king. This, according to Ellul, is the history of how Israel went from being an anarchist group of tribes to a centralized and politicized monarchy.[188]

Ellul also reminds us that for every king Israel had, they also had a prophet. As illustrated in many books of the Bible, the prophet was always a severe critic of the king and of the political system. These prophets were outsiders and provocateurs. They stood up for the poor and oppressed, and they always encouraged the people to serve God alone. Because the prophets spoke on behalf of God, Ellul takes them as clear examples of God's continual disapproval of political hierarchies and power.[189]

Ellul also refers to Jesus as an example of anarchism. If we look to the life of Jesus, we see that he had no regard for politics, he lived simply and was not materialistic, and he nonviolently resisted all forms of power. These principles were not only affirmed in his actions, but also in his teachings. Put succinctly, Ellul declares that in "Jesus' face-to-face encounters with the religious and political authorities, we find irony, scorn, noncooperation, indifference, and sometimes accusation."[190] Indeed, Jesus was a true example of one who resisted all earthly authorities—a true anarchist.[191]

Owing to these biblical examples and others, Ellul argues that Christian anarchism consists of resisting all forms of violence and refusing to participate in systems of power. This entails creating anarchist communities and institutions within the world of technique. As we know, Christian anarchism is predicated on a belief

188. Ellul, *Anarchy and Christianity*, 47–49.
189. Ibid., 51–52.
190. Ibid., 71.
191. Leo Tolstoy also argues this in *Government Is Violence: Essays on Anarchism and Pacifism*, ed. David Stephens (London: Phoenix, 1990), 69.

in a loving and free God who continually works to liberate people, whereas the world of technique is constantly enslaving and oppressing. Yet, according to Ellul's dialectic, it is possible to live in the realm of necessity and also remain free. This can be done only through seeing reality as it is and refusing to engage in the machinations of technique. The strength and hope to do this come from an active relationship with the living God.[192]

Harmony

According to Ellul, the cosmos is not inherently harmonious or balanced. Rather, it is "an immense battlefield."[193] Likewise, in the human sphere, there is political, economic, and psychological warfare everywhere. Even human history is marred by recurring and disturbing violent events. From Ellul's perspective, humanity moves forward on the basis of opposing and clashing dialectical forces.[194]

However, Ellul believes that when the cosmos was originally created, it existed in a state of harmony. The earth and its inhabitants lived for a short period of time in harmony with each other and with God. In fact, Ellul calls the residents of the earth "the partner of the Divine."[195] However, just as the Adam and Eve myth tells us, humans broke their partnership with God. "When this correspondence was broken, disorder came, diversity became exclusiveness, and plurality became competition. Human beings were no longer in harmony with nature."[196] This incongruity has never ceased; Ellul maintains that the earth is still dominated by similar violence, war, and death.

192. Ellul, *Humiliation of the Word*, trans. Joyce Main Hanks (Grand Rapids: Eerdmans, 1985), 268–69.
193. Ellul, *What I Believe*, 47.
194. Ibid.
195. Ibid., 49.
196. Ibid.

We continue to live in a realm of profound disunity, suffering, and despair. Ellul believes that it is the task of the Christian to try and make the earth humane and harmonious once again.[197] Ellul persuasively argues that one of the principal tasks of the Christian is to work for balance, an equilibrium that has been lost because of the values of technique. Thankfully, we can choose to reject technique's values, and in doing so, balance can be restored.[198]

In contrast to his descriptions of the world's imbalance, Ellul describes harmony in a few ways. First, harmony is equality. Because there can be no justice without equality, the struggle for harmony is also the fight for justice. This fight is the vocation of Christians and those who recognize the pernicious effects of technique. Second, harmony is not a permanent state. It is always temporary, and we see examples of its fleeting nature throughout human history. Like the sunset—an example Ellul is fond of—harmony comes and goes. It is beautiful and awe-inspiring when it is here, but it always vanishes quickly. Even though temporality is a characteristic of harmony, Ellul believes that we should nevertheless work toward bringing it into being as often as possible, while recognizing its fragility and its grave importance.[199]

Harmony is also an "exact correspondence between . . . being, having, and doing."[200] In this sense, it is wholeness. Ellul maintains that being is inextricably linked to having. In other words, it is impossible to live without nourishment, shelter, and especially relationships. Likewise, one's life is empty if one is not actively engaged in the creative process, which Ellul calls "doing."[201] Being creative can include raising children, constructing a house, writing

197. Ibid.
198. Ibid., 51.
199. Ibid., 51–52.
200. Ibid., 54.
201. Ibid.

a book, or a number of other acts. In any case, being, having, and doing are all inseparable and are central to what it means to be a human. Moreover, all three are necessary in order for one to live in harmony.[202]

Finally, Ellul says that harmony is the balance of humans *with* themselves, others, and nature. This is the opposite of alienation; it is integration of all aspects of the earth. It is precisely for this reason that the violence of technology, politics, and propaganda are so diabolical—they all act against harmony. Still, technique blinds most people from understanding harmony, instead disguising it as technological advancement or reducing it to the rhythm of nature. Those who are aware of their freedom in Christ must therefore see harmony in its full and vital essence, and must act in ways that increase the balance of the earth.[203]

Reconciliation

The utmost form of harmony is reconciliation, which cannot be understood without recognizing the dialectical nature of reality.[204] Many have failed to truly comprehend the nature of technique and have thus fallen prey to it. Because the realm of technique is a realm of necessity, even those who do apprehend it must live within its constraints. Technique has become totalitarian. Every aspect of the material realm is interlinked with it. However, as we have seen, Ellul believes that there is also a transcendent realm acting as a counterbalance, namely the sphere of the Wholly Other. It would be a mistake to believe that the two realms are equal. The milieu of technique is limited by physical constraints, while the arena of

202. Ibid., 54–55.
203. Ibid., 55–56.
204. Ibid., 214–23.

the spirit—of Christ—is unlimited and completely free. Despite this disproportion, the two spheres exist in dialectical tension with each other. Yet Ellul maintains that eventually, everything—including the realm of necessity—will be reconciled with God, in a perfect state of harmony. "Today," Ellul writes, "we live in division and contradiction the life that one day will be unity, balance, and peace. We live in tension the life that promises a flowering. We live in dialectic what will be the calm of the lotus flower."[205] This is a bold and important claim—one that might seem preposterous or illogical upon first glance. However, by recalling the characteristics of Ellul's dialectical worldview, we see that the notion of future reconciliation and reunion flows consistently from Ellul's thought. For one, the dialectical reality embraces everything: all components of each realm are part of it. This wide embodiment both implies and foreshadows the wholeness that comes with future reconciliation. In addition, Ellul's dialectic includes a God whose love and presence are completely all-encompassing and eliminate nothing—not even the realm of technique and its lack of freedom. Echoing Ellul's belief in universal salvation, these aspects of his dialectical worldview foretell and correspond with a future reconciliation and unity.[206]

According to Ellul, the work of redemption has already been completed in the death and resurrection of Christ. It simply has not been fully realized yet. Reconciliation is a process that will be finalized in a state of *anakephalaiosis* or recapitulation. The doctrine of anakephalaiosis was a prominent aspect of the theology of the early church, having its origin in the epistles of Paul.[207] Church fathers such as Irenaeus of Lyons especially emphasized this doctrine. According to thinkers such as Irenaeus, anakephalaiosis denotes an

205. Ellul, *Humiliation of the Word*, 269.
206. Ellul, *What I Believe*, 207–9.
207. Eph. 1:10.

eschatological process involving a new humanity that is governed by Christ.[208] This is the final aspect of salvation—the culmination of human history—and will unite all beings with God.

Ellul adopts the doctrine of anakephalaiosis as evidence of a future reconciliation.[209] He argues that ultimate redemption is not merely for humans but for all things "in heaven and on earth."[210] As such, his view of anakephalaiosis is a "cosmic view of reconciliation."[211] Moreover, Ellul upholds that this final state of existence is the logical outcome of God's omnibenevolence.

Ellul also argues that God does not simply reconcile humanity in the abstract, but that God does so for all of humanity in their individuality. All people in their concrete, particular forms will be redeemed and reunited with God in a future state of existence. This includes each and every person with their individual memories, hopes, fears, and faults. This is very different from certain mystical or Neoplatonic doctrines that state that only the essence of a person remains after death. *Ellul maintains that every single aspect of the entire cosmos will ultimately be made whole by God.*[212] Our present earthly cities are dominated by technique, propaganda, and politics. They are the concrete embodiment of necessity. They also represent everything that is opposed to God. However, even our earthly cities will be redeemed and eventually re-created as a new city of God. In stark contrast with Augustine's well-known city of God—which the

---

208. See Andrew P. Klager, "Retaining and Reclaiming the Divine: Identification and the Recapitulation of Peace in St. Irenaeus of Lyons' Atonement Narrative," in *Stricken by God? Nonviolent Identification and the Victory of Christ*, ed. Brad Jersak and Michael Hardin (Grand Rapids: Eerdmans, 2007), 422–481; see also Justo L. Gonzalez, "Anakephalaiosis," in *Essential Theological Terms* (Louisville: Westminster John Knox, 2005), 6–7. Paul Tillich also has an interesting discussion of anakephalaiosis in his *Complete History of Christian Thought*, ed. Carl E. Braaten (New York: Harper & Row, 1968), 44–46.
209. Ellul, *What I Believe*, 214.
210. Ibid., 215.
211. Ibid.
212. Ibid., 214.

saint often equated with the Roman Catholic Church—Ellul's city of God is the inclusive place where God will restore harmony to all at the end of time.[213]

The doctrine of anakephalaiosis, when understood in the light of reconciliation, provides a clear picture of the final form of dialectic. The final unity entailed by this dialectic is also logically consistent with Ellul's dialectical biblical hermeneutic. We can now see that Ellul's theory of dialectic provides a remarkably consistent and thorough interpretation of reality. It is also quite optimistic. Ellul's work ultimately points to a future state of peace and harmony, free from the chains of necessity.

Summary of Ellul's Dialectical Theology

Ellul's theology provides the counterpole to his philosophy and sociology. His Christian beliefs center around the conviction that the Wholly Other, through Christ, brings freedom to a realm of necessity. Through faith in Christ, one can encounter and live in freedom; without it, freedom is impossible on this earth. This assertion, however, does not make Ellul an ideologue or a fundamentalist. He is quite open to honest discussion of alternate views, as his work demonstrates. Also, as we have seen, Ellul's universal soteriology is radically inclusive and provides a sympathetic outlook concerning other religious and philosophical views. In any case, Ellul is firm and steadfast in his convictions concerning technique and the truth of the Word of God.

Ellul maintains that God is fully known only through revelation. Conversely, it is organized religion that creates images of God based on human knowledge. Only through the revealed Word of God—the

---

213. See Ernest L. Fortin, "De Civitate Dei," in *Augustine through the Ages*, ed. Allan D. Fitzgerald (Grand Rapids: Eerdmans, 1999), 196–202.

existential encounter with the Divine—can one authentically enter into a relationship with the Wholly Other. Ellul believes that this truth is affirmed throughout the Judeo-Christian Scriptures and that this revelation is unique to Judaism and Christianity. Furthermore, Ellul contends that religions (and the realm of technique, for that matter) are primarily based upon seeing, whereas authentic faith is centered on hearing. Seeing is the foundation of natural theology. Revealed theology, on the other hand, holds that the truth of God is heard or directly experienced by the individual. This is also one of the foundational convictions of dialectical theology. By truly listening to God's Word, Ellul believes that Christians can move away from the visual snares of technique, false hope, and empty religion. This will take time, discipline, and hard work, but it is required to develop a relationship with Christ.

Ellul does not present his readers with a systematic ethical system. He opposes moralizing in all forms and believes that most formal moral philosophies—Kantian, utilitarian, and so forth—lead to a restriction of freedom and individual responsibility. In contrast, Ellul maintains that one's moral behavior should flow freely from one's faith. For this reason, rather than outlining ethical rules and guidelines, he encourages his readers to *actively hope, resist violence,* and *form communities centered on scriptural principles.*

He also reminds us that, someday, the realm of necessity will no longer be a realm of violence, suffering, and death. Instead, it will exist as the "calm of the lotus flower": the place of wholeness and reconciliation. Those who take Ellul's views seriously will be given great comfort and peace of mind by this pronouncement.

Conclusion

Jacques Ellul—Dialectician and Prophet

As demonstrated in this presentation of Ellul's thought, his dialectical method is the essential thread that interlaces his theology and philosophy. Ellul saw reality as a whole, comprised of various conflicting factors. This viewpoint is mirrored in his work, which often seems contradictory or incomplete, but in fact is coherent. A full understanding of Ellul's thought is dependent on a solid grasp of his dialectical approach. Likewise, his dialectic can only be understood through a complete and intellectually honest examination of his distinctive writings.[1] This very task is what I hope to have accomplished in the pages of this introductory exposition.

At this point, a brief review will be helpful. Ellul's dialectical worldview was inherited from Marx, Kierkegaard, and Barth, but it is also a defining feature of Ellul, making him unique. Marx viewed the historical process as being pushed forward by the clashing forces of the material world. He concluded that the economic system and class struggle determined human consciousness. Marx also upheld that capitalism was a profound evil that led to exploitation and alienation in the modern world. Ellul learned a great deal from Marx, and

---

1. See Jacques Ellul, "On Dialectic," in *Jacques Ellul: Interpretive Essays*, ed. Clifford G. Christians and Jay M. Van Hook (Urbana: University of Illinois Press, 1981), 291–308.

he extended and developed many aspects of Marx's thought in his own work—though not uncritically. Ultimately, Ellul accused Marx of being an ideologue, an idealist, and a reductionist—especially concerning faith.[2]

Kierkegaard viewed humans as being constituted by freedom and necessity, possibility and actuality, rationality and irrationality. This dialectical anthropology had an enormous influence on Ellul. Also, Kierkegaard described Christ as "the Absolute Paradox" inserted into the world to provide freedom.[3] This view greatly informed Ellul's theology. However, Kierkegaard's dialectical convictions lacked the hope and optimism found in Ellul's writings.[4]

In a similar way to Kierkegaard, Barth made several important distinctions: revelation versus religion, the Word of God versus the word of humanity, and separation versus reconciliation. Ellul would make use of all of these particularities in his own way. Nonetheless, Ellul was bothered by Barth's ambivalence toward the evils of politics and technique, and well as his exclusively Christian scholarship.[5]

Ellul's central works concerned technique and its entailments. One can hardly emphasize with sufficient adequacy the importance of the concept of technique in Ellul's thought. For Ellul, technique is first and foremost a mindset—a worldview driven by an unfettered desire for efficiency and control. Technique has also become a "totality of methods rationally arrived at and having absolute efficiency . . . in every field of human activity."[6] As a worldview and methodology,

2. See Jacques Ellul, *Jesus and Marx: From Gospel to Ideology*, trans. Joyce Main Hanks (Grand Rapids: Eerdmans, 1988), 19, 55, 137.

3. Kierkegaard writes, "The greatest good, after all, which can be done for a being, greater than anything else that one can do, is to make it free. In order to do just that, omnipotence is required." *Journals and Papers*, trans. H. Hong and E. Hong (Bloomington: Indiana University Press, 1967–1978), 2:62.

4. See Jacques Ellul, *Hope in Time of Abandonment*, trans. C. Edward Hopkin (New York: Seabury, 1972), 304–6.

5. See Geoffrey W. Bromiley, "Barth's Influence on Jacques Ellul," in Christians and Van Hook, *Jacques Ellul: Interpretive Essays*, 32–51.

technique inevitably becomes linked with science, technology, politics, the military, education, and nearly every other sphere of modern society.[7]

Technique, which is characterized by rationality and artificiality, leads to an overemphasis on logic and science over arts and the humanities. It also leads to a loss of personal psychological and spiritual development as well as a devaluing of creativity. As Ellul puts it, technique leaves us living in a "logical dimension alone."[8] By providing an artificial environment in which humans live, technique also strips us of our relationship with the natural world. As a result of this artificiality, we begin seeing the world as an alien object. These entailments of technique are undeniably thriving today.[9]

Ellul asserts that technique, having crept into all aspects of society, is now progressing in a self-augmenting manner. Because humans have unquestioningly appropriated the mind of technique, and because technique is interlinked with all technology, it is free to evolve and progress automatically. This automatism points to Ellul's argument that technique has created a closed system—a realm of necessity. Individuals are no longer free to act on their own accord; instead, they must follow the dictates of technique. People must adopt the latest technology, politics, and education in order to simply survive. Thus, technique has ensnared humanity and continues to do so.[10]

One of the clearest examples of this entanglement is seen in propaganda. A necessary feature within the milieu of technique, propaganda is required for motivating the masses to put their faith in political and economic systems. Propagandists, whom Ellul also

6. Jacques Ellul, *The Technological Society*, trans. John Wilkinson (New York: Vintage, 1964), xxv.
7. Ibid., 7–11, 13–18, 280–84, 344–49.
8. Ibid., 79.
9. Ibid.
10. Ibid., 79–85.

calls public relations experts, use their knowledge of sociology and psychology to manipulate. They also apply their various techniques continually and universally via the corporate media. Ellul observes that this "psychological violence" locks people into a continual state of fear, anxious consumption, competition, and indifference toward others. For this reason, propaganda is one of the most pernicious aspects of technique and one that everyone should be aware of. Owing to mass psychological manipulation, nearly every aspect of society is seen through the lens of politics. The masses put their faith and confidence into the state; in turn, the state becomes a monopoly of power and violence.[11]

Technique, propaganda, and the state comprise the realm of necessity. According to Ellul, these three reciprocally interlinked factors are destructive, demonic forces that must be resisted. Ellul believes that we can fight against these powers, but we need faith in order to do so. As a requirement for effectively resisting necessity, faith brings Ellul's theology into dialogue with his philosophy.

For Ellul, faith in Christ is the only proper and substantive response to the realm of necessity; it is the only way that individuals can gain freedom and begin to live fully. While technique is founded on sight, the sphere of freedom is heard—rather than seen—through individual, direct experience with the Divine: the Word of God. This encounter inspires faith, and only this can bring true value and purpose to one's life. Furthermore, Ellul maintains that without faith, history can have no meaning. "If I step outside faith, the human adventure has no orientation of its own. It is not true that history as such has meaning."[12] Through faith in the Word, one can begin to live an

---

11. Jacques Ellul, *Violence: Reflections from a Christian Perspective*, trans. Cecilia Gaul Kings (New York: Seabury, 1969), 98.
12. Jacques Ellul, *What I Believe*, trans. Geoffrey W. Bromiley (London: Marshall, Morgan, & Scott, 1989), 15.

authentically significant and free life—even within the constraints of necessity.[13]

While this faith depends on the experience of God, the Wholly Other is ultimately unknowable and free, not subject to human laws of rationality or logic. Ellul emphasizes the Trinity as a primary symbol of God's revelation. Herein, God is fully transcendent and completely immanent, divine and human. God also embodies the four principles of dialectic, which comprise the four fundamental constituents of reality itself. As such, Ellul maintains that only through the Trinitarian lens can one see reality as it is.[14]

While Ellul upholds that Christ is needed in these ways, he continually defends universal salvation. God's love encompasses everything, and Christ's sacrifice atoned for *all* sin, universally. For these reasons, and following from the logic of dialectic, Ellul affirms that all things will be reconciled with God. This knowledge should give one a sense of profound hope.[15]

According to Ellul, hope is not only acquired through faith; it is also an ethical imperative for Christians. Hope is an act of freedom, and its primary forms are perseverance, prayer, and realism. Because this age is one of God's abandonment and silence, our necessary response is to protest through perseverance and prayer. Through these primary expressions of hope, one can enter a living relationship with God. This bond provides a framework for seeing and understanding the world in a realistic rather than an idealistic way. For Ellul, this realism is also a form of hope. Free from ideology and obfuscation, this worldview sees the realm of technique and its bonds of necessity, recognizing that there is only despair in this realm. By

13. Ibid., 23–29.
14. Ibid., 167–87.
15. Ibid., 214–23.

looking to the sphere of freedom and the future promise of Christ's reconciliation, one can find and act in hope.[16]

Aside from hope, another Christian duty Ellul defends is the resistance of all forms of power. This includes refusing to engage in acts of violence, despite the fact that the realm of necessity is dominated by it. Because Christ absolutely rejected any use of violence, so should his followers. Violence not only contradicts the life and message of Christ, it also denies that reconciliation is possible, thus negating a fundamental aspect of reality. Finally, violence contradicts the Trinity, which is of central importance to Ellul because it so aptly illustrates God's desire to have a relationship with us. Violence destroys the possibility of this authentic relationship.[17]

According to Ellul, the absolute rejection of power is anarchism. Ellul encourages individuals to focus on their own families and immediate communities rather than on politics at large. By doing this, Ellul believes people can escape the entrapment of politization and propaganda, and can avoid supporting the state's violence. Ellul also persuades us to work within their communities toward a state of harmony between people and the earth. Rather than putting false hope in politics, it is by resisting its powers that individuals can create valuable differences in the world.[18]

Together, Ellul's theology and philosophy form a complete, coherent, and ultimately optimistic work. One cannot understand any part of his theology without a correct understanding of technique. Likewise, one cannot fully grasp his philosophy without first comprehending his theology. As Kaczynski exemplified, if one only reads and studies Ellul's philosophical work, he will seem pessimistic and even fatalistic. However, if read in conjunction with

16. Ellul, *Hope in Time of Abandonment*, v–x.
17. Ellul, *Violence*, 1–5.
18. Jacques Ellul, *In Season, Out of Season: An Introduction to the Thought of Jacques Ellul*, trans. by Lani K. Niles (San Francisco: Harper & Row, 1982), 195–98.

his theology—so full of hopeful and encouraging exhortations—Ellul's philosophy simply cannot be reduced to fatalism, as so many have tried to do. He writes, "Whoever accuses my analyses and research as negativism and considers iconoclasm and the criticism of . . . ideologies . . . to be purely pessimistic proves one thing: that he loves his chains. He is not ready to risk the adventure of freedom."[19]

Indeed, Ellul is ultimately an advocate of human freedom; he is in fact optimistic and truly believes that, with God's help, humans can live in freedom, even in the face of necessity. Ellul's work is intended to awaken people to the bonds of technique and to the spoken Word so that they can begin moving in the direction of liberation.

It is not only the content of Ellul's work that is so needed today, it is also his concept of dialectic. Dialectic held Ellul's work in cohesion and provided a clear picture of the whole he described. Yet perhaps more important was its unique inclusivity and its intellectual honesty. Indeed, Ellul was an exemplary interdisciplinary thinker.

Ellul was also a modern-day prophet.[20] In fact, this is perhaps the only adequate title for Ellul. We must take his words seriously and continue to reflect on them. His call to reject the powers of technique and to live in freedom is now needed more than ever. It is my desire that this exposition will move its readers closer to Ellul and to the hope he advocates.

---

19. Jacques Ellul, *The Humiliation of the Word*, trans. Joyce Main Hanks (Grand Rapids: Eerdmans, 1985), 268.
20. David W. Gill, "Jacques Ellul: The Prophet as Theologian," *Themelios* 7, no. 1 (1981): 4–14.

References

Works by Jacques Ellul

Ellul, Jacques. *Anarchy and Christianity*. Translated by Geoffrey W. Bromiley. Grand Rapids: Eerdmans, 1991.

———. *Anarchie et christianisme*. Lyon: Atelier de Création Libertaire, 1988.

———. *L'Apocalypse: Architecture en mouvement*. Paris: Desclée, 1975.

———. *The Betrayal of the West*. Translated by Matthew J. O'Connell. New York: Seabury, 1978.

———. *Contre les violents*. Paris: Le Centurion, 1971.

———. *A Critique of the New Commonplaces*. Translated by Helen Weaver. New York: Knopf, 1968.

———. *L'empire du non-sens: L'art et la société technicienne*. Paris: Press Universitaires de France, 1980.

———. "The End and the Means." In *The Presence of the Kingdom*, translated by Olive Wynon, 49–78. London: SCM, 1951.

———. *L'espérance oubliée*. Paris: Gallimard, 1972.

———. *The Ethics of Freedom*. Translated by Geoffrey W. Bromiley. Grand Rapids: Eerdmans, 1972.

———. *False Presence of the Kingdom*. Translated by C. Edward Hopkin. New York: Seabury, 1963.

———. *Histoire de la propaganda*. Paris: Presses Universitaires de France, 1967.

————. *Hope in Time of Abandonment*. Translated by C. Edward Hopkin. New York: Seabury, 1972.

————. *The Humiliation of the Word*. Translated by Joyce Main Hanks. Grand Rapids: Eerdmans, 1985.

————. *L'impossible prière*. Paris: Centurion, 1971.

————. *In Season, Out of Season: An Introduction to the Thought of Jacques Ellul*. Translated by Lani K. Niles, based on interviews by Madeline Garrigou-Lagrange. San Francisco: Harper & Row, 1982.

————. *Jesus and Marx: From Gospel to Ideology*. Translated by Joyce Main Hanks. Grand Rapids: Eerdmans, 1988.

————. *Living Faith: Belief and Doubt in a Perilous World*. Translated by Peter Heinegg. San Francisco: Harper & Row, 1983.

————. *The Meaning of the City*. Translated by Dennis Perdee. Grand Rapids: Eerdmans, 1970.

————. *Money and Power*. Translated by LaVonne Neff. Downers Grove, IL: InterVarsity, 1984.

————. "Needed: A New Karl Marx." In *Sources and Trajectories: Eight Early Articles by Jacques Ellul That Set the Stage*, edited and translated by Marva J. Dawn, 29–48 Grand Rapids: Eerdmans, 1997.

————. *The New Demons*. Translated by C. Edward Hopkin. New York: Seabury, 1975.

————. "On Dialectic." In *Jacques Ellul: Interpretive Essays*, edited by Clifford G. Christians and Jay M. Van Hook, 291–308. Urbana: University of Illinois Press, 1981.

————. *Perspectives on Our Age: Jacques Ellul Speaks on His Life and Work*. Translated by Joachim Neugroschel. Toronto: Canadian Broadcasting Company, 1981.

————. *Politique de Dieu, politiques de l'homme*. Paris: Éditions Universitaires, 1966.

———. *The Political Illusion.* Translated by Konrad Kellen. New York: Vintage, 1967.

———. *The Politics of God and the Politics of Man.* Translated by Geoffrey W. Bromiley. Grand Rapids: Eerdmans, 1972.

———. *Prayer and Modern Man.* Translated by C. Edward Hopkin. New York: Seabury, 1970.

———. *The Presence of the Kingdom.* Translated by Olive Wyon. London: SCM, 1951.

———. *Propaganda: The Formation of Men's Attitudes.* Translated by Konrad Kellen. New York: Vintage, 1962.

———. *Reason for Being: A Meditation on Ecclesiastes.* Translated by Joyce Main Hanks. Grand Rapids: Eerdmans, 1990.

———. *The Subversion of Christianity.* Translated by Geoffrey W. Bromiley. Grand Rapids: Eerdmans, 1986.

———. *La Technique ou l'enjeu du siècle.* Paris: Armand Colin, 1954.

———. *The Technological Bluff.* Translated by Geoffrey W. Bromiley. Grand Rapids: Eerdmans, 1990.

———. "The Technological Order." In *Philosophy and Technology*, edited by Carl Mitcham and Robert Mackey, 86–106. New York: Free Press, 1972.

———. *The Technological Society.* Translated by John Wilkinson. New York: Vintage, 1964.

———. *The Technological System.* Translated by Joachim Neugroschel. New York: Continuum, 1980.

———. *The Theological Foundation of Law.* Translation by Marguerite Wieser. London: SCM, 1961.

———. *To Will and to Do: An Ethical Research for Christians.* Translated by C. Edward Hopkin. Philadelphia: Pilgrim House, 1969.

———. *Violence: Reflections from a Christian Perspective.* Translated by Cecilia Gaul Kings. New York: Seabury, 1969.

———. *What I Believe*. Translated by Geoffrey W. Bromiley. London: Marshall, Morgan, & Scott, 1989.

Ellul, Jacques, and Patrick Troude-Chastenet. *Jacques Ellul on Politics, Technology, and Christianity*. Eugene, OR: Wipf & Stock, 1995.

Other works

Augustine. *The City of God against the Pagans*. Translated and edited by R. W. Dyson. Cambridge: Cambridge University Press, 1998.

Barth, Karl. *Church Dogmatics: A Selection*. Translated and edited by G. W. Bromiley. Louisville: Westminster John Knox, 1961.

———. *Church Dogmatics*. Edited by G. W. Bromiley and T. F. Torrance 4 vols. Edinburgh: T & T Clark, 1956–77.

———. *The Epistle to the Romans*. Translated by Edwyn C. Hoskyns. Oxford: Oxford University Press, 1960.

Barth, Karl and Emil Brunner. *Natural Theology: Comprising "Nature and Grace" by Professor Dr. Emil Brunner and the Reply "No!" by Dr. Karl Barth*. Translated by Peter Fraenkel. Eugene, OR: Wipf & Stock, 2002.

Bianco, Anthony. *Wal-Mart: The Bully of Bentonville*. New York: Crown Business, 2007.

Bimber, Bruce. "Three Faces of Technological Determinism." In *Does Technology Drive History?*, edited by Merrit Roe Smith and Leo Marx, 79–100. Cambridge: MIT, 2004.

Bloch, Ernst. *The Principle of Hope.*Vol. 1. Translated by Neville Plaice, Steven Plaice, and Paul Knight. Cambridge: MIT, 1995.

Bromiley, Geoffrey W. "Barth's Influence on Jacques Ellul." In *Jacques Ellul: Interpretive Essays*, edited by Clifford G. Christians and Jay M. Van Hook, 32–51. Urbana: University of Illinois, 1981.

Bultmann, Rudolf. *Faith and Understanding.* Translated by Louise Pettibone Smith. Philadelphia: Fortress Press, 1987.

Chase, Alston. *Harvard and the Unabomber: The Education of an American Terrorist*. New York: Norton, 2003.

Christians, Clifford G., and Jay M. Van Hook eds. *Jacques Ellul: Interpretive Essays*. Urbana: University of Illinois Press, 1981.

Clendenin, Daniel B. *Theological Method in the Theology of Jacques Ellul*. Lanham, MD: University Press of America, 1987.

Cohen, Gerald. *Marx's Theory of History: A Defense*. Princeton: Princeton University Press, 2000.

Come, Arnold B. *Kierkegaard as Humanist: Discovering My Self*. London: McGill-Queens University Press, 1995.

———. *Kierkegaard as Theologian: Recovering My Self*. London: McGill-Queens University Press, 1997.

———. *Trendelenburg's Influence on Kierkegaard's Modal Categories*. Montreal: Inter Editions, 1991.

Davies, Brian. *The Thought of Thomas Aquinas*. Oxford: Clarendon, 1993.

Debord, Guy. *Society of the Spectacle*. Detroit: Black & Red, 1983.

Dennett, Daniel. *Brainstorms: Philosophical Essays on Mind and Psychology*. Cambridge: MIT, 1981.

Dively Lauro, Elizabeth A. "Universalism." In *The Westminster Handbook to Origen*, edited by John Anthony McGuckin, 59–62. Louisville: Westminster John Knox, 2004.

Dreyfus, Hubert, ed. *Husserl, Intentionality, and Cognitive Science*. Cambridge: MIT, 1993.

———. "Nihilism, Art, Technology, and Politics." In *The Cambridge Companion to Heidegger*, edited by Charles Guignon, 289–316. Cambridge: Cambridge University Press, 1993.

———. *What Computers Still Can't Do: Critique of Artificial Intelligence*. Cambridge: MIT, 2000.

Dusek, Val. *Philosophy of Technology: An Introduction*. Oxford: Blackwell, 2006.

Eagleton, Terry. *Why Marx Was Right*. New Haven, CT: Yale University Press, 2011.

Eller, Vernard. *Christian Anarchy: Jesus' Primacy over the Powers*. Eugene, OR: Wipf & Stock, 1999.

———. "Ellul and Kierkegaard: Closer than Brothers." In *Jacques Ellul: Interpretive Essays*, edited by Clifford G. Christians and Jay M. Van Hook, 52–66. Urbana: University of Illinois, 1981.

Fasching, Darrell. "The Ethical Importance of Universal Salvation." *The Ellul Forum* 1 (1988): 5–9.

———. *The Thought of Jacques Ellul: A Systematic Exposition*. London: Edwin Mellen, 1981.

Feenberg, Andrew. *Questioning Technology*. London: Routledge, 2000.

———. "What Is Philosophy of Technology?" Transcript of lecture for Komaba students, June 2003. http://www.sfu.ca/~andrewf/komaba.htm.

Fortin, Ernest L. "De Civitate Dei." In *Augustine through the Ages*, edited by Allan D. Fitzgerald, 196–202. Grand Rapids: Eerdmans, 1999.

Foucault, Michel. *Power/Knowledge: Selected Interviews and Other Writings, 1972–1977*. Edited by Colin Gordon. New York: Vintage, 1972.

Fromm, Erich, ed. *Marx's Concept of Man*. New York: Continuum, 2004.

———. *The Sane Society*. New York: Holt, 1990.

Fuller, R. Buckminster. *No More Secondhand God*. New York: Doubleday, 1971.

———. *Utopia or Oblivion: The Prospects for Humanity*. Zurich: Lars Muller, 1998.

Giedion, Siegfried. *Mechanization Takes Command: A Contribution to Anonymous History*. New York: Norton, 1975.

Gill, David W. "Jacques Ellul: The Prophet as Theologian." *Themelios* 7, no. 1 (1981): 4–14.

———. "My Journey with Jacques Ellul." *The Ellul Forum* 13 (1994): 7.

———. "The Dialectic of Theology and Sociology in Jacques Ellul: A Recent Interview." Unpublished interview and paper given at the American Academy of Religion Annual Meeting, November 21, 1988.

———. *The Word of God in the Ethics of Jacques Ellul*. London: Scarecrow, 1984.

Goddard, Andrew. *Living the Word, Resisting the World: The Life and Thought of Jacques Ellul*. Carlisle, UK: Paternoster, 2002.

Gonzalez, Justo L. "Anakephalaiosis." In *Essential Theological Terms*, 6–7. Louisville: Westminster John Knox, 2005.

Grant, Ian Hamilton. "Postmodernism and Science and Technology." In *The Routledge Critical Dictionary of Postmodern Thought*, edited by Stuart Sim, 65–77. New York: Routledge, 1999.

Guthrie, Charles, and Michael Quinlan. *Just War: The Just War Tradition*. New York: Walker, 2007.

Habermas, Jürgen. "Technology and Science as Ideology." In *Toward a Rational Society*, translated by J. Shapiro, 81–122. Boston: Beacon, 1971.

Hanks, Joyce Main, ed. *The Reception of Jacques Ellul's Critique of Technology: An Annotated Bibliography of Writings on His Life and Thought (Books, Articles, Reviews, Symposia)*. Lampeter, UK: Edwin Mellen, 2007.

Harris, Errol E. *Formal, Transcendental, and Dialectical Thinking: Logic and Reality*. Albany: State University of New York, 1987.

Hastings, James, and John Selbie, eds. *Encyclopedia of Religion and Ethics*, part 19. New York: Kessinger, 2003.

Heidegger, Martin. *Being and Time*. Translated by John Macquarrie and Edward Robinson. New York: Harper, 1962.

———. "Die Frage nach der Technik." In *Die Technik und die Kehre*, 5–36. Tubingen: Neske, 1954.

———. *Discourse on Thinking*. Translated by John. M. Anderson and E. Hans Freund. New York: Harper, 1966.

————. *The Question concerning Technology and Other Essays.* Translated by William Lovitt. New York: Harper, 1977.

Holmes, Robert L. *Basic Moral Philosophy.* Belmont, CA: Wadsworth, 2003.

Hunsinger, George. *How to Read Karl Barth: The Shape of His Theology.* New York: Oxford University Press, 1991.

Jay, Martin. *Force Fields: Between Intellectual History and Cultural Critique.* New York: Routledge, 1993.

Johnson, Howard A. "Kierkegaard and Politics." In *A Kierkegaard Critique*, edited by Howard A. Johnson and Niels Thulstrup, 74–84. Chicago: Gateway, 1967.

Jones, Steven E. *Against Technology: From the Luddites to Neo-Luddism.* London: Routledge, 2006.

Juenger, Friedrich Georg. *Die perfektion der technik.* Frankfurt: Vitorio Klostermann, 1946.

Kaczynski, Theodore. *The Unabomber Manifesto: Industrial Society and Its Future.* Berkeley: Jolly Roger, 1995.

Kant, Immanuel. *Fundamental Principles of the Metaphysics of Morals.* Translated by T. K. Abbott. New York: Prometheus, 1987.

Kaufmann, Walter, ed. *Existentialism: From Dostoyevsky to Sartre.* New York: New American Library, 1975.

Kierkegaard, Søren. *Attack upon "Christendom."* Translated by Walter Lowrie. Princeton: Princeton University Press, 1968.

————. *Either/Or: A Fragment of Life.* Translated by Alistair Hannay. New York: Penguin, 1992.

————. *Journals and Papers.* 6 vols. Translated by H. Hong and E. Hong. Bloomington: Indiana University Press, 1967–78.

————. *Philosophical Fragments.* Translated and edited by H. Hong and E. Hong. Princeton: Princeton University Press, 1985.

Kinna, Ruth. *Anarchism.* Oxford: Oneworld, 2009.

Klager, Andrew P. "Retaining and Reclaiming the Divine: Identification and the Recapitulation of Peace in St. Irenaeus of Lyons' Atonement Narrative." In *Stricken by God? Nonviolent Identification and the Victory of Christ*, edited by Brad Jersak and Michael Hardin, 422–481. Grand Rapids: Eerdmans, 2007.

Kuhns, William. *The Post-Industrial Prophets: Interpretations of Technology*. San Francisco: Harper & Row, 1973.

LeFevre, Perry, ed. *The Prayers of Kierkegaard*. Chicago: University of Chicago Press, 1956.

Long, Michael G., ed. *Christian Peace and Non-Violence: A Documentary History*. New York: Orbis, 2011.

Lovekin, David. *Technique, Discourse, and Consciousness: An Introduction to the Philosophy of Jacques Ellul*. London: Associated University Press, 1991.

Lukács, Georg. *History and Class Consciousness: Studies in Marxist Dialectics*. Translated by Rodney Livingstone. Cambridge: MIT.

Lyotard, Jean-François. *The Postmodern Condition: A Report on Knowledge*. Translated by Geoff Bennington and Brian Massumi. Minneapolis: University of Minnesota Press, 1978.

MacDonald, Gregory, ed. *All Shall Be Well: Explorations in Universal Salvation and Christian Theology, from Origen to Moltmann*. Eugene, OR: Wipf & Stock, 2011.

Marcuse, Herbert. *An Essay on Liberation*. New York: Beacon, 1969.

———. *One Dimensional Man: Studies in the Ideology of Advanced Industrial Society*. Boston: Beacon, 1964.

———. *Technology, War and Fascism*. Vol. 1 of *Collected Papers of Herbert Marcuse*, edited by Douglas Kellner. New York: Routledge, 1998.

Marlin, Randal. *Propaganda and the Ethics of Persuasion*. New York: Broadview, 2002.

Marx, Karl. "Economic and Philosophical Manuscripts." In *Marx's Concept of Man*, edited by Erich Fromm, 73–151. New York: Continuum, 2004.

―――. *Grundrisse: Foundations of the Critique of Political Economy.* Translated and edited by Martin Nicolaus. New York: Penguin, 1993.

Marx, Karl, and Friedrich Engels. *The Communist Manifesto.* Translated by G. S. Jones. New York: Penguin, 2002.

McCormack, Bruce L. *Karl Barth's Critically Realistic Dialectical Theology: Its Genesis and Development: 1909–1936.* Oxford: Oxford University Press, 1995.

Merchant, Carolyn. *The Death of Nature: Women, Ecology and the Scientific Revolution.* New York: HarperOne, 1990.

Miranda, Jose. *Communism in the Bible.* Translated by Robert S. Barr. New York: Orbis, 1982.

Mitcham, Carl. "Notes toward a Philosophy of Meta-Technology." *Techne: Research in Philosophy and Technology* 1, nos. 1–2 (1995): 3–5.

―――. *Thinking through Technology.* Chicago: University of Chicago Press, 2004.

Moltmann, Jürgen. *Theology of Hope: On the Ground and the Implications of a Christian Eschatology.* Translated by James W. Leitch. San Francisco: Harper & Row, 1967.

Mumford, Lewis. *The Pentagon of Power.* Vol 2 of *The Myth of the Machine.* New York: Harcourt Brace Jovanovich, 1970.

Müntzer, Thomas. *Revelation and Revolution: Basic Writings of Thomas Münzter.* Edited by Michael G. Baylor. Bethlehem, PA: Lehigh University Press, 1993.

Neher, André. *The Exile of the Word: From the Silence of the Bible to the Silence of Auschwitz.* Translated by David Maisel. Philadelphia: Jewish Publication Society, 1981.

Pascal, Blaise. *Pensées.* Translated by A. J. Krailsheimer. New York: Penguin, 1995.

Peters, F. E. *Greek Philosophical Terms: A Historical Lexicon.* New York: New York University Press, 1967.

Pitt, Joseph C., ed. *Techne: Research in Philosophy and Technology* 1 (1995).

Plato. *Republic*. Translated by C. D. C. Reeve. Cambridge, MA: Hackett. 2004.

Pojman, Louis B. *The Logic of Subjectivity: Kierkegaard's Philosophy of Religion*. Tuscaloosa: University of Alabama Press, 1984.

Popper, Karl. *The Open Society and Its Enemies*. Vol. 2 of *Hegel, Marx and the Aftermath*. Princeton: Princeton University Press, 1971.

Porquet, Jean-Luc. *Jacques Ellul: L'homme qui avait (presque) tout prevu*. Paris: Cherche Midi, 2003.

Ricoeur, Paul. *Essays on Biblical Interpretation*. Philadelphia: Fortress, 1980.

———. *Hermeneutics and the Human Sciences*. Translated and edited by John B. Thompson. Cambridge: Cambridge University Press, 1980.

Roochnik, David. *Retrieving the Ancients: An Introduction to Greek Philosophy*. Boston: Wiley-Blackwell, 2004.

Sartre, Jean-Paul. *Existentialism Is a Humanism*. Translated by Carol Macomber. New Haven, CT: Yale University Press, 2007.

Scharff, Robert, and Val Dusek, eds. *The Philosophy of Technology: The Technological Condition*. Oxford: Wiley-Blackwell, 2003.

Searle, John. *Minds, Brains, and Science*. Cambridge: Harvard University Press, 1986.

———. *Rediscovery of Mind*. Cambridge: MIT, 1992.

Shaw, Jeffrey. "Illusions of Freedom: Jacques Ellul and Thomas Merton on Propaganda." *The Ellul Forum* 47 (2011): 20–21.

Stump, Chad and J. B. Meister. *Christian Thought: A Historical Introduction*. New York: Routledge, 2010.

Sudduth, Michael. "John Calvin." In *The History of Western Philosophy of Religion*, edited by Graham Oppy and Nick Trakakis, 47–64. New York: Oxford University Press, 2009.

Tillich, Paul. *A Complete History of Christian Thought*. Edited by Carl E. Braaten. New York: Harper & Row, 1968.

————. *Perspectives on Nineteenth and Twentieth Century Protestant Theology.* Edited by Carl E. Bratten. New York: Harper & Row, 1995.

Tolstoy, Leo. *Government Is Violence: Essays on Anarchism and Pacifism.* Edited by David Stephens. London: Phoenix, 1990.

Vahanian, Gabriel. *Praise of the Secular.* Charlottesville, VA: University of Virginia, 2008.

Van Vleet, Jacob. "A Theoretical Approach to Mass Psychological Manipulation: Jacques Ellul's Analysis of Modern Propaganda." In *Censored 2012: Sourcebook for the Media Revolution,* edited by Mickey Huff, 313–24. New York: Seven Stories, 2011.

Virilio, Paul. *The Aesthetics of Disappearance.* Translated by Philip Beitchman. New York: Semiotext(e), 1991.

————. *The Information Bomb.* Translated by Chris Turner. New York: Verso, 2000.

————. *The Lost Dimension.* Translated by Daniel Moshenberg. New York: Semiotext(e), 1991.

————. *The Original Accident.* Translated by Julie Rose. London: Polity, 2005.

Volti, Rudi. *Society and Technological Change.* New York: Worth Publishers, 2000.

Watkin, Julia. *Historical Dictionary of Kierkegaard's Philosophy.* Lanham, MD: Scarecrow, 2001.

Watson, Francis. "The Bible." In *The Cambridge Companion to Karl Barth,* edited by John Webster, 57–71. Cambridge: Cambridge University Press, 2000.

Welch, Claude. *In This Name: The Doctrine of the Trinity in Contemporary Theology.* Eugene, OR: Wipf & Stock, 2005.

————. *Protestant Thought in the Nineteenth Century.* Vol. 1, *1799 – 1870.* New Haven, CT: Yale University Press, 1972.

————. *Protestant Thought in the Nineteenth Century.* Vol. 2, *1870 – 1914.* New Haven, CT: Yale University Press, 1985.

Wilkinson, John A. "Introduction." In *The Technological Society*, by Jacques Ellul, ix–xx. New York: Knopf, 1964.

Winner, Langdon. *Autonomous Technology: Technics-Out-of-Control as a Theme in Political Thought*. Cambridge: MIT, 1977.

———. "The Enduring Dilemma of Autonomous Technique." *Bulletin of Science, Technology, and Society*, 15, nos. 2–3 (1995): 62–72.

Zerzan, John. *Future Primitive and Other Essays*. New York: Autonomedia, 1994.

———. *Running on Emptiness: The Pathology of Civilization*. Los Angeles: Feral House, 2008.

Zerzan, John, and Alice Carnes eds. *Questioning Technology: Tool, Toy or Tyrant?* Philadelphia: New Society Publishers, 2001.

Index

73–74, 76, 158–60, 171,
179n92, 200–1, 210–1, 214,
217, 230

Searle, John, 112n127, 231
Seeing, 4, 64–69, 185, 205, 211
Sin, 58, 73, 158, 199, 203, 217
Socialism, 12–13, 186, 197
Substantivism, 80, 83–84

Technique, 3n10, 4, 7, 8n1,
13–16, 19, 28, 34, 36–40,
42–43, 59, 63–66, 69–71,
76–77, 79, 84–112, 114–5, 121,
125–7, 129, 131–6, 140, 142–3,
145–53, 155–8, 160–4, 167–9,
179, 181–3, 187–8, 190, 193–8,
200, 204–11, 214–9, 223, 229,
233; as consciousness and
ideology, 15–16, 77, 87–89,
121, 143n51, 147, 193; as
method, 84, 86, 131, 158, 214;
as realm of necessity, 36–37,
39, 42n48, 64, 69, 71, 76, 84,
89, 104, 107, 126–7, 135, 145,
148n64, 157, 187, 193–4, 205,
207–8, 215–6; alienation and,
13–16, 37, 69–70, 158, 207; as
science, 86–87, 105–6; as tools,
85–86; as total environment,
89, 135; consequences and, 14,

69, 94–107, 121; efficiency
and, 13, 36, 65, 84, 86–90,
94–95, 98, 101, 104, 108–9,
114, 129, 133, 148–50, 152,
188, 194, 214; means and end,
84, 109–15, 221; politics and,
4, 14, 70, 89, 93n54, 105,
126–7, 146, 148n66, 149–50,
152, 167–8, 198, 207, 209,
214–6; propaganda and, *see*
Propaganda and technique;
value and, 13, 64, 87, 87–88,
90, 95, 108–10, 114, 129, 147,
148n63, 151, 206
Teilhard de Chardin, Pierre, 62,
81
Tillich, Paul, 41, 61n59, 209n208,
231

Universal salvation, 4, 13, 33,
43n49, 57, 59, 60n56, 73, 208,
217, 226, 229
Utilitarianism, 88, 97, 188, 211

Virilio, Paul, 101–103, 232

Watson, Francis, 53, 232
Winner, Langdon, 93n54, 233

Zerzan, John, 83, 100n83, 233

Lightning Source UK Ltd.
Milton Keynes UK
UKHW020625090621
385191UK00006B/177